SWALLOWED ALIVE!

Fighting for Life in Alaska

Volume 1

Larry Kaniut

Anchorage, Alaska

Paper Talk
Larry Kaniut, 4800 Natrona, Anchorage, AK 99516
Email: kaniut@alaska.net
Web site: www.kaniut.com

Printed in the United States of America

ISBN 978-1955728102 (paperback)
    978-1955728119 (ebook)

ALASKAN AUTHOR Logo, Copyright 2022 Sharon Aubrey, used with permission.

Acknowledgments:

Thank you to all those who responded to and allowed me to interview them or receive their stories.

Thank you to the many reporters and their publications which provided information over the years.

Thanks to Sharon Aubrey at Relevant Publishers LLC for formatting this book and designing the cover.

Disclaimer:

Different spellings occur, such as snow machine or snowmachine; snowmobile or snowmachine; dry suit/drysuit. In some cases the European spelling is used.

In some cases The Associated Press appears, whereas Associated Press may appear elsewhere—both are the same.

Some may question the inclusion of some material in this book—that it does not represent the theme of being swallowed alive, however reviewing it may go a long way toward keeping the reader from danger.

DEDICATION

The Men:

In a country as vast and varied as Alaska, men go out...but they do not always return...

This book is dedicated to those who sought adventure, either consciously or subconsciously, but were swallowed alive by the wilderness.

It is also dedicated to that plucky band of rescuers who ventured out to save the lost, or the suffering...in many cases even some of them were swallowed alive, giving their lives in the most noble of efforts in order to provide succor.

INTRODUCTION

"I had wondered if the Inlet would swallow me up. I've lived here all my life and most people who crash in the Inlet or get stuck in its mud never get out of it. From duck hunting and hooligan fishing experiences as a kid, I had realized how easy it is to get stuck." -- Bob Elstad, Alaskan plane crash survivor, Page 284, *Danger Stalks the Land* (author: Larry Kaniut)

Alaska's vast wilderness, punctuated by diverse topography, variable weather and unpredictable animals, creates a playground that embodies adventure, and, all too often, misadventure. This wilderness playground is very fickle. She teases and coerces. Many are her wiles. Her clothed beauty, disrobed, reveals her dangerous and disastrous ways. She is known to literally or figuratively swallow men alive.

In her arms man encounters a multitude of dangers that could include animals (bears, wolves, coyotes, cougars, crocodiles, sharks, snakes); lightning strikes; severe cold; becoming lost; falls; aviation related events; gunshot tragedies; poor or mis-planning; improper knowledge and/or water conditions.

Swallowed Alive is a collection of stories and anecdotes capturing serious outdoor experiences primarily in Alaska. As long as man ventures into wilderness country, tales will be told of the tragedy and/or the foibles he faced. If you are nose to nose with danger and challenging Alaska's treacherous terrain and terribly cold temperatures with hopes of returning to civilization, you'd better have your ducks in a row...because nature ain't fooled. This collection includes those who perished as well as those who lived to laugh at their experience.

The title *Swallowed Alive* is all too telling of many who faced danger and were literally swallowed alive by Mistress Wilderness:

Cynthia Dusel-Bacon survived a black bear which tore and ate her flesh;

Reuben Lyon and Dennis Long watched as their pilot succumbed to the water;

Steve Keiner and a 17-year old youngster disappeared into glacial crevasses;

one person perished under the snow-laden roof of a ramshackle cabin;

Patrick Hallin vanished beneath the waters of Turnagain Arm while windsurfing;

Cook Inlet claimed another when his anchor rope pulled him overboard.

You can never trust yesterday…the situation may have been safe then…but this is a new day.

These are not isolated cases. On a regular basis one hears over the electronic media or reads in the print media of one or more persons in Alaska turning up missing or perishing in the wilderness. On the morning news August 24, 2000, for instance, I heard about a missing plane with four aboard being found on the side of a mountain. Following that story was one about a man who rented a kayak Sunday, August 20, was reported missing on Tuesday and was found floating in a saltwater bay beside his broken kayak Wednesday. It is not uncommon to hear of numerous outdoor tragedies every week in Alaska. (APPENDIX 2 NEWSPAPER HEADLINES This list is a smidge of headlines that appear on a regular basis in Alaska's newspapers)

But the bottom line is for the outdoor adventurer to go prepared or risk being swallowed alive.

The "Mountain":

It is often said that men climb mountains because they're there. And so it is with those who challenge the outdoors. Alaska is not the only "mountain" men have scaled or sought to conquer… there are other venues. The "mountain" is the challenge facing all outdoor adventurers who push the envelope. Some are more greatly challenged or confronted by the mountain than others. There is risk in the arms of Mistress Wilderness…risk in the form of geography, animals and weather. But when one is lost or in need of rescue, the message is always the same…

The Message:

To the rescuee: "Never give up."   "Fight on."

To the rescuer: "Rescue the perishing." "Let it not be said of me that I did not try." "Without the risk there is no reward."

The Measure:

Some men set a standard of excellence of Herculean proportions. They raise the bar high enough to challenge those of us who remain. What is the value of an adventure? The price of an adventurer? The cost of rescue? What is the lesson to be learned? How can we cope with the injury or loss of a friend or brother? Is the price of trying too great?

The Meaning:

Often the reward of rescue is the return or the eventual restoration to health of the rescued. Sometimes the reward is merely a combination of the return and the effort expended. Frequently the only reward is in the failed effort. The failure does not overlook the knowledge that the effort was expended…that an exhausting and thorough search or retrieval was accomplished. Unfortunately sometimes the winds of ill fortune blow across the land, depriving man of his desired results.

The Mentality:

Men who face the mountain, be they adventurer or rescuer, must steel their bodies, minds and spirits to the task, face the endeavor, determine to achieve and expend their highest and most noble effort to accomplish safe return.

Contents

SECTION 1 DRAMA

Twenty-two Hours

by Larry Kaniut

They heard it coming. Like a freight train rumbling out of the mountains and roaring across the tundra for miles, the wind galloped in waves. Each time it threatened to tumble them from their perch and into the deadly cold water below.

The two friends sat atop the airplane floats. Normally the float surfaces would be beneath the water, the plane above; however the plane lay below them, upside down on the bottom of the lake. Fortunately the water was not very deep and the floats thrust above the surface high enough for them to sit on the bottom of one.

Their only protection from the chilling air was the small, dismantled tent they had managed to save from the plane's interior. They kept it wrapped around them. But the wind ripped at this meager defense and it was all the pair could do to keep the tent fabric in place.

Night had fallen over the lake and the Alaska sunrise was still many hours away. Reuben Lyon and Dennis Long clutched each other as they clung to the pontoon of the overturned airplane. They were slowly freezing to death.

It was October. It was Alaska. It was cold!

They weren't exactly sure where they were; the pilot who had that information died when the Cessna 206 flipped and sank. Lawrence Wooten made it out of the cabin but never got to the surface. Now he lay submerged in the frigid waters near the lake bottom, 10 feet below the two men on the plane float.

The two survivors knew they were on a small lake somewhere close to Lake Iliamna, Alaska's largest body of fresh water, some 90 by 25 miles in size. The trio had left Anchorage to do some caribou hunting and had flown a couple of hours southwest.

At about 5 p.m. that day, Wooten had reduced power for a landing on the lake surface. Though there was a wind, it appeared steady and Wooten set the single engine Cessna down on the water.

Just then a gusty side wind hit the aircraft and flipped it.

As the 206 went over and began to sink, "It was like fast slow motion," recalled Lyon with that perception of time peculiar to accident victims. "Once it hit the water, it sank real fast and the water was real, real cold."

The plane's cabin was already full of water by the time Long and Lyon struggled through the door on the pilot's side—Lyon first. Beyond that, neither man remembers much about those moments. Neither remembers seeing pilot Wooten actually escape the plane.

But when the two got to the lake surface and clutched the upside-down floats, they realized Wooten wasn't with them. Climbing onto the floats, the men looked down and saw Wooten through the distortion of the lake water. He was clear of the plane but was submerged and apparently lifeless.

Soaked and thoroughly chilled in the 20- to 30- knot winds, the two men did not go after their companion. Their instincts wouldn't permit them to reenter the cold water—no matter how much they wanted to.

"After we saw the pilot, he was for the most part dead," Dennis Long remembered. "He was Reuben's friend for a long time, and (Reuben) kind of went crazy—he was yelling 'That's my friend down there, that's my friend down there!' and all I could do was yell back 'He's gone—he's gone.'"

"You think about this constantly, and its' hard to get it out of your mind," Long said. "But still you get the same answer: There's not much you can do risking anybody else to go back in this water, when from what we saw there was no sign of life."

Now, with the long night ahead of them, it was all the two men could do to save themselves. The temperature sank below freezing and kept on dropping. The wind showed no signs of slowing.

They were dressed in the lightest of clothes and they were wet. Both men suffered minor injuries in the crash; that, combined with the painful cold, was inducing shock in both of them. Moreover, they had nothing to eat.

Most importantly of all, they had no life jackets, no raft and no means of getting safely to shore.

The men estimated shore to be somewhere between 75 and 125 yards away. They struggled with the decision whether or not to swim for it. But within minutes of the crash the cold had begun to eat their strength away. Lyon said, "Of course we were wet, and the wind was blowing on us, and we were losing our strength pretty fast. The way the water was and the wind blowing and what we had on...neither one of us knew how far it would be until we could touch bottom."

The decision was made—neither could face the prospect of going into the water.

So the pair settled in for the night, with the knowledge that no one would report them missing. It was only Friday. Their families would not be looking for them since their arrival was not expected until after their weekend hunting trip.

Both officers with the Anchorage Police Department, Long and Lyon used to work the graveyard shift at the courthouse together. The hours had been long and boring, and plenty of times they had fought to stay awake. That experience would prove invaluable as they struggled to survive.

"We knew that he had to stay awake all night long in order to stay on the float," Lyon said. "We knew that if we dozed off, we'd lose our balance and fall into the water—and it would be all over."

Lyon was raised in Stevens Village on the Yukon River, where his father was a Bush pilot. A memory came back to him now: once, one of his father's companions had died after falling asleep in sub-zero weather.

"That's one thing you've got to do in cold weather, is stay awake," he said. "The key to the whole thing for us was to stay awake, because if you go to sleep, you'll never wake up again."

The two men caught each other dozing off time and again, but their sleepiness was the fatigue of hypothermia. They fought it back with conversation.

They discussed the options they would face in the morning; they talked about family and work; they wondered aloud whether the Cessna had an emergency locator transmitter and, if so, whether ELTs worked while submerged in water. They prayed—they prayed a lot.

Periodically, Lyon remembered the loss of his friend, whose body lay just a few feet below them in the darkness.

"Reuben kept on reverting during the night to saying, 'Larry… he's gone.'" Long recalled. "Hell, that was his friend. It was really agonizing."

It was so cold that the two men screamed in pain. They didn't have enough room to shift their hunched-up sidesaddle positions on the narrow underside of the float, and their legs began to cramp severely.

When dawn came, they didn't even notice. With their tent wrapped around them and Lyon's thin jacket pulled over their heads, they huddled together, not looking at the world outside their shelter.

One of the few things the two men could do on that unnamed lake was tell time because Lyon had a watch. More than twelve hours had passed.

By then, Long had lost all sensation from the knees down. He believed they were frozen. One consolation was that his feet didn't hurt any more.

About 11:30 A.M. the worst that could happen did. Lyon lost his balance, slipped from the float and fell through a layer of new ice into the lake water. Long struggled to help him back up onto the pontoon.

The situation was deteriorating. Both men wanted desperately to think of some kind of flotation device they could make that would allow them to get to shore. But suffering advanced hypothermia, they could barely think at all.

The cold water merely solidified their decision to stay with the float and not attempt reaching shore. Lyon was deeply chilled and the incident reminded both of them that going into the water again would mean "instantaneous freezing," in Long's words.

The midday sun shone, but provided no warmth. They saw their deaths approaching. In nearly 24 hours they hadn't heard a single aircraft. They were entirely alone, and weakening. It was below freezing. The wind clawed at them relentlessly.

"We figured we had by the time nightfall came to live, that we'd be dead by morning because our condition was deteriorating that fast, not only physically but mentally," Long said. "The biggest thing was trying to keep our minds straight, not go bonkers."

The day began to wane as the low southern sun started down, making longer shadows and casting a pallor of fall over the lake and nearby shore. The two men on the float prayed some more.

Time crawled.

Then, suddenly, Long threw off the jacket covering their heads. He reached into his shoulder holster, pulled out his .357 Magnum and started firing into the air.

He had heard the sound of an airplane. Ridiculous as it seems now, he was trying to attract the pilot's attention with the sound of pistol fire, an impossible hope as the engine noise within the cabin drowns out all other sounds besides intercom radio dialogue.

Lyon's watch indicated the time was 12:42 P.M.

When they caught sight of the plane, they waved Lyon's bright red jacket in the air. The plane changed course and came toward them, soon nodding its wings in acknowledgment.

As the aircraft disappeared into the distance, the two men realized their ordeal was not over.

"I told Reuben it would be an hour to an hour-and-a-half before they got a chopper to us," Long said. It turned out to be an hour and forty minutes, the longest hour and forty minutes either man had ever spent.

The chopper arrived at the lake, hovered over the pair of men for a few moments, then went to shore and landed. Inexplicably, it took off again and disappeared.

"This old boy here went a little ballistic, knowing a helicopter came that close and then left," Long said about himself. "I started to cry. I just couldn't handle that he got so close and left again. My mind was fried.

"We could hear someone yelling at us from shore, but we couldn't hear what they were saying—we didn't come out from under the tent.

"I think we were going pretty quick. We just kept on telling each other that we had to hold on a little bit longer."

Soon the helicopter returned and descended to within a few feet of the two stranded men. State trooper Curt Harris dressed in a survival suit, jumped into the lake, climbed up onto the float and muscled Long onto the chopper's skids. Long remembers the intense agony as his legs were unfolded for the first time in 22 hours.

The chopper shuttled him to shore, set him down and returned for Lyon. On shore, rescuers stripped Long's clothes off and put him in a sleeping bag.

By now, the two recall, there were airplanes "all over the place." The silent tundra had turned into a bustle of rescue activity. Long and Lyon believe that by the time all was said and done, about 150 people—mostly from the village of Iliamna—aided them in some way or another.

When their oral temperatures were taken in Iliamna, Lyon's was 94 degrees; Long's was 93. The two men were evacuated to Providence Hospital, where Lyon stayed for five days, and Long for eight.

Both men initially were listed in serious condition. They were treated for back injuries and severe hypothermia, while Long also suffered cold injury to his feet. They wouldn't be back on their police beats for several weeks.

In retrospect, the two men agree on one thing above all: if they had been carrying some survival gear on their persons, they would not have come so close to death.

Both say they won't get back in a floatplane without wearing carbon dioxide-type inflatable vests. In the event of a watery crash landing, survivors must have a way to stay afloat and/or get to shore.

Marine-type flares would have given them greater peace of mind. Had they heard a plane in the middle of the night, they might have been able to attract its attention.

And food. Had Long and Lyon had some trail mix, candy bars or other high-calorie sustenance in their pockets, they would have been much better armed against the cold.

Extra clothing would have been helpful, too, they say, although both warn that if they had been wearing a lot of bulky clothes at the time of the crash they might never have escaped the aircraft at all.

State troopers at the scene are convinced that if the pair had tried to dive for Wooten, they would have perished as well. Yet their inability to rescue their friend haunts them.

Later, both men would emphasize that if they had had access to their gear, everything would have been different. But it was stored in the Cessna's floats, right beneath them but impossible to get to, blocked by a barrier of frighteningly cold water and doors that were held fast by screws.

"Some lessons have come out of Larry's death," Long said, "If a lesson can be learned that could help other people under similar circumstances or change the way people think, there'll be some good come out of it—and that's all I'm hoping."

After his release from the hospital, Lyon spoke of the pilot, his close friend for more than a decade, "People will always do whatever they can to help us not feel guilty about what happened, but that doesn't ease my mind any."

Long, consigned to a back brace and armchair during his convalescence, spent his time trying to come up with a design for airplane floats that would have yielded up their contents in the Iliamna emergency.

The floats of Wooten's Cessna 206 had doors secured with four screws apiece. If the float covers had been equipped with latches that release, the men might have been able to access some of their provisions without spending too much time in the water.

Long and Lyon are all too familiar with the floats on a Cessna 206. They spent 22 hours huddled on top of the underside of one.

"We're not talking about the top, where it's flat," he said. "We're talking about the bottom—it's about 12 inches wide.

"If you ever get a chance, take a look at the float of a 206—upside down."

Fortunately, these men were found before Alaska could swallowed them alive.

SOURCE NOTE:

Rewritten account of Reuben Lyon and Dennis Long, "Survivors recount chilling 22-hour ordeal," by Joe Bridgman, *The Anchorage Times*, Sunday, November 4, 1984

Hike Turned Deadly

by Zaz Hollander

This story represents what happens without proper clothing and a fire starter—wool, rain gear, mag stick probably would have saved these guys...a small fee for life. LK, 7/7/05

Anchorage Daily News, July 6, 2005

As things went wrong, hike became deadly.

HYPOTHERMIA: Helicopter probably saved cousin's life.

By ZAZ HOLLANDER, *Anchorage Daily News*, July 6th, 2005

WASILLA -- Richard Kelley awoke Monday morning to find his 20-year-old cousin, Hezekiah Kelley, cold and still. It was the second rain-soaked night the two had spent outside, lost and wandering the rugged backcountry of the Talkeetna Mountains.

Richard knew Hezekiah was dead.

The slightly built 19-year-old in baggy cotton clothes remembered his father's advice: If you get lost, follow a stream until you hit a road.

That's why he was miles down Peters Creek -- at least 12 miles from the hut where the cousins started a quick hike Saturday -- when state parks ranger Kym Miller spotted him from the helicopter that probably saved his life.

The Kelleys' story illustrates the skills of scores of rescuers involved. But it also shows just how wrong things can go -- and how fast -- for people ill-prepared to deal with the fickle terrain and weather of Alaska's wilderness, even at the height of summer.

Neither Richard nor Hezekiah, both of Wasilla, carried rain protection or food. No compass. No map. They wore tennis shoes, not boots. One wore jeans and one wore cotton pants -- clothes that can get soaked, then provide more chill than warmth.

The 17-year-old girl who watched the cousins disappear over a ridge Saturday afternoon didn't report them missing until Sunday evening. Ultimately, the Kelleys were out for nearly 30 hours in fairly constant rain and clouds before the rescue got under way, several search participants said.

By then, hypothermia had likely set in, especially for Hezekiah.

"They were completely soaked," said Alaska state troopers Sgt. Craig Allen of Palmer, who helped recover the body Monday from a boulder field above Peters Creek. "You don't need freezing temperatures to have hypothermia," he said. "It's a deadly environment -- even though it seems like it's summertime everywhere else."

Kelley family members, as well as the girl who reported the cousins missing, could not be reached Tuesday.

Richard Kelley told his story Monday afternoon to ranger Miller as they flew the high reaches of Peters Creek, looking for the gap on a snowy boulder field where his cousin's body lay.

The whole thing started Friday night when the cousins, with a male friend and Hezekiah's 17-year-old girlfriend, made the easy 1.5-mile hike to the Lane Hut at the end of Archangel Road, according to interviews with state parks officials and troopers.

The group slept In. Around 2:30 p.m., the cousins announced they planned to "climb a mountain" nearby. Hezekiah's girlfriend watched them disappear around a ridge.

Richard said the two climbed to the top of a nearby peak and started playing in the snow. Then they got distracted. Somehow, they ended up descending about 2,000 feet to Purches Creek, on the Willow side of the ridge.

At some point, Richard told the ranger, they realized they couldn't see the hut any more and knew they had gone the wrong way.

Searchers later spotted tracks from a high ridge above the hut: one person slid down, the other stepped. The tracks led to a big hole in boulders jumbled on a slope below, a sun-melted spot in front of one big rock. That's where the cousins spent their first night.

Meanwhile, the two people with the Kelleys slept at the cabin. The girl wondered when they didn't come back Saturday night, but later told Miller "those guys have played tricks and disappeared on her before."

Sunday morning, the girl drove the male friend into Palmer for church. She came back to the hut and spent the day yelling for the cousins.

That day, the Kelleys decided to cross Purches Creek heading north and go uphill into the Peters Creek drainage, thinking that was the Archangel Valley they had come from. They spent the day chilled and wandering, climbing steep passes only to realize they were still off track. Clouds sometimes obscured all vision, at times reaching the ground, other times clearing.

Hezekiah's girlfriend called 911 at 6 p.m. Sunday.

Rescuers descended on Hatcher Pass. Volunteers from the Alaska Mountain Rescue Group and Alaska Search and Rescue Dogs joined the troopers and state parks staff. Several troopers searched the ground on all-terrain vehicles, and the air from a helicopter and a Piper Super Cub.

Sunday night, the search focused on the area around the hut.

As rescuers tromped through pouring rain, the cousins huddled together miles away, high above Peters Creek in a "cave" beneath car-sized boulders. Water dribbled into the opening. Snow covered the floor.

Monday morning, Hezekiah was dead. Richard started to walk out.

Miller somehow spotted Richard from a troopers helicopter piloted by Mel Nading headed down Peters Creek to pick up a volunteer dog team. The ranger, a veteran mountaineer and pilot, wasn't looking for Richard. But she glimpsed a flash of blue on ground that should have been brown.

Nading brought the helicopter near the ground, but there was no place to land. As the pilot hovered just above the ground, Miller stepped onto a skid, then jumped down. She helped Richard climb into the helicopter.

The ranger and pilot probably saved Richard's life -- frail, hungry and rattled, he wouldn't have survived another night out, Miller said.

"It was heartbreaking when we found him. He grabbed onto me just like a 4-year-old and cried and cried and cried," she said. "I held him and told him it was gonna be OK now, but we really needed to find Hezekiah and we really needed him to show us where he is."

The helicopter made a second trip to recover Hezekiah's body.

"They didn't realize how serious the mountains can become so quickly," Miller said by phone Tuesday, back in her office at Finger Lake. "They just struck me as being very young... and unfortunate."

A Man and a Knife

by Larry Kaniut

What would it be like to be pinned to the ground by a tree? If you were unable to free your leg and yourself from that position, what would you consider doing to escape? One man was faced with that decision, and he met the challenge.

Don Wyman had finished his shift. He was a bulldozer operator at a strip mine in Jefferson County. The expansion of the mine called for removal of trees and overburden. Because Don wanted the logs and had permission to remove them on his own time, he worked alone July 20, 1993.

Don hung his hat in New Bethlehem, Pennsylvania. He was a 37-year old outdoorsman. He'd developed a reputation for his mental toughness and strength of will. His experience included many outdoor activities and he was considered by his friends as tough as rawhide. Over the years he'd developed the will to live.

As Don began clearing trees, he approached an oak. To avoid kickback his normal procedure called for knocking down the tree with his cat then pushing it to the road for easy access—where he cut off the root wad and make it easier to move the tree to his property.

He dropped an oak tree. Don pushed the tree downhill to the mine road. Near the road, he dismounted the cat and took up his chainsaw. He began cutting through the 26-inch diameter tree to remove the root wad. He made his first cut from the underside of the tree partway through the trunk. Then he began a cut from the top, expecting the cut to intersect the bottom cut. He noticed that the bottom cut was pinching and both sides of the cut were coming together.

Don thought the stump was trying to roll downhill and he failed to notice the top part of the tree was wedged between other trees. The wedge produced a "bow" in the trunk, much like an archer's bow. The tree was actually trying to spring uphill. The root wad anchored the tree and produced powerful force. When the point of that force was released, the pressure would explode.

When Don cut through the bulk of the tree from its bowed position, its torque caused an end to snap at him almost like a giant arrow. The tree launched itself at Don like a giant battering ram, hitting him and throwing him backwards ten feet through the air before pinning him to the ground. He was barely able to move. His left leg was shattered. He had no way to get help.

"When I sawed deep enough for it to break free, the spring in the tree drove the trunk at me like a Mack truck. It knocked me 10 feet, broke both bones in my lower left leg, and smashed my foot into the ground. My instant reaction was to push the tree off of me, but of course, that didn't work. I was pinned. I could see that the broken bones were protruding against my pant leg about seven inches below the knee. But the rest of my leg and foot were under the log." 2

Although alone, he yelled for help. It was something to try while clearing his head and thinking of other options.

Don tried to dig his leg out from under the tree.

Because of his experience afield, he knew he had options. He'd grown up hunting alone because his father, a steel worker and truck driver, had little time to go into the woods with Don (at one point a game warden brought the 16-year old home thinking he should not be in the woods without adult supervision).

Don's chainsaw was running 5-feet away. He hooked it with a branch and pulled it to him. He turned it off to conserve fuel. Don was pinned to his right side as the tree pressed from his left. His precarious position did not allow him to twist into a position in which he could bring the chainsaw into play against the tree. And since he wasn't sure how much spring the tree had left in it, he wasn't so sure he wanted to cut into it, nor to have someone else do so in fear of risking further injury.

Wyman kept yelling, aware that no one was around to hear.

He knew his wife Janet would not expect him home for another four to five hours as he normally came in when his work was finished after dark.

Don's focus in the woods while hunting was always one thing— to get game. If his technique proved unsuccessful, he immediately opted for changing strategy. He was not one to wait around when something wasn't working.

With his bare hands he clawed at the confining dirt beneath his leg. Maybe I can dig myself out.

Within moments he was down to hardpan and could not dig any deeper. He was unable to dig with a stick and turned to his chainsaw. The saw was effective. Three times he hit rock, and the chain came off. But each time he disassembled the saw, carefully keeping track of its parts, and reassembled it to continue the digging. In time he ran out of fuel. At that point he took the bar from the saw and dug with it.

When he'd dug as much as he could, he saw his foot smashed between the tree and bedrock.

Panic showed its head, but he fought it. There has to be another way. I won't give up.

Previous outings had steeled his will to face hardship with a full cylinder in his six-gun of life...he refused to quit, even when the final bullet left the cylinder. He recalled a couple of memorable moments when he had faced Mother Nature.

Once he and a buddy had gone into the forest in late February when the mercury hovered at −15 degrees. They had no tent. They had warmed rocks near the fire until they were hot. Then the men buried the rocks in the dirt and covered them with hemlock boughs. They placed their sleeping bags on the platform above the heated rocks which produced heat and kept them comfortably warm during the night.

Another time Don went hunting small game without food or a tent, challenging himself in a dual with Mother Nature. Although others disagreed with his philosophy, he felt he could always survive in the extremes he faced.

This was one of those extremes.

Thoughts of his family raced through his mind and he prayed. He looked about, trying everything he could think of to escape his predicament. He'd exhausted everything else. What can I do? What else can I try? He contemplated the idea that dead limbs fall from trees. He wondered what a raccoon would do with its paw caught in a trap.

Wyman had been pinned beneath the tree for an hour. He knew it would be at least four more hours until his wife would suspect a problem with his failure to return home. He knew it would be longer than that before help arrived. He considered the idea that shock might overtake him or that he might bleed to death from the compound fracture.

Then it came to him. He knew what he had to do. Cut. His only option was amputation. And he would be the surgeon. He said later, "I could leave my leg here and live." 2

He withdrew his pocket knife from his pocket. It wasn't much of a knife, more of a grease-removal tool he used to clean the cat's grease fittings. It had a 3-inch blade. When he attempted to cut through his pants leg, the blade wouldn't cut.

He found a piece of sandstone and used it as a whet stone, running the knife blade across it. It was nothing he hadn't done on many deer hunts. Before long he cut through his pant leg.

Once through the cloth, he observed the fracture, "When I saw how bad it was, with bones sticking out and my foot smashed, I knew what I had to do. I pulled the starting cord out of my chain saw for a tourniquet. Of course, a tourniquet causes damage when it's on too long. I tied it right above where it was really bad so I'd lose as little leg as possible. Then I cut my skin, sort of scratched it with the knife, to see if there was any feeling. It didn't hurt too bad. So I tried it again a little deeper. That hurt! I doubted I could do it." 2

Knowing that those who fail to persist, fail, he decided to cut around the shattered bones and through the torn flesh 6-inches below the left knee.

"Finally, I decided there was no other way to stay alive. I got myself in a determined state of mind, grabbed my leg with my left hand, resolved not to pull back, and I started cutting where the bones were already broken. It hurt terribly every time I hit a nerve or vein. My muscles jumped like frog legs in a frying pan. But I kept cutting across the top. And then I cut up from underneath until the knife came through and I could pull away.

"Blood was spurting from arteries, so I laid the chain saw wrench across the tourniquet knot, tied another knot over it, and twisted until the spurting stopped. I gave my leg one last look and crawled 140 feet up the hill to my bulldozer." 2

Holding the tourniquet with his left hand, he hobbled along on his right foot. Seriously handicapped by the loss of his left lower leg, the loss of blood and with his energy waning, he attempted to climb onto the supporting arm of the blade on one side of the cat. Failing two or three times to get onto the arm did not dissuade Don. He kept trying. And he finally succeeded in climbing atop the arm.

From there he crawled up the front of the track and dragged himself toward the cab. He reached it, climbed onto the seat of the monster earth mover and started the engine. He threw the automatic transmission into gear. "I was relieved to be on a piece of machinery that would take me someplace. My truck was a quarter of a mile away." 2

When he reached his truck, his standard 4-speed transmission created a new problem. He wasn't sure how he'd shift, but that didn't deter him. He grabbed a file to engage the clutch, shifted into first gear and left for the highway.

In his quest for help, he stopped at two houses. Both seemed deserted, so he drove along his way. At the third place a girl played in the yard. Wyman pulled up and yelled, "Get your dad, I'm bleeding to death." 2

From his dairy barn John Huber, Jr. approached the "yelling madman" cautiously, wondering what was going on. Wyman held up his bloody stump which looked as if it had been blown off by a shotgun. The dairyman rushed inside to call paramedics.

Huber said later, "He was so sharp and mentally strong." 1

Wyman figured they could economize his time and enhance his chances of survival if they drove toward the ambulance. He asked Huber which direction they were coming from. Huber didn't know so Wyman told him to "Go back and ask the dispatcher. It's faster if we meet them halfway." 2

When Huber returned, he slid behind the wheel, started the vehicle and sped off. Huber drove so fast that Wyman asked him to slow down, suggesting that he didn't want to die in a car wreck.

Volunteer firefighters beat the ambulance to the crossroads where Huber and Wyman met them. Wyman drew a map to the location of his missing leg and climbed onto the wheeled stretcher. Ever alert to the possibilities of his continued self-rescue, he refused to take a sedative—he wanted to remain conscious just in case someone else made a mistake.

He did allow them to give him morphine at the hospital. He said, "They had to wash the leg and clamp the arteries. Boy, that hurt! Soon after, they took me to the operating room and did a nicer job than I had. My leg followed me to the hospital by a half-hour, but the doctors said it was too late, they couldn't reattach it. In fact, they said it was probably best that I had cut it off. With all the broken bones in the leg and smashed foot, I would have been hospitalized from six months to two years. It would have taken many operations to reconstruct the bones. Even then, I may never have walked as well as I do now." 2

The Advanced Prosthetic and Limb Bank Foundation decided to allow Wyman to participate as one of 100 amputees in their new "Sense-of-Feeling" technology. Wyman was fitted with a leg from Sabolich Prosthetics and Research Center in Oklahoma City. The prosthetic leg had sensors at the bottom of the foot. He said, "I know when a rock is under my foot. So I can avoid sliding. And it greatly helps my balance to know when the foot touches ground." 2

Don's wife Janet said later, "The only thing he can't stand is being cooped up inside—he'll do anything to stay outdoors." 2

Those who knew Don Wyman attested to his spirit and will to live. Although it was a surprise for them to learn that he'd lost his leg, they seemed to feel that his self-amputation fit him to a "T." They would expect no less of his independent spirit and determination.

Don was back at work within three months of the accident. His story traveled the nation and beyond, amazing people unknown to him. But those who knew the real Don Wyman all along—his wife Janet, son Brian, boss David Osikowicz and friends, figured him to be a man who would have fit in well with the hardiest of Old World explorers, mountain men of the Old West or Klondike era gold seekers.

SOURCE NOTES:

1. "Man cuts broken leg off with knife," *Anchorage Daily News*, pg. A5, July 22, 1993

2. "A Choice for Life," Larry Mueller, *Outdoor Life*, pp. 62-66, July 1994

At The Lake's Mercy

by Larry Kaniut

Man dies after driving truck into lake, troopers say

SKILAK: 9-year-old survives 17 hours in cold after dad helps him, family dog to shore.

TATABOLINE BRANT, *Anchorage Daily News*, March 3, 2004

I rewrote this newspaper article June 2021 and titled it *At the Lake's Mercy.*

Call the culprit drowning or hypothermia. Skilak Lake has claimed the lives of more than two dozen people by way of one or the other. The 10-mile-long lake is popular among hunters and anglers and numerous cabins line its shores. Like many remote waterways in Alaska, parts of Skilak Lake are used like roads in the winter months by vehicles and snow machines.

Crossing the ice was normal during winter months...nothing new. Forty-two-year-old Autumn Doxsee, her son Miles Richardson and friend John Connell III, both 17, pulled a U-Haul trailer from the lake's boat launch. Approaching Caribou Island, the ice cracked beneath them, partially submerging their truck. The three occupants climbed out of the sinking vehicle onto the ice, wet and cold, and walked to an island cabin where Robert Klotz Jr., 49, gave them shelter. After they had warmed up, he helped them to their cabin, not far away. When Autumn discovered the empty cabin, she thought that her husband had stopped at another cabin or turned back. They spent the night. Around 10:30 a.m. Tuesday with the GMC missing, a multi-agency search was launched.

Alaska State Troopers said the family was ferrying supplies from their home in Kenai to their cabin on Skilak Lake and had made several trips. Traveling in separate vehicles—A U-Haul and a GMC pickup—about an hour and a half apart.

Adrien Doxsee, 56, and his son Ryder, 9, drove onto the lake in a pickup truck with their dog Pebbles around 10:30 p.m. Monday night. They left from a boat launch on the lake's north shore and headed west. Troopers say tracks suggest Doxsee drove straight off the ice into open water where the Kenai River drains from the lake.

Doxsee climbed out one window and his son broke and climbed out of another window. The pair and the dog made it to the edge of the ice, but the boy could not pull himself up. While ice kept breaking beneath him, Ryder's father pulled him up onto the ice. They reached shore where they huddled with Pebbles in order to stay warm, surrounded by trees. Doxsee gave his son a lighter to make a fire and told him he was going back to the truck to get something. At daylight, the boy went down to the ice and found his father dead. He returned to the trees with his dog.

Around noon on Tuesday, a wildlife trooper searching in a plane spotted Doxsee's body on the ice. He had apparently died of hypothermia. His truck was found about 30 minutes later, submerged about 10 feet under the ice but still visible.

The Kenai Peninsula Borough's Central Emergency Service's dive team began looking for Ryder while other searchers canvassed the lake's shores. When no bodies were found in the truck, the searchers redoubled their efforts on land.

Around 3:30 p.m. -- some 17 hours after the accident -- a trapper on snow machine, working with searchers, spotted Ryder and Pebbles on the southwest shore of the lake, alive. The boy was wearing a snow machine suit and a down jacket. He was conscious but hypothermic, stated Sgt. Craig MacDonald said. The boy was rushed to Central Peninsula Hospital, where he was reunited with his mother. Central Peninsula Hospital reported that Ryder was recovering Tuesday from hypothermia and frostbitten feet.

Pebbles fled from rescuers but U.S. forestry officials will try again to catch the dog.

Date With Death

by Larry Kaniut

I first heard about Paul Coleman over the radio news about Wednesday the eleventh of November, 1992. As always my ears perked up and I wondered and hoped that searchers would find him. His disappearance was compounded by the fact that his insulin and syringes were found in his pickup.

I wanted to help in the search but had committed to take Laura Lee (sister) with Pam (wife) and me to Lewiston, Idaho, on the 13th. The following week the official search was called off. I wanted to help out, but I was committed to help Pam wrap up her Christmas shopping prior to leaving for Anchorage the 20th. When I heard the news during the week, I decided to go help on Saturday the 21st.

I called Larry Coleman the evening of the 20th to make sure I could get to the searcher rendezvous efficiently the next day. He informed me that I needed to go to mile 31 east of Estacada and turn left at the marker to space 1 of the Silver Bow RV Park. He told me to look for Bruce or Barbara Coleman or Curtis Bunch. I set the clock for 5:40 in anticipation of a little over an hour's drive.

I got up and awakened daughter Jill (as she'd requested--wanted to make me breakfast and lunch, but I told her I had some things in my pack already). I headed out in a driving rain and wind, listening to the radio for news as I traveled 99W to I-5 to 205 and ultimately the Estacada off ramp.

Black enshrouded everything, rain hammered the land, puddling on the roadway. There was little traffic. As I rolled along, country and western sounds honkey tonked from the radio--Tanya Tucker belted out "Two Sparrows in a Hurricane" and Alabama crooned "I'm in a Hurry and Don't Know Why." The weather man warned of strong 60 or 65 mile per hour winds along Oregon's north coast with strong gusts to be felt in the Portland-Cascade Mountain areas. At the I-5 overpass at Tualatin, I got my first glimpse of light--layered gray clouds blanketed the eastern sky.

Windshield wipers rhythmically thumped. I increased my speed to 65 and the Suburban shuddered side to side with sporadic wind blasts. A ghostly eighteen-wheeler loomed ahead, crowned with amber lights and lumbering along, water spewing from its tandem wheels.

I kept a steady speed toward Estacada and when I'd left her eastern boundary, I enjoyed the rural scenery in the lightening dawn- -farms, barns, outbuildings. Highway 224 snaked along, large trees dotting the shoulders. After half dozen miles the 45 mile speed limit evolved into 55, and I stair stepped up into the Cascades through a few fog patches.

I didn't see the milepost at 32 but caught the RV sign out of the corner of my eye and made a hasty turn, zoomed up the asphalt to the park, discovered three or four dozen vehicles scattered along the roadway near camp trailers. A guy told me to head up to the recreation center.

I slogged through the muddied ground under the fir trees to the center. A Red Cross wagon and an ambulance were parked outside. I entered and discovered a gathering of nearly fifty people--mostly men. Two guys were informing the searchers about the search plan. Spread before Curtis Bunch (?) was a large black and white topo map with grease pen markings designating the area that had previously been searched.

A lady (maybe his sister ?) came in showed the searchers a syringe like Paul's and made some comments about it and being careful. Announcements were made about where to get pancakes for breakfast and sandwiches to take along.

Two groups of seven men were to work together in a grid search where Paul's pack had been found. I caught a ride with Robert O'Brien, a builder from Aurora, and we joined a caravan of eight other vehicles driving east toward Detroit. Ten miles before we got to a mountain road we encountered snow along the roadway (and hit one thirty to fifty yard stretch of four inches in the road).

Due to a miscommunication we lost Greg, our leader. After several minutes he appeared and we went on ahead. By the time we reached the search area a mile and a half from the highway we were in six to eight inches of very wet snow, and it was about 10:30 a.m. We exited our vehicles, put on our raingear and walked down a side road, spread out twenty feet apart and started into the woods. There were fifteen of us spread out over 100-120 yards.

A flagger was on the end to mark our path, and we kicked along in the snow for a half mile to the next road. Then we regrouped, moved another length up the road and started back for the first road. We covered more territory and regrouped about noon. After a brief consultation it was jointly agreed to eat lunch, warm up and resume the search after returning from a newly located base camp closer than the RV park.

We drove back down the mountain into snowless country, found the new camp, pulled in to a roaring camp fire. The Red Cross wagon was dispensing chili, hot dogs, coffee, hot chocolate and pop. As Robert and I surmised, the search was over for the day. It was after 1 o'clock; and we figured we wouldn't get back on the road until 2; it would be an hour to the search area, and we'd have only a half hour to search.

It was disappointing to us as we had wanted to continue the search. Robert and I had mentioned we could gobble a sandwich at the search area, eliminate the long drive to and from base camp and stay with our objective. But the officials chose to return to camp.

We left that camp for the original base camp and checked out. At that time we learned from a woman that Paul's car had been moved from his hunting area (or at least somewhere up the highway where he had made a phone call to his wife) to a lower area (Memaloose) which had been the object of the original, thorough search.

In introspection, I was amazed by the apparel and mind set of those who came to assist in the search. Their volunteerism was admirable, however their wilderness skills were greatly lacking.

At least three men did not have gloves. One wore tennis shoes. Most wore rubberized-LL Bean type rubber boot packs. A third wore Helly Hansen type rain gear. Others wore rubber coats; one had a GI olive drab coat; many wore fabric coats. I was the only one wearing a poncho.

People periodically wrung rain water from their gloves as it continued to rain hard the entire time.

SOURCE NOTES:

From *The Oregonian*, February 2, 1993, appeared the article "Missing hunter's body found," by Dennis McCarthy and Steven Amick.

This article highlighted the recovery of Paul Robert Coleman's body and theorized about the cause of his death. The body of the 28-year-old Portland man was found on the bank of the river by a man and his son while they prepared to pan gold near the confluence of the north and south forks of the Clackamas River.

Deputy medical examiner Jeff McLennan indicated there was no evidence of foul play. It was uncertain whether Coleman's death was caused by his inability to medicate himself with insulin. A diabetic, Paul Coleman left his insulin in his pickup ten miles southeast of Estacada. It was found the day after his proposed return from the hunting trip. The pickup was originally parked a mile upstream from where the deceased was found.

Captain Donald A. Vicars of the Clakamas Country Sheriff's Office theorized that Coleman "might have fallen from a steep embankment above the river and become entangled in some tree." Vicars said "the victim could have been picked up by the river when the water was high from winter storms and carried to the spot where his body was located." Vicars theorized, "it would have been very possible to have missed Coleman because of the steep terrain and the trees and bushes, making it difficult to get tracking dogs to the area." (page B-3)

I was saddened by the loss of this young man and wish he could have been found. His loss further decries the need to have a partner when you go into the field, because, all too often, the common place evolves into catastrophe.

Berry Bad Trip

by Larry Kaniut

This is a rough draft of which I listed several possible titles. I thought it might be interesting for the reader to get a view of the process of "writing" a story. You may wish to see a few other rough drafts in the appendix of Swallowed Alive, Volume 2. In the fall of 1992, I interviewed Dennis. I drove from Lewiston, Idaho, to Dennis' place near Troy, Montana, hoping the hour time zone change wouldn't mess me up. His story follows, in his words.

Possible titles:

A Mountain Tragedy	Getting on with Life
You Can't Take it Back	Mistake on a Mountain
Berry Trip Gone Awry	One Man's Mistake
Know Your Target	Know What You're Shooting At
Tragedy in the Woods	

Chapter quotes:

"I struggled-frantically stabbing with my elbows and pulling... stab, pull; stab, pull...I felt no pain, but my mind was bombarded with thoughts..."

"'Vengeance is mine saith the Lord'. I'll let Him deal with that because I'm pretty busy with the important things in life."

A solitary figure sat beside the forest access road, taking in the grandeur of the surroundings. It was another gorgeous Montana Big Sky day. The fact that he'd just rolled his truck and had to hoof it back to camp wasn't so depressing in light of his freedom and gratitude for life. It was a great day! He was happy to be alive.

Dennis Williams had left camp that morning to pick huckleberries. He was a 47 year-old self-employed seed collector. He headquartered in a mobile home on the Montana-Idaho state line, but he spent days on end camped in the woods to facilitate his work. Ten years previous he had left his office overlooking the Windsor Bridge in downtown

Detroit. He'd been burnt out on the politics of working in the human services field as a psychologist. With a vague concept of going to the West Coast, he left Michigan behind in search of some alternative things for his life.

The same day Dennis rolled his truck and on the same road, two hunters bounced along in a pickup truck. They were Larry Bowman and Rodney Cymbaluk. The 38-year-old Bowman maneuvered his pickup down Southside Road just north of Troy, Montana, talking with his 40-year-old buddy Rodney Cymbaluk. The country teemed with deer, bear, mountain lion and elk. Bear abounded in this vicinity (a hundred bear have been shot within twenty miles of here). It was opening day of bear season. Bowman and Cymbaluk scanned the roadside and forest in search of their prey. The sun had dropped behind a mountain, and they knew dusk was not far off. Their plans to fill a tag were inching closer.

It was September 7, 1991. Wearing a pair of light forest green, denim pants and a long sleeved brown and white checkered shirt Dennis Williams rolled up his sleeves because it was so hot. His other attire included a white T-shirt, a baseball hat and lace up, light tan woods boots.

He jostled along in his old International Harvester pickup looking for huckleberries. He was about ten miles out of Troy on Southside Road which follows the Kootenai River downstream to Bonner's Ferry, Idaho. It was a typical single lane, dirt mountain road used by the U.S. Forest Service, loggers, hunters, berry pickers and other outdoors people. Five miles from his base camp, he played thoughts across the big screen of his mind, about his past, seed prospects and his future plans.

When I went to college, I debated whether or not to go into forestry or psychology. Kind of a strange combination. Back in the '60's forestry was a very hard thing to get involved with. For instance Michigan Technological University, an engineering school, was the only formally registered forestry school in the state of Michigan. I was tired of numbers and all that stuff. I wanted to do something else. So I did.

I spent every free moment in the woods or in the garden. Every summer while I was going to school I landscaped. Since I've always been into nature, it just seemed to dovetail into my lifestyle. Now, jokingly, I say I can get trees to talk to me.

Suddenly I'm jarred alert to the business at hand. Failing to make a slight turn, my pickup left the shoulder of the road and struck a tree.

I fought the wheel and jammed on the brakes. The truck did not respond. I bounced down the embankment, careening off fir trees. In a heartbeat my pickup turned over, smashing onto its top. The windows shattered and gas spewed from the tank of the still running engine. Knowing that my lit cigarette could ignite an explosion given the right circumstances, I scrambled from the truck cab through the passenger's window. How could I know that the truck's left front hub had fallen apart, rendering the vehicle unsteerable?

Fortunately the only damage was to my truck. I headed down the road for my base camp. I'd gone probably three quarters of a mile when I decided to take a cigarette break. I sat down on a rock beside the road in a clear, straight stretch that couldn't have been a hundred and fifty yards long. Grass grew probably eight inches to a foot high on that east slope.

I had just lit my cigarette when I heard a vehicle approaching. I went, "Haaa. Boy! It's really going to be great. I'm gonna get a ride to camp." Theoretically woods people help others.

It was maybe six, six-thirty in the evening. The sun was over the edge of the mountain. It wasn't dark yet, but after six o'clock in September it starts getting dark really quickly. It had been a really hot day, probably 90 degrees in Troy; and it was probably still in the 70's where I was.

I looked down the road to my left and saw the vehicle coming with its headlights on. The vehicle stopped. Then it started forward again. I just looked down the road and thought, "Well, they see a deer. They're gonna shoot the deer or take a picture of it." It was legal hunting hours.

The truck came forward five, ten, fifteen yards...and eased to a stop.

I didn't move. I didn't know where the deer was. I figured if I stand up and scare it off, these guys will get ticked off and won't give me a ride back to camp. I turned back and was looking directly across the road.

I heard a shot and simultaneously a bullet ripped into my left knee cap. The bullet mushroomed and hit my right leg at mid-thigh, all but blowing it off—the leg was hanging by a thread of meat and skin. "Holy shit! I better hide," I thought.

When you're sitting on a rock in grass, there's no place to hide. My only hope was to get to the timber across the road, so that's where I headed. I dropped into the grass and started crawling, using my elbows to paddle-drag myself across the dirt road.

I struggled-frantically stabbing with my elbows and pulling...stab, pull; stab, pull...dragging two useless legs and trailing a stream of blood. I felt no pain, but my mind was bombarded with thoughts... Who's shooting? Why are they shooting at me? Can I hide? Will I live? What will I do in the woods when I get there?

I was almost a third of the way across the road when I was hit again. I couldn't believe it. I had taken a slug in the back. I decided I better just be still...I was still alive and still conscious. And I was not pleased!

I'm thinking, "Ah, shit. What's going on here?" I didn't move or do anything. I held my breath. I heard the vehicle coming. I was lying in the road diagonally with my back to the vehicle. I thought, "I wonder if they're going to come up here and finish me off or what the hell's going on?"

But I wasn't moving. I didn't want to move at all. If I move one more time, they shoot me one more time; and then I'd be dead. The way those bullets were tearing chunks out of my flesh I thought, "Oh, man, this is not cool."

I heard men's voices through the open windows of the pickup. I heard something about, "Oh, my God, it is a man!" Then I heard the door open.

I thought, "Maybe I can look now and see if he's gonna kill me. At least I can see who's gonna kill me." I looked over there and the guy didn't have a gun. It was Rodney Cymbaluk. He came running up and yelled, "Oh, Jesus Christ..." He said, "Oh, my God, it is a man, it is a man!"

I said, "You got that part right, buddy. I don't think I'm going to make it down off the hill. Will you tell some people..." I was gonna give him my last will and testament right there. There's blood all over the place and blood's comin' out of my legs. I was just a mess.

So they said, "Oh, yeah. You can make it. We'll take you down to Troy."

I said, "I don't want to go to Troy!"

Five miles away, near my camp there's a water truck (used for watering the roads), and it has a really big time CB. Not only that, there's a paved road all the way into Bonner's Ferry. We could call on the CB and scoot right into Bonner's Ferry. So we had an argument, but I wasn't in much condition to argue. And Cymbaluk said, "We'll get you down off the hill. You're gonna make it."

I said, "Okay."

I asked him," In the process then, how we gonna stop this leg from bleeding? You got any rope?"

Cymbaluk says, "Yeah, we got some rope. Bowman goes to the truck, cuts a chunk off and ties my shattered leg off, making a tourniquet out of the rope.

I said, "Okay, now my left one. I don't think we can do much about it right now."

The driver Bowman says, "Ah, yeah we can," and rips off his shirt and used it as a compress.

They picked me up, put me in the back of the truck and down the road we went lickety split. Cymbaluk was back there with me. He was holding me and talking to me all the time, "Jesus Christ, I'm sorry. I thought you were a bear. I thought you were a bear. I had no idea."

By the time we got into Troy it was pitch black. We stopped where the driver saw somebody that he knew. I assumed it was the Silver Spur, a restaurant-bar. I heard Bowman yell, "Hey, we've got a gunshot wound in the back. Get in and call."

We ended up at the ambulance station downtown. They patched me up as best they could in the back of the pickup and asked me if I could walk. I was still conscious and said, "Oh, yeah. I can walk." (I've got one leg shot off and one broken; and I got up and, assisted by ambulance people, walked to the ambulance).They had removed the tourniquets and replaced them with air splints.

The helicopter from Sacred Heart in Spokane, Washington, was delayed a little bit, so the paramedics thought maybe what they ought to do was run me to Libby. At the Libby hospital, the medical staff did some basic first aid and asked me what my blood type was.

I had no pain in my legs nor my back—they were numb—until they got me to the hospital in Libby. Then people started prodding and poking me. I was surrounded by doctors and assistants. They were looking for a vein for an I.V. and trying to get my blood pressure. The doctor taking my blood pressure said, "This guy isn't gonna make it. I've got blood pressure 10 over 30."

I was talking to another doctor who told me to scream if it hurt. "You're damned right it hurts!" I screamed. It was something else.

By now I was experiencing major pain from the air splint on my right leg. All the pressure stopped at my groin. None of my injuries hurt, but my leg at the top of the splint was killing me. I told them, "Come on, man, you want to take this thing off!"

I screamed and hollered at people for a while. One lady said, "The helicopter's coming for you." I'd never been wounded, never been in a helicopter, never flown, nothing. So I told her that I wasn't really too keen on flying to Spokane. She told me I was in no shape to walk.

She must have been embarrassed because after she that, she said, "I'm sorry."

I started laughing and swung at the oxygen mask they were trying to put on me. I said, "Get it away from me. I want to talk." I kept swinging at it. I've got one broken leg; one leg's blown off; one damned arm I can't even move. I've only got one arm to swing with.

I was screaming and hollering. I didn't care what they thought. I was claustrophobic. I was hyper-ventilating. I was in shock. The whole nine yards. All I knew was that I didn't want that oxygen mask on me. I knew if they put that on my face, I was gonna die. I yelled, "Get it away from me!" I was pretty wild.

The nurse said, "How about if I just put it there for a couple of seconds; and I won't strap it to your face?"

I said, "That'd be cool."

The helicopter picked me up, and I'm kind of fighting this flying. I'm frightened. Finally I relented thinking, "Oh, shit, if I made it this far, I must be able to make it the rest of the way."

They wouldn't let me go to sleep. I kept telling them if I could only close my eyes and take a little nap...but they kept jostling me to keep me awake. It was about seventy-five minutes by helicopter to Sacred Heart.

They wheeled me in and started doing the same stuff they'd done at Libby. They were going to do blood type. And they wanted to know what happened. I got tired of telling people what happened. It seemed like all 4,138 employees asked me the same question.

First off, a doctor tried to take my thoughts away from my leg wounds. He's going, "You've got a blood vessel in your shoulder just about ready to go."

The bullet missed that major artery by 3/16ths of an inch but the shock coagulated the blood. The impact of the bullet missed the main artery going down into the right arm—it produced a blood clot that shut everything off, resulting in insignificant blood loss compared to what I lost in my legs. That's the reason I didn't bleed to death. Three sixteenths of an inch more and kiss it goodbye. I wouldn't be here.

They finally put me under. Eighteen hours later I awoke and was pretty immobile. My left leg was in a cast from my groin to my toes.

My right one was, obviously, not even a leg—they'd chopped it off. I couldn't move my leg, and I could barely use my left hand.

My wife and I were estranged at the time. When I became conscious in intensive care and opened my eyes, there's my wife and my best friend, Pat. That was pretty wild. Pat smoked, and I just kind of looked up, reached out with one hand, grabbed her hand and started sniffing it for the tobacco. They figured if I wanted a cigarette, I was going to make it.

After two days they decided they couldn't do anything more for me in intensive care, so they moved me to another floor. I got telephone calls from sharks, lots of attorneys, television producers, newspaper and magazine people.

I did agree to do an interview with People Magazine (September 30, 1991) because most of the press coverage was totally inaccurate. I wanted the story told accurately for people to know what was going on. The photographer and the writer came to Sacred Heart even before the medical staff operated on my left leg a second time to insert pins. The article was pretty accurate; I insisted on that.

That article and the constant barrage of questions from everybody helped me to deal with my accident; but being a psychologist helped me too.

It was like people were forcing me to deal with it, like every nurse that came in wanted to know about it. Charge nurses were the ones who wanted to take care of me. Always the top person on staff. You wonder who was my doctor on the rehab? It was the director of rehab. Who was my physical therapist? The director of physical therapy. People treated me with kid gloves. And I'm going, "Okay, this is cool."

A week later they put some pins in my left leg to stabilize my femur. Then I started getting phantom pains big time in my amputated right leg. I had to go on some strange medication. After the first month in the hospital I could move around a little bit. By the time they could actually weigh me I weighed 137 1/2 pounds. I'm 6' 1 1/2" and weighed 160 pounds before the accident.

The second month in the hospital I spent in rehabilitation and got a prosthesis. Learning to walk with a prosthetic device is hard when two joints are involved. You have to account for both the ankle and the knee joints, so it's more difficult than allowing for just the ankle joint. I hiked around and learned to walk on it really well I thought. About the first of November, when I'd been there a couple of days less than two months, they kicked me out of the hospital, said, "There's no reason for you to be here anymore."

When I left the hospital, I didn't go back to my mobile home. One of my friends had a month's business in California and Arizona. He asked me to stay in his house. As it turned out, he wasn't gone for a month—he was gone four months. So I spent the winter care taking his country house between Troy, Montana, and Idaho.

Of course I was not in the best of shape when I got out. I was really under weight. I could eat prodigious amounts of food, and it didn't make any difference—I never gained a pound until March, and then I put on twenty pounds in the next few months.

I could walk fairly well with my prosthesis and a cane when I left the hospital. I was a little hesitant of snow and ice, but at least I could get around, and I didn't fall too much.

I still have pain, but it's intermittent. I get some really bad days where I get probably five hundred jolts a day. Sometimes it feels like about two thousand volts of electricity hit me down there in the foot that I don't even have. And it'll go right to my big toe. Sometimes I'll be sitting here and people watch as I jerk with pain. They go, "Whoa, you must have had another one of them little zingers."

And I go, "Boy, did I ever."

To date my financial losses including medical bills, lost wages and earning capacity are at least $150,000. I had seed orders of approximately $100,000 last year. Needless to say I didn't get too many of them. I had some seeds harvested before the accident, but they went to waste because I wasn't around to take care of them.

I'm not a veteran, didn't belong to the National Rifle Association and had no insurance. Fortunately the social workers and financial advisors at Sacred Heart talked me right through that, and we got lots of that stuff covered through public assistance.

I moved to Troy the first of April and immediately started going into the woods collecting seeds and mushrooms. I was still getting letters and calls (eight months after the accident) from people who had read or heard about me. People from veterans' hospitals read the thing in People Magazine and wrote me wanting to know how I could be so positive, resilient and non-combative.

They wrote, "I was sitting here feeling sorry for myself; and I guess all you want to do is go back to living."

And I'm goin', "Yeah, I see the alternative is no fun, man."

I received marriage proposals. I got some of the most bizarre requests you'd ever want to read...people wanted to take care of me the rest of my life. Hundreds, hundreds, hundreds of letters. People even sent money. It was pretty strange.

Several attorneys called me wanting to take my case. The attorneys that I talked to at any length understood me when I said, "I think it's more important for me to get on with the business of living than it is for me to drag this thing out."

Besides here's what happens in a court of law. I can sue the guy. Yeah, I'm gonna win. It's a given. So if he has an attorney worth his salt (and he did), the attorney will tell him, "The day that judgment is against you, file bankruptcy...or in the process you put all this stuff in your wife's name or your parents' name." The guy who shot me was worth a few bucks plus his insurance.

I went to Libby and gave a deposition to Cymbaluk's attorney. He said, "Weren't you a little alarmed when you saw two guys standing outside the truck with guns pointed at you?"

I looked him right square in the eye and said, "You tell me they were standing outside. I looked! They weren't outside the truck. Them s--- a b-----s shot me out the window because they didn't have their doors open. They didn't open the door on that truck until they got to me."

I could read his mind, "Oh, oh. I don't want this guy on the stand."

I asked the attorney about Cymbaluk's "it is a man" comment (when the hunters approached me in the truck), and he said, "There is some debate. As they got closer to you, they realized that perhaps it didn't quite look like a bear after all."

I did settle with Cymbaluk's insurance company, homeowner's policy of all things. And I was satisfied with that. Most of my medical was covered. I've got just a couple of odd bills that are floating around yet from that, nothing really significant. I've got two, maybe three thousand dollars something like that out of around $75,000 in medical bills.

The settlement with Cymbulak, the guy who shot me, gives me enough money to live on for many, many years. I mean not high on the hog. I can't eat steaks every night, but then I'm not a steak man anyway. They pay me for the next fifteen, twenty years through his insurance company. (As a matter of fact I need to get down to the post office right now cause there's a check for the first of November.)

Bowman's insurance company thought there was a little fault there, and they were getting a little worried because I wasn't in any hurry to sign a release. They dangled a carrot and I took it. I started this business officially so I could buy a couple of reliable vehicles and some reliable cleaning equipment. I sunk more than $15,000 into the seed business.

I guess I don't really bear those people any animosity, but what I would really like to see is for them never to hunt again. I think that shooting someone in a similar situation is inexcusable. The law in Montana reads such that Cymbulak got penalized to the full extent of the law.

He got fined a thousand dollars and had his hunting privileges taken away for two years. I don't think that's fair. I think two years is a crock—go rob a bank or shoot a moose. Shoot a grizzly bear—they take away your birthday. And shoot me? And it cost you a thousand dollars? And you can't hunt for two years?

As far as giving suggestions to others, my experience with scopes is that they collect light, they don't disperse it. Had I been hunting with open sights, I would not have shot. Both these guys had scopes.

Had I known I was the target, I would have made a lot of noise and let the hunters know I was a man. My suggestion to hunters is that they always make sure what's behind their target; and always know what you're shooting at.

Satchel Paige said, "Never look back because whatever's chasing you might be catching up." Although I'm not a Christian, I try to live a reasonably moral life—makes me feel better. "Vengeance is mine saith the Lord." I'll let Him deal with that because I'm pretty busy with the important things in life.

Sometimes my lack of mobility makes for frustrating days. I can no longer gather seeds wherever I want to, and it takes a long time to get the ones I can get to.

Fortunately, I do have other skills that provide me relief from that frustration. I like marketing (you have to not only collect and clean seeds, but you also have to sell them), teaching (here's the most efficacious way to collect those fruits, etc.) and writing (have to do catalogs, collector's guidelines and day to day business correspondence).

Some advantages of being "stove up" (which may give you an inkling of how I cope):

People don't ask me to help them move anymore.

I only have to cut five toenails.

I don't have to change my right sock.

I save water bathing.

So often our plans go awry. On September 7, 1991, on Southside Road near Troy, Montana, two paths crossed. One party was hunting wild game. One was picking huckleberries. The hunters did not get their game; the berry picker did not get his berries. Neither party knew about the other. But within minutes circumstances changed the men's plans. And their lives will never be the same.

Lying Low

by Glen Guy

Glen Guy formerly sang with Glen Campbell and was performing 7 nights a week from May through September at the Sourdough Mining Company in Anchorage. One day surrounded by tourists as I signed books across the street from the restaurant where Glen entertained, he strode over. The grizzled looking Old Sourdough pulled a long barreled hog leg from its leather holster, pointed it at me and said, "There ain't room in this town for both of us."

Tourists stood in stunned disbelief...before he asked me to substitute one night for him so he could have a break.

After many years' dedicated service to the Mining Company, Glen and his wife have taken his show on the road promoting his new activity, Prospectors for God.

Son-in-law Brad Risch and I spent a weekend in Fairbanks, Alaska, with our friend Glen for a book signing. Known by his stage name as Dusty Sourdough, he told us that he'd been a pilot during the Viet Nam war. I was quite surprised but amazed when he told us about his experience—shot down twice, the first time by small arms fire before punching out over water and being rescued within 15 seconds; the second time...well that's Glen's story which follows.

I flew in an A 4 squadron, VMA 223. My actual assignment was 1969 but we didn't get there until 1970 when I was 25-years-old. I was originally flying out of Kwan Tre. There were a lot of rockets at Kwan Tre at that time, planes being parked in bunkers saw hangars still get taken out. There were quite a lot of losses to the Marines on the Constellation.

They asked for volunteers for the Constellation. I had carrier training and I preferred being on a carrier to being rocketed every night. I got assigned temporarily to the USS Constellation. I liked it so well I asked for permanent duty there.

We were assigned several sorties a week. We were flying in areas that were very dangerous—for one thing we were beyond the reach of rescue helicopters and if we got shot down, they would have to figure ways to get us out.

We consider an A 4 a light bomber fighter and it was very agile. Even when they came out with the F 15's, we still used the A 4 for training purpose because it was so much more agile. It was small compared to all the other fighters. If you had any problems with an A 4, it's going to go down very fast. It doesn't have very good glide characteristics.

After several missions off the Constellation, I had been very lucky it seems like. I avoided getting any real hits. I had small arms fire hits…nothing ever destroyed my confidence. I think all fighter pilots are very confident.

It was the start of monsoon season. It rained heavily in the north quite a bit. We had a lot of our missions scrubbed because of the weather. Finally we got the okay for a mission that we were flying and we took off with six planes in a flight. Two of them came back because of mechanical problems, which left us with four.

We were flying into a valley that we knew was protected by surface to air missiles, SAM's. The flight leader was in the first pass. We were dropping straight ordinance trying to take out a bridge. That was before the laser guided bombs and stuff. It was all up to the pilot. Our flight leader went in and took a direct hit before he even got to the bridge.

And I was right behind him and I saw that he had made it out, his chute had opened. I went ahead and—dropped…not that I could do any damage. When I saw the bridge, you'd have to be really lucky to hit the bridge. It was such an angle that you couldn't get a good straight run at it. I pulled up and someone behind me hollered "missile's on the way!" By the time I turned around, looked back behind me, I saw stuff was really flying…and I was out of control.

As far as I was concerned, I took a direct hit. It had clipped me in the tail section but the missile didn't go off—I happened to have a sheer problem. What happened was not only did that take me out of the sky but it ignited a lot of fire but nothing blew up. I had already jettisoned all my bombs and we had flown in far enough that we didn't have any external fuel tanks, all we had was what was in the wings.

The little bit of glide that I had, I glided on up into the valley and I was ejecting because the plane was already tumbling and coming apart. There was no control. I had a fire in the cockpit. Hydraulic fluid had caught on fire, burnt my whole left hand. When I hit the ground, I knew right away that I was deep enough in northern territory that I was more or less going to be captured.

I wasn't ready for that. My education…my degree is in wilderness survival plus with the training in wilderness survival in the military in the SARs class, I thought I could evade them long enough to get somebody there to rescue me even though we were way too far in for a helicopter to make it and get us out. So I started heading north. I thought if I keep going north, I'd be moving away from them because they'd be coming toward me trying to capture me. So I started north.

The first day I had evaded the initial stage and I realized that they knew all the routes out but probably they weren't paying too much attention to the routes going deeper in and didn't know their way around any better than I did. Coming out they would have had ambushes set up and probably would have captured me within twenty-four hours.

I never walked a straight trail. You couldn't to begin with. I had no idea where I was going or how far I was going north before I started turning back. All I wanted to do was head toward the coast if it was south. When I started out, I had no plan. All I knew was that I was not going to be sitting in a prisoner of war situation. It wasn't in me to have that happen. I know everybody believes that. I knew that I was not going to be captured. I would not surrender my .45 at that particular time or the weapons that I picked up along the way.

I had a serious problem. My hand was burnt down to the meat and I had to do something with that. I didn't have a whole lot of meds. Survival is about a three day thing normally for any planes shot down. If you're not found in three days, you're pretty much written off. I didn't know at that time that I'd been written off.

I had to do something with my hand; it was getting infected. I had to find water. When you're up in the mountains, the highlands, you don't get to see that very often in the war movies and everything. They show you all the muddy water; but they have pristine streams just like we do. I finally got a little bit of a break, during the day I would find some place where I could lie with my hand in the water and still be in good enough surroundings that I couldn't be detected by somebody trying to find me.

I don't know if you've ever had a burn or not but that cold water feels really good. I kept thinking about washing it out, getting it cleaned. I spent hours with my hand lying down on a stream. I would lie with my hand in the stream until it shriveled up. It looked like an old man's hand. It started clearing up. There were a lot of plants that seemed medicinal. I found some that I thought would work, just putting it on there. Within about four weeks or so my hand started feeling…and it looked good and everything was still moving. So I figured I was over the bad part.

At nightfall I sought out monkey trees. I knew that not only our military stay away from them but also the enemy stayed away from them. In a monkey tree once you get up there and they quiet down, they treat you like you're one of them. They just ignore you. I had one befriend me as a matter of fact. He hung out with me for a long time. I wanted to keep him. I would hide up in the trees and if anybody or anything were sneaking around anywhere close, the monkeys would go off. That was a warning for the people not to come underneath it. They wouldn't come underneath, look up and see me. I'd find a crotch in a tree and that's where I slept.

After being on the ground and seeing some fresh tiger tracks, I thought I needed to be aware that there were tigers. I had a tiger follow me for a while. That's when I thought of finding a rifle because I did not want to deal with a tiger with a .45.

I managed to move off a lot of the trails. Up there, in that part of Viet Nam, they didn't have a lot of booby traps they have down in the areas. It was mostly North Vietnamese Regulars up there, not a whole lot of VC. They would every now and then send squads of regulars into these Montenyard villages. To be truthful with you, I survived for eight months but I wouldn't have if it wouldn't have been for Montenyards. They really took care of me.

I was being chased more than once by small units of military. I would get into some of these Montenyard villages and they would hide me out. I've seen some things happening... because they knew I was up there and they couldn't ever find me because of the villagers who sacrificed their lives. A lot of them did sacrifice their lives. I would hide out. They would feed me. They'd take care of me. I lost a lot of weight. I was only like a hundred thirty-one pounds anyway when I entered the military. I was probably down to about ninety-six, ninety-seven pounds. They fed me. I remember them sacrificing a lot.

Some villages, I believe that however they communicate, a lot of places knew who I was when I was coming. After a period of time jungle stories go around I guess and they knew when I told them who I was they all smiled and shook their heads. They tried to communicate. By then I'd learned how to speak a little Vietnamese, you have to. You communicate with just a little bit of pidgin English and your reputation precedes you. Most of them wanted me in and out of their village because if the NVA showed up, they would turn the villages upside down if they even had an idea that I'd been there. I survived mainly because of them and what I had learned in college, how to survive in the wilderness, how to move about. People would envision that I was being Rambo but I was scared every day.

Spiders and snakes. We had some BIG snakes, really big snakes. We had spiders over there that were the size of dinner plates. I'm highly allergic to bee stings. I worried about bees the whole time I was there. One of the little critters I saw a couple of weeks after was probably about four or five inches long, flying. Looked just like a bee. It was solid black and around its butt was a red stinger hanging out. I just knew if that ever stung me, I would probably die.

Like I say, it was monsoon season so it was never dry. I had jungle rot on my feet, no dry socks, no dry boots.

Three North Vietnamese guys were chasing me. They were really relentless. They just kept after me and kept after me. I know that they knew how to track really well—these guys were obviously trackers. I figured with the rains and mud and everything I could walk and there would be no footprints. But they were still following me. I finally decided they were either going to kill me or I was going to have to kill them. I had to figure out some way to get them off my trail.

I waited until the rain got really bad and I stopped and circled back around. There was a trail going up the mountain and there was another one that was kind of "Y"-ing off. I thought that must be one that's going down, for whatever reason maybe I can go down and come back up and catch up to them from the back.

It did work out that way. When I went down and started back across, I started back up the trail. These guys had evidently given up for the day and they had set up their little bivouac area—they had something very similar to our ponchos that the military uses to put together to make a shelter out of it. They had set up a shelter to cook their rice and dried fish.

By then I was eating anything; it didn't make any difference. I was really hungry so I approached them and relieved them of their rifles. They had three rifles actually. Two of them I could have stood in front of them and they probably couldn't have shot me. It didn't look like those two...one of them had a fairly new AK 47 and had four clips for it. So I ended up getting that and ate their dinner and went on down the trail.

That was probably the most spectacular and Rambo part I did. The rest of it was a stroll through the jungle. It was about eight months long. When I went back and looked at maps and did my debriefing, they wanted to know where I'd been. I could look at a map and say, "This is where I was shot down. This is where I ended back up." But the territory all the way up this way and back down, it was really hard.

The Montenyard villages don't have names and there's a lot

more up there than people think. These little people know how to live and feed off the land. They've been in war for three thousand years, forever it seems like. There are probably fifteen or twenty families in the village. Some of them were destroyed because of me. Some of them, the North Vietnamese would come in and steal all their rice.

As I got closer back south, I'd have to deal with the VC. There was probably an informant and they kept finding out that I was still alive. Most of them weren't the bravest people in the world. They didn't want to confront me.

I probably looked absolutely terrible. And I did. I was as brown as you can imagine. I had been sunburned. It would rain and the sun would come out. I had blisters and I was pretty rough looking. My hair was snow white and I had hardly any uniform left at all. Eight months and I was wearing sandals. My boots had wore out, they had rotted out. There was nothing heroic or beautiful about surviving. I smelt bad. I looked bad. I was dirty with dysentery and some other things that were probably going through my system. I had about every kind of fungus on me that you can think of when I finally got out. Unbelievable stuff. Some of it was curable by mountain medicine, herbs and roots took care of it.

One morning I heard voices and they were speaking English. I had heard a lot of Vietnamese; some of them could speak perfect English. One of the NVA that I confronted was educated at UCLA. It was not uncommon to find people that were our enemies that could speak perfect English. Vietnamese, whether they were farmers, mayors of these little villages, the head chief, it didn't make any difference. I did not trust any of these guys. So I was very cautious. I was making my way down the trail and I came upon the army A team. I knew when I saw them what they were. I had actually snuck up on them. If I would have been their enemy, I could have killed them without any problem.

Of course they wanted to know who won the last World Series and I didn't know. I'm no baseball fan. I don't care who won the last World Series. I told them where I was from and we finally got on the same page. They called in the dust off and I was taken to Japan for debriefing. Didn't take long, about a month. They reassigned me back to the Constellation.

With all the debriefing and stuff, I went through questions after questions. I was in the hospital where I put weight back on and got back to normal and got rid of all the funguses and stuff that I had growing on me as well as in me. It was debriefing almost every day. I had anywhere from captains, COs, to light colonels debriefing me. Of course, the shrink wanted to talk to me.

He asked how I'd managed to survive by myself. First of all, I was by myself all the time. I think one of the things that puts people in POW camps and people that are left alone like that, the first thing you have to do and it sounds conceited or self-centered, you've got to really like yourself. You find out about yourself when you're by yourself. Not when you're at that level. Even today I like going out into the woods and spending time alone. I like to be by myself.

There was nothing heroic or beautiful about surviving. I knew that I was not going to be captured.

Second sortie out the second time small arms fire got me this time. I managed to bring it out over the water and when I got my feet wet, I punched out. They had me out of the water in fifteen seconds

They tried to brand me as being a coward. I figured three times is a charm. They couldn't kick me out. I'd already been decorated. It was obvious I was not a coward. So they chose to send me off to… in Twenty-nine Palms to be the executive officer there. They ended up turning me into a drunk, Larry. I spent every day at the O Club. If a CO wanted to see me, he would have so send someone down there to get me. I didn't care much what they were going to do. I was just waiting for my time to be up. I resigned my commission but I wasn't going to do it until my time was up. I got out three months early. They cut a deal with me and I signed release papers on my resignation.

I graduated from college and went to OCS and went to Pensacola in the Marine Corps. I didn't go into the Marine Corps as a fighter pilot. They don't guarantee you anything when you join the Marine Corps. In officers corps you have to be qualified but I had flown small planes before so I had an aptitude for flying. I thought …second lieutenants at that time were…left and right. Pretty short life expectancy.

I thought if I could get into schools, so I started applying to all the schools at OCS when schools came up on the bulletin board. So I signed up for all of them, didn't matter what it was. I wanted to prolong this long enough for the war to be over. I'd been going to schools. It wasn't that I didn't want to fight, I just didn't want to get killed. I was doing my best to serve my country and at the same time getting an education to get out of the war. I didn't want to die.

I ended up pre-selected for flight training. You want a funny, humorous part. We all believed in order to fly fighter jets you had to be in the top ten of your class. After our basic training in aviation at ground school, I was picked for the fighter training. I thought alright I'm one of the smarter ones. I found out that they were just short on pilots for A 4's. You had to be small to fly an A 4 because it is so tight. I was five-foot-six a hundred and thirty-one pounds. I fit the bill whether or not my skills were better than anybody else's. I ended up doing fighter training.

My grandpa introduced me to flying. For some reason I always wanted to fly. In high school I was wiping planes down, doing whatever I could for free. I didn't have any money. I just found favor with some of the instructors and they started giving me manuals and books and stuff to learn. Then they started taking me up whenever they had some spare time. Outside Olympia, Washington.

Don't Cross that Water

by Larry Kaniut

I stood at the overlook at mile 95.5 on the Seward Highway east of Anchorage. I gazed across the swirling brown water. I knew some of the details. I wondered about the others.

Derek and his father had invited me to go with them. But I'd refused. Carl had asked me the previous summer to go gold mining with him. I assured him that I'd be happy to go but not over water. Maybe we could get an air taxi to drop us off or we could walk in overland. But not on the water of Turnagain Arm.

Now Derek was gone.

He'd make no more trips.

On Thursday night, June 25 (?), 1999, our daughter Jill was working on a wedding cake. Robin Helvey was visiting her when the phone rang ten minutes after 11. Robin asked, "Who would call this late?"

I suggested, "Probably Ben," knowing that our son Ben went to work at 5 a.m. in LA and that it wasn't he.

It was our neighbor Carl Snyder who asked, "Can you do me a favor?"

"Sure," I replied. "What can I do for you?"

"Could you pick me up at Columbia Regional?"

"Sure," I said. Thinking that perhaps he'd cut himself with an ax while working at his woodpile I asked, "Are you okay?"

"No. Dereck's gone."

"Ohhh, no!" I gasped automatically. I couldn't believe it. They must have gone gold mining after all. I told him I'd be right there.

When I went into the hospital, I met Carl and told him I was sorry. He limped to the Suburban and on the way home explained the misadventure.

Derek had invited me on Monday to canoe across Turnagain Arm on a gold mining jaunt. I loaned him an article about some veteran canoeists who had recently crossed on calm waters and asked Derek if he were an expert. He said no and took the article which I told him to share with his dad.

Seems they took the canoe, parked at the edge of the Seward Highway on the Bird Creek flats and started across. Unfortunately the outgoing tide had other ideas. Funneling its high tide waters on their way out, the water flowed into river-like channels and dumped them into its icy maw. As Carl was flushed by the current toward Cook Inlet, he said he saw Derek standing on a sandbar clad in his shorts. He assumed Derek jumped into the water to save his father. Carl washed up on the south shore but Derek did not make it.

Ugashik–Overboard

by Frank Kufel

My first few years teaching and coaching in Alaska, I heard many stories. I gobbled them up. My principal Frank Kufel told me one that stuck with me. Little did I know in the late 1960's that I'd end up in 1968 test fishing in Bristol Bay for the same Alaska Fish and Game Department that Frank had served and, again in 1979, commercial fishing the same waters of his near tragedy, which he shares here.

In the summer of '67, I was employed by ADF&G to work on a test boat at the mouth of the Ugashik River. My partner was an old Copenhagen chewing Finn from Astoria, Oregon, named Poisby. We had been supplied with an old, refurbished double end sailboat that had an engine installed and a roller in the stern. Poisby was an "old salt" and I was a "greenhorn" to this type of fishing. Our job was to set out our nets during each tide to determine the strength of the red run. After we pulled each set (from the boat), we would call our catch numbers in to the local commercial fisheries biologist and he would determine whether or not there would be opening for the commercial boys who were anchored all around us just waiting for the opportunity to fish.

Because the little cabin on our boat was more cramped and uncomfortable, it had been arranged that we eat our meals at a tender that was anchored nearby to purchase fish when the fishing opened. This became a daily ritual. Pull up to the tender, tie up, leaving enough slack in the rope for our boat to remain aside the tender as we ate. When we were ready to go back to work, we'd pull the boat up, jump on, start the engine, untie and do our work.

Often, Poisby chose to sleep on the tender rather than on the cramped wooden bunks in our cabin. It was one of these times that he chose to sleep on the tender that the accident happened that I would remember the rest of my life. Just like many times before, I would drop him off then go out and anchor to spend the night. In the morning I would go up to the tender and tie up.

This was the tricky part as the water ran swift and dirty. Because of the current, I had to approach the tender from downstream. In order for me to get the rope from the bow of our boat to the tender,

I had to leave some throttle to keep our boat against the tender's bumper then race forward, grab the line and jump onto the tender and tie off.

I remember that it was a dreary day and the tide was racing in. I nudged the bumper, gave our boat some throttle, ran up, grabbed the line and jumped for the tender. Thankfully my feet hit solidly and I tied the 1 ½ inch Manila line to the cleat on the tender and gave enough slack for our boat to ride behind. I was dumbfounded when all of a sudden a huge boil of water churned that threw the bow of our boat violently to the starboard, snapping the mooring line as though it were thread. This brought the stern of our boat up against the stern of the tender. Fearing the loss of our boat, I jumped for the stern, hoping to hop right in but in the micro-second that I was in midair, another furious boil from beneath swung the stern away from the tender.

I grabbed desperately for something and managed to grab the gunwale. There was our boat, moving under power out into the tide with me hanging desperately to the side. I had hip boots on—would they fill with water and pull me under? I could see a flurry of frantic activity around me as fishermen were jumping into their boats from the tender to offer me help.

The water was freezing cold yet I felt nothing. What made matters worse was that the gunwale I had a hold of was 5-inches inside of the actual side of our craft, providing an entire surface to walk on around the entire periphery—awkward to say the least.

I knew that I was alone and in order to survive, I had to rely on myself. The December prior, I had become the father of a new son, Eric, born on December 23rd. About all that I remember is seeing his picture in my mind. It filled my entire thought. You can't leave that baby without a daddy. The words raced and repeated through my brain.

In the meantime the boat is really moving through the current, still under power. I remember trying to pull myself up but couldn't. My boots were weighting me down and I just didn't have the strength to pull myself aboard.

In desperation, I managed to get one leg out of the water and with every ounce of strength I had, I got it up and into the boat. With that, I had a purchase and managed to pull myself to safety. I remember lying on the bottom of the boat exhausted and near shock.

Help soon arrived and I was taken to the tender, warmed, fed and safe. What saved my life was Eric's picture and the fact that when I received my first pair of hip boots, my best friend McCarthy (like my second father) told me, "Whenever you get boots, always cut out those things that snap to your calves because if you ever fall in the water, you boots will fill and drag you down." My boots fluttered behind my ankles held to me only by my feet. If I had snapped them to me, I would have died. Thanks to Eric and Mac, I was able to continue to work but never remained on the water again alone.

Shark Attack

by Eric Larsen as told to Larry Kaniut

When I first read about Eric Larsen July 3, 1991, I wanted to pursue his story from the angle of its rarity and of man's will to live. I called information then contacted him in his hospital room requesting his address so that I could send him a copy of one of my books and my intentions. I assured him over the phone that the land sharks would soon be arriving in large schools and suggested that perhaps we could write his story for Reader's Digest. He replied that "they were already here." So much for the major players' ability to respond instantly.

Over the years I've lost contact with Eric but am enclosing his story as I think he would have wanted it to be written. Primarily to state that sharks do not regularly seek humans as prey and that the news media does not normally endeavor to tell the victim's story (the way he'd like it told).

Imagine sitting on a surfboard, dangling your legs and hands in the water. You're facing north and looking over your left shoulder for a wave. It's a pleasant and peaceful morning but you feel some apprehension because you're alone. One second you're on your board, the next you're in the water. A great white shark has you in its massive jaws.

What do you do?

My brother Nick and I decided to go surfing and planned to leave early on Monday, July 1, 1991. He was on vacation and I was on a leave of absence from my job. We got up about 5:30 in the morning and went out to Davenport in my Toyota 4Runner truck for "dawn patrol." We arrived later than I had wanted to due to the fact that I had slept through my alarm wrist watch. It was already light when we were suiting up. We both were wearing full length wetsuits, booties, and web fingered gloves due to the cold water

Having worked with the Bridger Bowl Ski Patrol in Montana where I acquired an Advanced First Aid and CPR certificate, I modified my attitude towards taking risks in the outdoors. When I first started patrolling, I thought that taking more risks meant that you were "advancing" in your efforts--a person who knew more and was more experienced was a person who was in a position to take more and bigger risks.

Since watching and listening to the professional ski patrolmen however, I have concluded that this was a false perception. I learned that the people who are really "in the know," do things essentially the same way every day, day in and day out, with very minimal risk, accomplishing a very dangerous activity in such a way that it is very safe and routine.

When we arrived at the beach, we saw a couple of guys out in the water and we spent some time observing the surf. We had a quick talk about how we would enter and exit the surf zone and where we would position ourselves to wait for the waves. We stretched out and checked leashes. I always try to put my leash on in the same way, so that I can remove it quickly should it snag and hold me underwater. I discussed this with Nick and we practiced unleashing. We timed out a couple of sets and then hit the water at 7:20 a.m.

Nick rode my 8' 2" Agua tri-fin in a long board shape while I used a 7' Taylor tri-fin short board.

We bobbed around for a while and waited for the intermittent waves. Conditions were not very good. We were on the "outside," trying to ride the rights—after picking up a wave, the normal move would be to make a right turn. Nick caught a couple of waves, which he rode on his chest. I only stood up one time, and did not get a very good ride. I had not been surfing much due to canoe commitments and was not surfing well, especially on my short board.

I observed seals a number of times that morning. It may have been the same seal, seen repeatedly. About thirty to forty-five minutes prior to the attack a seal came close by and I slapped the water with my glove.

A boat was seen not too far offshore. This boat left after the emergency response happened. It is suspected that the boat may have been discharging some fish entrails (chumming) into the water in hopes of attracting a shark.

About 9 a.m. Nick indicated he was not feeling very good due to taking on salt water while being held under by waves. Since the other guys had gone in and I was out there alone, I planned to follow Nick in, after catching just "one more wave." It wouldn't take long to surf the hundred and fifty yards to shore.

About twenty minutes later I was sitting on my board facing north and looking over my left shoulder for the next wave. My legs and wrist were dangling in the water. Although I had surfed the area many times including once alone, I felt some apprehension about being out there alone, the only one in the break. Since the surf was small, I was not too worried.

While awaiting a wave I had the feeling that I was in the presence of a very large marine mammal. I felt sort of a strange quality to the water in that it seemed to be swirling a little and I felt like I was being spun around. I remember hoping that an elephant seal or whale had come up under me.

I felt a clamping force on my left leg and looked down to see the shark's jaws on my leg. The shark had come up between my legs, under my board and clamped onto my left leg. My left knee was pointing into his mouth and his teeth were biting in just above the ankle and about six inches below my buttocks. I looked down at the jaws and gum line. I remember a distinct visual image of large triangular white teeth, and a very red gum line.

I remember my first thoughts being, "How can this be happening? Shark attacks are very unlikely!" Then I concluded that I needed to deal with the situation somehow, because it was happening to me, unlikely or not. The shark was motionless for a few seconds and lacking any better ideas, I tried to pry him off my leg by placing my left hand on his top jaw, and the right hand on his bottom jaw. This was futile due to not being able to get much mechanical leverage and the strength of the shark's bite. At this point I should have hit the shark on the snout with my left hand.

The shark opened up slightly and I was able to extricate my leg. I think the shark flicked his tail and came at me. At this point I think I was pushed off my board into the water. Since my hands were essentially in his mouth, he got both of my arms in his mouth at this point. The left arm was in up to the elbow, and oriented for maximum thickness. The right arm was in at about mid-forearm, oriented flat. My impression was of a fairly large cavern inside his mouth.

I was able to pull the right arm out. At this point, I was still near the surface, sort of thrashing around. I remember a lot of bubbles in the water. I pulled back in my right arm and used it to hit the shark with a "hammer blow." By this I mean that my right arm hit with the little finger next to the shark's skin, along with the forearm. I was very "pumped up'" with adrenaline at this point, and hit with sufficient force that I later had a lot of muscle soreness and tightness in my (uninjured) right shoulder. The effectiveness of my strike was limited by difficulty in winding up and hitting underwater.

The shark released my left arm and I remember thinking that I was coming out of this maybe okay. My next recollection is of a violent pulling on my leash, which was attached to my uninjured right leg. The shark was somehow entangled in my leash and pulled me under for a few seconds. The sensation was very violent. It was like being hooked to a ski boat. I came free and got to the surface. I got a fast breath and got right onto my board in one motion. On the first attempt, I happened to hit almost exactly the right spot on my board and I started to paddle in.

I remember trying to stay calm, paddle very efficiently and thinking that everything had to go right from this point onward if I was going to make it. I was surprised at being able to paddle almost normally, even with my arms being very ripped up due to the injuries. This is due to the fact that the flexor muscles and tendons were relatively intact, whereas the extensors were damaged.

I remember looking down at my left forearm and noticing the yellowish fatty tissue. At the shark seminar I attended the instructor mentioned that sharks were supposedly attracted to yellow color. I surmised that this is because seals have a lot of fat, and it might be yellowish, like mine. I also observed blood trails coming off my arms. I remember looking over my shoulder for an oncoming fin.

I was about 150 yards offshore at the time of the attack. About two thirds of the way in I was able to catch a small wave and ride it in on my belly. I got to the shore and picked my board up and carried it over some small rocks. I set it down and looked at it quickly to check for dings or bites. I remember thinking that I should probably not worry too much about it. I started to feel weak, so I sat down and looked at my arms. I could see blood spurting out of the left arm near the crack of my elbow. I clamped the wound closed using my right hand and elevated the left arm. I was feeling very weak and at this point the thought occurred to me that I might die soon.

The beach was empty and I was around the corner of a small cliff from some beach houses. Nick was up at the truck at this time, over a mile away and out of sight. I knew that nobody would see me for at least a half hour, perhaps more. I concluded that I was going to have to walk up the beach to the houses or to where Nick could see me. At this point I had a sensation of some important events in my life passing before my eyes, like a movie projected at one hundred times normal speed. I tried to motivate myself by thinking about how I had motivated myself in long distance canoe races.

Walking was difficult due to the fact that the shark had transected (completely cut in half) my left quadriceps lateralis muscle. This is one of the main walking muscles. I knew that crawling was out of the question due to the possibility of getting sand into the wounds on my arms. I lost energy at least once and had to sit down. I did not want to pass out because then I would have released the grip on my left arm wounds and a lot of bleeding would have occurred.

I got to a point near the houses and started to yell as loudly as I could. I was yelling, "Help, SOS." I saw someone come out of one of the houses and I yelled at him. I was very anxious at this point. I told the person to call 911 right away. This person turned out to be Ben Burdette, a 16-year-old surfer who lives in the house near the beach.

Ben's mother, Michelle Tummino, came out, with some towels. She indicated that she did not know much about first aid. I instructed her to apply a pressure point to my brachial artery, to apply direct pressure using the towels to the wounds, and to elevate my good leg to drain some blood into my abdomen. I think I also asked her to keep the left arm elevated. She asked me what I did for a living and I told her that I was a programmer on leave of absence, and that "real surfers don't have real jobs."

I asked someone to go up and get Nick at the truck. He came down and saw that I was pretty cut up. I told him I was glad that he was there. At this time, the paramedics and emergency response people started showing up.

The last blood pressure they got on me was 50 over 30. They started oxygen and fluid IV's on both arms. They used mast trousers which inflate and then compress your legs to force more blood into your abdomen and brain. I felt a lot better when they were on. Nick was holding an oxygen mask on my face since I felt like I wasn't getting enough oxygen without his pushing it against my face.

The Army had a helicopter ready to land and everybody put on goggles to protect eyes from blowing sand. It was a Huey. At the time we took off, it was unclear to me (and Nick) where we were going. We landed at Dominican Hospital in Santa Cruz.

Essentially they slammed the doors shut and took off. This resulted in a very fast response. I think that the elapsed time between the 911 call and when I was in the air was only forty-five minutes. This is very fast, given the fact that Davenport is fairly remote. It is also good that a helicopter was available, due to the Fourth of July holiday traffic.

I am also told that the Stanford Life Flight helicopter was unable to land on the sand. The army guys landed close and picked me up. They had a winch that they could have used to send down and pull up a litter, as well as the capability to put a medic in a wet suit directly into the water. The Army unit that provides this service (free of charge) will be relocating within the next year or so, and at that time it is unclear how these vital services will be performed.

A lot of X-rays were taken in the emergency room (of me, transition). While I was being moved around and positioned for these, I got a lot of pain. A couple of ER guys helped me out by holding my arms in a static position relative to my body while I was being repositioned. This helped a lot. While waiting for surgery, I started to get very cold due to having lost all the blood. They turned on warming lamps and I started to feel a lot better. These two guys were starting to really perspire. They were local surfers. I thought it was so good that they were willing to hang in there and give me some good moral support even though it had to be very uncomfortable and hot under the lights.

I don't remember much about the surgery, since I was under general anesthetic. I think I took 350 sutures internally and 135 staples externally to close thirty inches of wounds. I received three units of blood. The doctors decided not to give me more blood to reduce the risk of hepatitis and AIDS. I was placed on iron pills and told to eat hamburgers and drink orange juice. This is my normal diet anyway.

The surgeon that worked on my arms (Dr. Tomlinson) had treated three shark bite patients previously. He had been a doctor in the military stationed at Tomales Bay. He had a very fast, precise and accurate method of operating and dealing with situations. I think he might have developed this as a result of dealing with a lot of patients in a military hospital. One move he made that was pretty good was when he was removing a drain (a section of tubing installed to allow fluids to drain from the repaired wound), and observed that it was not quite normal. Later, he made a short exploration and found that a section of the drain had indeed broken off inside my arm during the removal process. He removed the extra section of drain. Had it been left in, it would have caused complications. This is a case where expertise, and experience proved invaluable A less experienced surgeon might have missed this.

My first memory is of waking up in intensive care and talking to my nurse. I think her name was Tracy. I told her the shark story. We spent a lot of time that first night trying to get a sand grain out of my eye. Dr. Tomlinson was able to quickly remove it the next morning. I took this as evidence of why surgeons deserve to make the big bucks.

Tracy asked if I wanted to watch TV. I remember seeing a clip advertising the National Geographic specials which showed a diver testing a chain mail wet suit. The clip showed a shark clamped onto the diver's arm. I think I changed the channel!

The worst pain and problems were in being able to urinate. I had a lot of problems. They pulled out a Foley catheter that was inserted into my penis. I had trouble relaxing with all the nurses fluttering around. A local surfer and doctor, Dr. Scott, was visiting me, and he was able to apply a sort of relaxation-hypnosis technique which allowed me to urinate over 1000 CC's. This is about a quart! I felt a lot better. Dr. Scott is a general practitioner. Even in the ICU with all the high technology equipment, there is still no substitute for the human touch.

I got pretty good care when I was transferred to the normal part of the hospital. One of the best things I got was a massage. I was able to sleep very peacefully for about three hours after this. I got physical therapy from a guy who had been in the Navy. He had worked with the Navy SEAL teams. It was good to work with him, since he motivated me to get out of bed and walk up and down the hall with my walker.

I remember very distinctly the first time I was cleared to walk around unsupervised with my walker. I was able to brush my teeth myself for the first time, and it took about twenty minutes. I had to get the brush and the toothpaste and a cup for the water as separate operations. It felt very good to make small steps towards being more self-sufficient.

It was very hot the week I was in the hospital, but not too bad in Santa Cruz. The sun would beat in the windows in the late afternoon, so I would roll in my wheelchair over to the deck area and get some sun and fresh air. I would lift my casts over my head to let the blood drain out, then hold them down to let the blood drain in. It felt good to hold my arms up in the cool evening air.

Doctors make you survive and live, therapists make you healthy and normal. I enjoyed PT, and I had a very good physical therapist, Susan Happe. She knew a lot of things. I was in physical therapy for about six weeks.

Although the attack occurred on Monday, but the real feeding frenzy took place on Wednesday when the hospital finally allowed a press conference. There were about fifty journalists with TV and still cameras. I was completely encircled. I think it went well. One newspaper account described how I "calmly described the attack." Given the drugs I was on at the time for pain, I would have been very calm about just about anything.

I conclude after my experience with a lot of TV, newspaper and magazine journalists that a person has the attention of the press as long as he is saying something the press perceives to be a good story. I thought that I might be able to use the spotlight to give some attention to environmental issues such as offshore oil drilling on the northern California coast or over fishing of sharks, or mindless killing of sharks by "sport" fishermen.

In general the press did not carry these stories. They were basically only interested in the attack itself. Possibly the worst press was a TV show called "A Current Affair" which had a interview with me interspersed with footage of a simulated shark attack. This footage portrayed sharks as mindless, blood thirsty killing machines. One of the shark researchers I talked to indicated that he always got upset when he saw things like this in the media because the sharks are not actually showing natural behavior. They are showing artificial behavior in the presence of bait.

I spent over six hours with the crew from "A Current Affair," and the segment was cut down to about ten minutes.

I received no money for my exposure to the media, however I did receive some gear. I got two free wet suits, one from O'Neill and the other from Hotline. O'Neill gave me a T-shirt, some booties, gloves and a new leash. I agreed to appear in an ad for Rip Grip, and received some free product in return. The ad should be fairly humorous since the essence of it is that the whole thing is a publicity stunt by a low budget company.

The fundamental lesson is that a person has very little control over what appears in the press, and once you talk to a reporter, you are taking your chances. The standard of truth and accuracy of press coverage is not the same as that of the engineering world. What is discussed in the interview and what appears in the article may be very different in emphasis. Facts can be presented in a very slanted way.

As a result of all the publicity, I got a lot of letters and phone calls from people I had never met. A number of people called who had been in terrible accidents and recovered. A woman called who had been attacked by a bear. A number of people wrote in with religious messages. I got one photo from a model. One woman wrote me a number of very nice letters because she thought I looked attractive on TV.

An important question is: when shark attacks are statistically rare, why did the shark choose to bite me at that time and place?

Years go by when no shark attacks occur. The exact reason for the attack is something that can never be completely known, but a number of theories arise.

This simulates the sound of a fish's tail slapping the water and will occasionally draw a seal up close to investigate. The sound was unexpectedly loud, and may have attracted the shark since they are reputed to have very good low frequency hearing.

This has never been substantiated.

The underside of my surfboard is pure white. This may have looked like the white underbelly of something delicious. I was also wearing a wetsuit with black sections on the legs, and black booties with white bottoms. This coloration may have mimicked that of a seal to some extent.

I was alone in the water. This may have caused the shark to proceed, when he might have been deterred with more surfers in the water.

I vaguely recall someone saying that at that particular time of year, the elephant seal pups are taking their first swims up at Anyo Neuevo (four to five miles north). It is possible that extra sharks might be in the area to gobble these seal morsels. I am not really very sure about this.

One of the shark researchers I talked to mentioned that in a shark attack on an elephant seal, the shark will sometimes bite and then come back when the animal has weakened by bleeding. The fact that I got right onto my board and paddled out of there may have been significant.

Also seal bones are rather porous and "crunchable," whereas human bones are dense and hard. When the shark bit into me, he left striations (tooth marks) on my bones. Encountering my bones may have given him a clue that I was not a seal and possibly hard to digest.

A number of precautions have been suggested by the experts for avoiding shark attacks:

Don't enter waters known to be frequented by large sharks.

Don't swim, surf or dive alone.

Avoid murky water or water with sand churned up

Don't go too far offshore or near channels or drop offs.

Don't go into the water near seal colonies.

Avoid the water at dawn, dusk or at night.

Short surfboards are worse than long boards since they look like a smaller seal from below.

Note that I was in violation of all these precautions.

Four factors were very important for my survival: 1) the emergency response team, 2) my physical condition, 3) my mental condition and 4) my First Aid knowledge.

First, the emergency response and medical system works very well in the Monterey Bay/Sanata Cruz area. Had this happened in Mexico, things might have worked out very differently.

Second, I was in very good physical condition. I had been paddling outrigger canoes almost every day for the two months prior to the incident, and I had been running a lot. This was important in my ability to paddle in and hike up the beach, even though I had lost a lot of blood.

Third, I was in good mental condition. I was relaxed and unstressed due to having been on leave from my job. Because I was relatively comfortable in the water from surfing and swimming a lot, I didn't totally panic, even when the shark pulled me under water when he was hooked in the leash.

Fourth, I had good basic knowledge of First Aid. I had learned this as part of my experience on the Bridger Bowl Ski Patrol. I had a (now expired) Advanced First Aid and CPR certification. I never expected to have to use it on myself.

One other thing that I think about is that the shark bit me, but didn't eat me, or bite off big chunks even though he could have. It might be more accurate to categorize what happened to me as a couple of bites, rather than an attack.

In retrospect the shark was almost gentle. As gentle as he (or she) could have been with his teeth. Once he concluded that I was not a seal, he swam off and left me alone. Humans should similarly give sharks some slack by not killing them for sport, or unnecessarily. Sharks are an important part of the natural environment. Any animal that is that big and that strong, deserves respect.

I have concluded that every day is important. Life is short, and every day is a chance to do something meaningful, and important. This can be surfing, or writing a new operating system for a computer. But in any case life is too short to spend a lot of time on things that are stupid, or don't lead on to anything else. Sitting in traffic and working on engineering projects that get discarded are two of the things that I hope to not spend much time on in the future.

Basically I think this incident resulted in a reinforcement of previous attitudes, rather than any new revelations. Life is deterministic, and a person has a lot of control over what happens. There is a need to be prepared and to be tough. All a person can do is to be as ready as he can be, and then go out and do whatever it is he was planning on.

Five separate emergency response organizations were involved. These were:

Davenport Fire and Rescue

California Department of Forestry

Santa Cruz Paramedics

U.S. Army 237th Medical Detachment Helicopter Crew

Stanford Life and Flight Helicopter Crew

I learned later that the Army guys were in their helicopter and doing a check when they got the call.

The Davenport Fire and Rescue guys were great. I went to a picnic that they held later on in the summer. In some years they have performed fifteen cliff rescuers. Their specialty is rescuing people that fall off the cliffs near Davenport. While I was at the picnic, a rescue call came in and they all suited up and went to rescue a woman that had fallen off a cliff to the north.

Extended Goat Hunt

by Larry Kaniut

After reading the story, I re-wrote it. It is a good story and I hope you enjoy it.

On Tuesday morning September 14, 1965, around 7:45 AM they left Cordova, Alaska, expecting to be back later that day.

Wind was moderate when they took off from Cordova's Eyak Lake in a single engine aircraft equipped with floats. Moments later they were flying through a slight drizzle over the Copper River Delta toward Yakataga. Hundreds of Canadian geese and all species of ducks cluttered the airspace and clouds prevailed. The Copper River flats draws a concentration of waterfowl migrating south.

The pilot and guide was Ralph Marshall. His passengers were Helen Burnett and Tom Brawner, 63-years-old.

Tom commented to his companions that the sights below made the flight worth it even if they didn't garner game and hadn't seen a brown bear to go after.

Ralph commented, "I'll show you something that is beautiful!" 1 They flew along the beach of the Gulf of Alaska observing the Bering Glacier, circling it at three or four unnamed peaks rising from their bases and completely surrounded by snow. As it turned out, this was Ralph's secret goat haven. Four or five years before, he had discovered the abundance of goats in the area.

Suddenly Ralph asked Tom, "How about a goat?

Tom told him he'd already killed one near Valdez.

Ralph told him he was allowed two and asked Tom if his was a Boone & Crockett trophy.

"No," Tom replied.

Ralph assured him that he could get him one that would go well up in the record book.

His attention captured, Tom asked Ralph how long it would take since he was eager to rejoin his wife in Anchorage. Ralph turned to Tom and said, "Two minutes."

With Tom's "okay" Ralph swung the plane toward his secret unnamed lake high in the mountains above the glacier. Almost before you could tell it, they had exited the plane and were stalking a large billy, one of the largest Tom had ever seen.

Helen remained in the plane, watching the progress of the men as they stalked the animal. Since the goat moved every time the men did, it seemed to Helen that the goat was aware of their presence. Before long it was at the peak of the mountain.

It looked like "now or never," so Ralph told Tom to hold about 24-inches above the shoulder. At the crack of the rifle, the goat tumbled down the mountain onto a snowfield and slid halfway to the hunters before it vanished from sight behind some ice. Ralph congratulated Tom as he rose to go after the downed goat, estimating the distance at 420 yards. Ralph worked the goat from the ice and estimated its weight at 200-250 pounds.

The men returned to the plane with the meat, cape and horns of the billy which wore 9 ½ inch horns. Ralph's custom called for taking off the lake with only one passenger, landing at a larger lake nearby then returning for the second. In this case Helen departed with Ralph around 1:30 p.m. Tom would wait on shore for Ralph's return.

About fifteen feet off the water a sudden blast of turbulent air hit the plane. Rather than chance not clearing the ridge across the lake, Ralph set the plane down to start over. As they turned to taxi back to shore for a longer run at takeoff, the right wing tilted at a strange angle. Helen was unable to see what was happening and crawled into the rear of the plane to retrieve life jackets.

They put the jackets on and exited the plane on the left float. They discovered that the lift strut and fittings supporting the plane on the floats had given way, snapping the cables and shoving the float up under the wing and fuselage where the prop had chopped through the front of the float.

Determining that the plane would not turn over, they sat on the float and paddled toward shore. As they neared the bank, Tom was awaiting them and they tossed him a rope. He pulled them close enough so that they could jump to shore.

Fixing the plane was not feasible. They secured it to the bank and discussed their options. There was no cover available nor wood nearby with which to build a fire. They did not know when someone would notice their absence and begin a search. They determined to travel to the larger lake where they could set up a shelter and have a fire. Foot travel necessitated crossing the glacier and obstacles in the form of crevasses hundreds of feet deep. In all likelihood they would have to cross snow bridges over these gaping holes.

They secured the plane with what ropes they could spare. Then, fearing the possibility of the plane's sinking, they unloaded their meager gear from the plane, stacked their extra rifles and cameras in plastic bags under rocks. They loaded a pack board with gear which included their goat meat, a small package of salt, one sleeping bag and cover, two ponchos, two raincoats, a parka and a large sheet of black plastic and a third of a bottle of whiskey.

The only other gear they had was their clothes and Helen's pack and a half of cigarettes. The threesome left the plane around 2:45 PM headed for the larger lake. Their greatest challenge would be safely crossing the intervening glacier.

Like other glaciers, this one was an accumulation of layers of snow that have built up over the years. As many other mountain regions, this glacier filled the bowl formed by numerous mountain peaks. Many glaciers resemble a glove, with fingers pointing in various directions, wending their way down slope.

En route they crossed rocky canyons

The glacier field that lay before Ralph, Tom and Helen was massive, stretching for miles and pockmarked with crevasses which can be anywhere from a few feet in depth to hundreds of feet.

As the threesome traveled the surface of the glacier, they constantly had to change direction or retrace their steps because their journey was blocked by a crevasse. Some crevasses required miles of walking in order for them to reach the other side and to continue their proposed route.

In some cases they were required to straddle snow bridges connecting one side of the crevasse with the other. Crossing crevasses on snow bridges necessitated running a rope from Ralph in the lead to Helen and on to Tom. Sometimes they were able to cross on hands and knees like walking a roofline on a house.

Helen said later that she was never so frightened in her life.

Crossing from their lake to the larger one took them a little over five hours. By 8 PM it began raining and they reached a large boulder at the edge of the glacier. Although it was dark, they were very pleased when they reached firmer ground.

They found a large boulder and fastened their plastic sheet to it and secured part of it to the ground before crawling under. They did not know then that they would stay there two days while rain poured from the sky and gale force winds shrieked. Their sleep consisted of nods.

They discovered that the running water they'd heard was coming from a huge torrent at the bottom of the sheer drop near where they'd taken shelter. Should they wish to continue, the only way was to cross the rotten ice connecting their safe ground.

After two hours of gathering brush they were able to get a fire started and to cook some goat meat. They felt like they could eat a small grocery store, including shingles and nails. As quickly as the meat was cooked, it was devoured.

They sated their hunger and continued cooking as a precaution against future fire difficulties. Their decision proved prophetic as it turned out that they spent periods of two days at a time before they could exit the shelter to cook.

Restroom facilities were plentiful with large boulders all about. That issue was compounded when they'd exhausted their last Kleenex, necessitating the use of green leaves.

With time on their hands they rearranged their shelter. At the top of the list was raising it so they'd have more room underneath. As long as they were there for the duration, they decided to be as comfortable as possible. By arranging the cover to one side of the boulder, the needed room was provided, though their sleeping area was a mere 4 by 6 and a half feet. Sleeping positions where even more tolerable where they could huddle together for more warmth. They discovered the joy of sharing a mummy bag with another adult. And they periodically used each other as pillows.

Helen lamented not having a tooth brush or hair brush. The three had no means of bathing in the ice cold water that would enable a lather, even if they'd had soap. Their camp became pretty lame in regards to body hygiene. Ralph's small comb was their only item of toiletry.

Going to sleep meant lying on the ground, either struggling to get into the sleeping bag or, in Tom's case, pulling the raunchy goat hide over him for warmth. Because the green hide was wet and rain continued to dampen it, it soured and smelled terrible.

When the smell was too great, Ralph would kill another goat to use that hide.

By the fourth day on the 18th they were getting more rain and wind. The following three days were so foggy that they couldn't see a hundred yards. They heard planes in the distance but the weather was a definite deterrent to any air search in their vicinity, even if people had a pretty good idea where they were.

The three settled into a routine. On good weather days they hunted more goats to supplement their food supply. They cooked it and enjoyed the weather, retreating to the shelter when the rain started, remaining there for a couple of days until weather improved. Then they repeated the process.

On the 22nd and 23rd the fog wasn't so bad. During that time they observed a small plane in the distance and a commercial aircraft high overhead. They entertained each other with their hunting and fishing stories and other experiences.

Helen ran out of cigarettes on the eighth day when she smoked one in two stages, thinking she had overcome her need for them. Fifteen minutes later she was craving just one more cigarette.

Two more goats succumbed to their rifles, the hide of one providing additional cover for Tom. By the end of their stay the hide smelled pretty potent.

The three used the whiskey bottle to carry water from the creek to camp. They used a small glass Helen had carried to contain and allow water to warm so that Tom could more readily drink it than the cold water which upset his stomach.

Wonderful and exotic food became the subject of many of their conversations. Someone constantly came up with a delicacy which fired their hopes though was unattainable in their situation. Helen constantly dreamed of a wonderful food she'd cooked, and about the time she was ready to eat it, one of her companions awakened her.

About the tenth day out the men were ready to strangle Helen when she teased them with food talk about baking apple dumplings and blue berry muffins on her return to civilization.

Somewhere around the 24th Tom sat up one night to reposition himself after having tweaked his neck. As he sat there smacking his lips like a hungry dog eating, Ralph sat up and asked him what he was doing. Tom replied that he was eating a fried chicken. Oh, boy.

Hope soared on the 24th and 25th which were clear and beautiful. Surely planes would come today. But such was not their lot.

Each person had his private thoughts and hopes. Each was concerned about his responsibility to those awaiting them. And, of course, Ralph felt terribly about the predicament he'd gotten Helen and Tom into.

Around noon on the 26th the sun came out.

On the 27th more rain and fog greeted the three. A rescue plane flying east passed over without seeing them. An hour and a half later the plane returned but was a considerable distance beyond their camp and over the glacier.

The 28th dawned clear and the group prepared to leave their camp. Four planes had flown a pattern over them, including one high flying 10th Rescue search plane. Since they hadn't been spotted, they chose to move to a more likely spot in hope of rescue. They would need an early start to cross the glacier and climb a steep mountain before reaching their destination.

They built a "help" sign with a big arrow pointing the direction they'd take. And they prepared a landing strip for a wheel-equipped plane, constructed on the ice from rock that they carried a considerable distance.

Tom reluctantly left his goat hide behind because it was too heavy to carry. They draped the white hide over a rock in hopes it would provide a signal to searchers.

Crossing the rotten ice they left the glacier behind at 10:45 AM. They started up the mountain, encountering elderberry bushes. They were excited to find brush which would provide some measure of firewood. The fire, however, brought a new problem—if they built a fire, they'd have to keep it going because they had only two matches left.

Around 1 PM Tom found nine salmon berries. He said they were so good they were worth $50 each, including the ninth one which was half rotten.

Meanwhile Ralph had scouted the top of the mountain and returned with the news that they could not proceed and would have to camp below their current position. They were halfway down when a plane flew over. Before they knew it there were two more planes. And then the sky rained aircraft, like a swarm of mosquitoes.

They reached a spot where they could build a fire and eagerly built one in hopes someone in a plane would spot them.

At 3:20 a C-130 lumbered over and discovered them. Tom said later, "I shall never forget its number—493 USAF.

"They dropped a survival kit that contained a radio that Ralph quickly assembled and began talking to the pilot." 1

The pilot said they had a paramedic on board. He could jump to provide medical assistance if needed.

A Cessna 185 followed the C-130 in on one run and dropped two objects. Helen was ecstatic to learn they were cigarettes for her. She found out later that the plane's passengers included three men from Fairbanks—her ex-husband Henry Jensen, Ralph's guide, pilot Jim Fredricks and co-pilot Jack Burnett. Henry surmised that the group might well be at Ralph's secret lake goat hunting.

It was 4:25 when the pilot of the C-130 reported that a helicopter stood by in Cordova, waiting for the weather to clear. He was unsure whether the chopper could come for them but told them he'd stay with them and report back in an hour with more definite information.

The group ecstatically opened the items the Air Force had dropped them. They found sleeping bags, warm clothing and food.

Their next contact with the Air Force pilot informed them that the chopper would come in the next day. In the meantime the C-130 dropped them another package of food in case the weather turned worse. He assured them he'd return no later than 6 AM the 29th.

They were thrilled with the food. Helen coaxed the men to put on warm clothing while she cooked them a hot meal from the C rations and pork and beans. Tom was served a large can of hot chocolate first. Then they ate heartily. Tom spent the night in two sleeping bags attempting to warm up.

At 6 AM the next morning the C-130 was back. The pilot cruised low overhead and asked if they'd slept well. He circled them for thirty minutes then told them the chopper had left Cordova and that he was returning to escort it to them.

The C-130 returned and advised them to pack their things and wait where they were until the helicopter had settled. Within a few minutes the chopper had selected a spot 300 yards from them and landed. A paramedic and crew member ran to meet them.

Overcome with the emotional shock of rescue combined with the stress they'd endured, Tom collapsed. They carried him to the whirlybird and they loaded their gear and crawled in for the trip out.

They were soon airborne for Yakataga air strip where Tom was transferred to the C-130 and rushed to the hospital in Anchorage to be treated for exhaustion and exposure. Tom said he would be eternally grateful for the personal care provided him by Captain Dale Cloy, M.D.

The chopper delivered Helen and Ralph to Cordova. They were greeted with welcomes from their friends. They returned the next day to Anchorage and met another welcome party. Helen went back to work as usual while Ralph arranged for parts to repair his plane.

A week later Ralph and Helen returned to the site of the accident only to discover that high water and probable strong winds had proved too much for Ralph's plane which vanished into the waters.

Part of the routine of their stay included hoping the weather would clear enough for search planes to look for them.

Aftermath

Tom said, "I do not relish another experience of this kind, but, if I do, I hope it will be with Helen Burnett and Ralph Marshall." 1

No one ever mentioned seeing the "help" arrow.

SOURCE NOTES:

1. "Two Minute Goat," Tom Brawner, *Alaska Sportsman*, April 1966, pp. 6,8,10 & 69

2. "Glacier Ordeal," Helen Burnett, *Alaska Sportsman*, April 1966, pp. 6,7, 9, 69 & 70

Floundering in the Wind & Waves

by Larry Kaniut

Floundering in the Wind and Waves

Frigid swim for life

'No one knew we were out there; there was no choice'

I've had a ton of stories in my computer a dozen or more years. In June 2021 I re-wrote Jon Little's piece from the *Anchorage Daily News*, July 13, 2002, Soldotna.

Cold, chilled saltwater clutched the man who faced the nearly impossible task of reaching shore…a mile and a half mile distant. Four-foot swells pummeled his body as he struggled on… calves cramping badly. He knew that his boat mates' lives depended upon his reaching safety and succor.

Ron Halsey was a 43-year-old Cook Inlet commercial fisherman whose skiff had sunk between the Kenai and Kasilof rivers, leaving him, his wife Debbie, 48, and crewmen William "Cody" McVay, 20, and Sam Gammon, 14, to fend for themselves in the waters.

Theirs had been the last skiff pulling nets in the Inlet on Thursday afternoon. The four had commercial fished aboard a 22-foot motorized skiff. They were set netting, catching salmon in floating gillnets anchored to the Inlet's floor. Strong southwest wind turned the Inlet choppy. As scores of other set netters along the Kenai Peninsula bluff between Nikiski and Ninilchik, they picked salmon from the nets, then stowed nets in the aluminum boat one by one. The fishing period ended at 7 PM and by law all gear had to be out of the water.

The crew untied one end of a net about 6:30 PM and was motoring up alongside it to untie the other end when the webbing tangled in the boat's outboard motor. It is about the worst thing that can happen. The net's pull drags the back of the boat down and allows waves to swamp the vessel.

Ron Halsey hurriedly tried to cut the line as his boat swung to the north with the incoming tide, but a couple of waves crashed over the boat's stern, filling it with water. The waterlogged vessel literally fell away beneath their feet, leaving the four floundering among gas cans, fishing corks and other debris. With only the bow above the water, the emergency radio, in a dry box, floated out of reach.

For a while Ron clung to an empty gas can. There was no help within sight. "No one knew we were out there. There was no choice: If I didn't make it, I didn't think anybody would ever know," Halsey said. He left the others and started swimming for help.

Visibility was limited. Whitecapped waves crowned blue walls of water in the early evening sunshine.

Wearing jeans, a T-shirt, cotton gloves and a life vest and resting one burning leg at a time, Halsey labored on. He incorporated every stroke he knew, from back-floating to dog-paddling and crawling. Finally, he felt the Inlet's firm sand beneath his feet. And only then did he feel cold. He just wanted to fall down and rest. Minutes ticked into hours, and he struggled fighting fatigue, to keep himself motivated. He wanted to give up.

But he staggered on, over the rocky high tide line in wet wool socks. He hiked a dirt road up the bluff and showed up, shivering, at the camp of fellow set netters Horace and Laura Blanchard.

The effort had taken him two and a half hours, and the Inlet's water temperature was about 50 degrees. Experts say an average adult should have been dead after that much time immersed in such cold water.

He shuffled into the Blanchards' camp about 9:15 PM and dialed 911. An Alaska State Trooper helicopter was dispatched, set netters launched skiffs, and Soldotna-based Central Emergency Services sent two rescue boats. Searchers found the rest of Ron Halsey's crew by 10 PM.

After Ron disappeared from view, his wife hunkered down with her back to the wind, her arms and legs tight to her body. Debbie still wore rain gear, from hip boots to a slicker, and she put her hood up against the gusts. She was okay. Not wanting to die but wanting to be found if she did, she slowly unclipped her life jacket and carefully re-clipped the top fastener around one of the buoy's ropes. She was halfway out of the water.

Time passed. As the Inlet's ferocious tides turned, the boat slipped beneath the water. With nothing to cling to, McVay and Sam floated south separately on the ebb tide. They passed buoys, but couldn't reach them. The outgoing tide carried the two crewmen down the Inlet, they talked, prayed and sang as their heads poked above the swells. They passed each other, back and forth. And they got colder and colder. "I couldn't feel my legs, and all the swells were coming over my head. I swallowed a lot of water," McVay said.

The current carried Debbie almost directly to another set netter's buoy. It was a pair of floating plastic barrels lashed together by rope. She climbed aboard the X-shaped rope between the barrels, and straddled it like a horse.

McVay kept Sam alert and they sang gospel songs, "Lord I Lift Your Name On High" and "Awesome God" as they were swept along. McVay limited his movements, but the younger deckhand was panicking. "I was trying to keep him under control because he was kicking," McVay said. "I said, 'God's with us. Everything's going to be OK. Stop kicking.'" Eventually, Sam floated past McVay one last time and disappeared from view about an hour before rescuers arrived.

The Blanchard's launched one of their fishing boats after Ron Halsey showed up, and were the first to find Debbie Halsey strapped to the buoys. She had no energy to move on her own. "I was thinking, 'I don't care if they pull every joint out of the socket, just pull me up'… Those boys, they saved my life."

A Central Emergency Services jet boat picked up McVay after two CES divers jumped from a trooper helicopter to attend to him and Sam.

Tim Cooper, a CES captain and one of the divers, helped put Sam onto another skiff operated by set netter Dean Osmar. Osmar had seen the chopper flying low and assumed the worst, so he and two crewmen cruised to investigate.

His crew, Ryan Roemmich and Bart Klonizos of Cody, Wyoming, threw themselves into resuscitating Sam, Cooper said.

One attempted mouth-to-mouth while the other worked the boy's chest all the way back to a Kasilof River dock and a waiting ambulance, Cooper said. "In just nasty weather, the boat was pounding all over the place. They kept on doing it, trying to give that guy a best chance."

Sam, a Soldotna resident, was declared dead at 2:32 AM Friday at Central Peninsula General Hospital.

The Halsey's and McVay are from Abilene, Texas. Tired and sore, they were recovering Friday at Ron's parents' home in Soldotna. Their faith in God tempered their fear of death and helped keep them calm as they dealt with the unforgiving wind and waves without a boat.

Trapped on the Beach

by Larry Kaniut

Frank W. Johnson decided to go trapping. When Frank needed help seal hunting, fishing or completing similar work, he had previously engaged in business with his friend The Kid. In the fall of 1971, they decided to partner up and go to southeast Alaska's Dry Bay, 50-miles south of Yakutat. What began as an ordinary hunting and trapping trip, turned disastrous.

Although the old timer had been reluctant, The Kid had assured him that game was plentiful, that he needed meat for his family and that he'd do all the work trapping and hunting. It sounded too good to be true, which should have raised some red flags.

The plan was for Frank to cook, take care of camp and keep The Kid company. The youngster figured they'd make $3000. Frank would be happy to go home with $500 clear. He had spent the bulk of his 79 years outdoors, so he knew very well what conditions they might meet, but still he decided one more winter wouldn't hurt, in spite of his better judgment.

Frank made arrangements with Dick Nichols to fly him, The Kid and their gear to the trapping area. Then he got busy rounding up $300 worth of food and supplies. They left for an Alsek River cabin on Dry Bay November 4, 1971.

When they first laid eyes on it, they knew they had their work cut out for them. The cabin would need heat. An oil drum was needed in order to construct a stove. The Kid spent the day hunting while Frank worked on bringing the cabin up to his standards. Even though The Kid reported ample moose and fur bearers in the vicinity, he didn't bring home any meat.

Frank encouraged his partner to build a few line camps right away. These were basically shelter lean-tos consisting of a ridge pole with evergreen boughs forming the "A-frame" roof. The lean-to would provide crude shelter overnight a day's trapping journey from the next one. Once the snow covered the roof, it would provide ample shelter for the trapper.

From what Frank could tell, The Kid never built a line camp, and by the time the plane returned two weeks later to check on the men, the youngster still had no meat in camp.

Ten days later snow arrived in a large dump. With all the snow on the ground the partners knew the wheel plane wouldn't be landing at the camp again until spring. Yakutat usually receives 130-200-inches of precipitation a year, but that year received 400-inches of snow.

Anticipating a few days in Yakutat at Christmas, Frank decided they could wait for the plane at the beach where it would be able to land at low tide. It was roughly six miles from the cabin to the mouth of the Alsek. They could walk overland or float downstream during high tide. Choosing to ride rather than walk, Frank began building a plywood boat.

Forty days after their arrival and before the boat was completed, The Kid seemed impatient and told Frank they should just go on and walk to Yakutat. Frank figured he had cabin fever (a condition wherein the sufferer felt trapped and needed to get away). He told The Kid they could readily hike to the beach or else take the boat when it was finished, but that it would be more prudent to catch the plane than to walk the fifty miles to Yakutat.

Since the trapping was abysmal—yielding only a marten, a squirrel and a weasel, their camp meat consisted of two ducks; the men were hardly speaking to each other. Frank thought maybe a trip to Yakutat was well advised.

They loaded some gear into the boat and started down river, which turned out to be rougher than either of the men had expected. Ice choked the river, requiring them to pull the boat over and around it.

The first day they reached only the halfway point. It took them all of the second day to cover the remaining three miles. They finally reached the beach that night.

Both men had good sleeping bags and tarps. The high tide came all the way up to the snow line. Because it was getting dark, Frank chose to build a snow wall for protection from the incoming tide as opposed to building a snow house.

That night Frank slept well. He was happy with his surroundings and felt he could have stayed a month. Food was not a problem. Had they needed more, they could have returned to their camp on the incoming tide. They had time since the tide was high.

The tide book indicated the tides were scheduled to be higher each day.

The next day following breakfast the men discovered a cabin that

Frank had left years before.

Sand had drifted against the door effectively blocking the window and door. Using tools he found at hand—a board, a gallon can and an ax—Frank began removing the gritty material in order to gain access.

In the midst of digging he felt a cold chill, felt slightly light headed and lay down to see if the feeling would go away.

Evidently, The Kid had had enough of the waiting game and while Frank rested, The Kid abandoned him. He hiked to a food-stocked cabin located between them and Yakutat where he was found in good health three days later.

Frank awoke to find his partner gone and a storm brewing. He felt he could safely stay at his beach camp another night and complete the cabin digging the next day.

During the night he awoke once and realized he needed air. He had taken a poke stick with him to his sleeping bag. This was an old habit. Often in the past he'd used similar sticks to open a breathing hole in snow if necessary. So he poked a hole to get air.

Daylight brought both the dawn and a dilemma. Frank lay on his left side unable to move his sleeping bag frozen solidly to the beach sand-gravel. An unexpected phenomenon had trapped him on the beach. Ocean spray had blown a thousand feet across the spit and settled on the hapless man. The settling mist froze, effectively "welding" Frank to the ground.

No matter how hard he tried, he could not move enough to apply any pressure to his sleeping bag. He lay there listening to the seas building, knowing that the tides would be higher that night. Thoughts about his chances of surviving the incoming tide flooded his mind and he wondered whether the tide would free him, drown him or take him out to sea.

His only hope lay in the tide's thawing the ice to enable his escape, or in the timely yet nearly impossible arrival of someone's coming to his rescue.

He went to sleep but during the night the heavy breakers washed over him, hammering his position for half an hour. Every receding wave brought cold, salt water into his sleeping bag through the breathing hole he'd opened. The water drained away through the open zipper.

The ice had softened some from the water's immersion. Although cold from the repeated dunkings, Frank began kicking at his tomb. He kicked, rested, slept and awakened to kick again for the next thirty-six hours.

The third night a higher tide brought bigger waves which kept Frank busy for three hours. First he heard the wave coming. Then it washed over his bag and drenched it. He managed to trap enough air in his bag between waves to allow him to breathe. The constant washing of the waves had nearly freed Frank's cocoon.

By noon he'd managed to kick a small hole in the bag and plastic tarp. Able only to free the lower part of his body, the icy grip still held him tightly. Knowing that the fourth night's higher tide would cover him and keep him from acquiring air to breathe, Frank was now desperate. The below-zero temperature caused the bag to freeze and he couldn't get back into it. He knew that the incoming tide allowed him only an hour and a half before his final breath.

That's when Frank heard the sound of an aircraft in the distance. As the noise drew nearer, it was the sweetest music he had ever heard. The noise came from two aircraft. As he later found out, one carried Dick Nichols and the marshal; the other was a Coast Guard plane.

The planes circled then landed. Before long helping hands freed Frank and carried him to a waiting plane which medi-vaced him to Anchorage's Providence Hospital. Frank spent nine months in the hospital and in a rest home. He lost five toes.

The long nights on the beach had given him time to think about his partner and their venture. He didn't think he'd be partnering up anytime soon with The Kid.

SOURCE NOTE:

"Encased In Ice, I Nearly Drowned," Frank W. Johnson as told to Ola M. Hughes, *ALASKA Magazine* February 1974, pages 31& 32.

Valdez Glacier Episode

by Larry Kaniut

On pages 22 to 24 of *Alaska Sourdough* (1956 Rand McNally and Company) Richard Morenus tells about an experience Slim Williams had roughly around 1900.

There had been an accident.

Four men stood at the lip of a crevasse looking down. Slim joined them. The crevasse was about four feet wide at the top. For the first few feet the glacier showed the white of the packed surface snow and the frost crust, then deeper inside it became ice, first light blue, then darker and darker, turning to lavender, purple, then black. No one could guess how far down this crack might go, for at that point the depth of the glacier was not known. Slim heard the bottom was at least half-mile down, lost in the blackness of millions of tons of ice that had existed for ages.

One of the men standing there had let a lighted coal-oil lantern down into the opening by a rope. The light flickered eerily against the shining faces of ice. Another of the men cupped his hands to his mouth and leaned forward and yelled into the opening. "Can you hear me, Tom?"

From the crevasse came an answer like a voice through a megaphone. "Yes, I can hear you plain. I can see the light of the lantern, too."

Slim understood the situation immediately. "Let me try to get him out," he suggested. "I haven't got this name 'Slim' for nothin.'" He was already peeling off his parka and fastening the noose of rope under his arms.

As Slim sat on the lip of the crevasse giving his instructions, one of the men said, "Hope you can make it, Slim. We couldn't get to him, but you're thinner'n any of us. Tom as a little fella, skinnier'n you even, by a lot. He wasn't much bigger'n a kid."

"Well, I'll go as far as I can," said Slim hopefully. "There may be side cracks or something that he could o' slipped into if he was a little fella. Can't tell. You keep the rope tight and let me down slowly. If I find I'm gettin' wedged, I'll tell you and you pull me up. Now, let me down."

He slipped off the edge, and the men paid the rope out gradually. At about twenty feet down he called to them to stop. He was almost six feet deeper than the others had been able to go.

Slim talked with the imprisoned man. He could hear him clearly, and he learned why he could not see him. Just as he had feared, there was a side crack, which he could feel with his feet. Without a doubt the man had fallen directly down, then his body had slipped through this opening . There was no knowing how far or how deep he had fallen, but Slim knew that rescue was hopeless. He called to the men above to pull him up.

The four waiting men spoke almost at one time, "How about it, Slim? Did you get to him? Can we get him out?"

Slim slipped out of the rope noose and into his parka before he answered. Then he looked at the four hopeful faces and slowly shook his head. "There's a side crack down there he somehow slipped into. I talked with him, and his voice was like he was in a big hall. I was almost wedged so tight I couldn't move, and I wasn't even anywhere near him, so I don't see any way to get to him."

"He'll die!" said one of them. "We can't let him die down there like that."

Again Slim shook his head. "Nothin' anybody can do. It won't be bad. He'll just get cold, and finally he'll go to sleep. I'm awfully sorry, fellows. I wish I could've done more."

Slim went back to his work, completed his haul to the glacier summit, and by dusk was back where the accident had taken place. One man was still there. "The others went on," he told Slim, "but I stayed and talked with him until a couple of hours ago when he said he didn't feel any pain or anything and he was getting sleepy and was going to take a nap. He hasn't said anything since." Nor would he ever speak again. Cold, numbness, sleep, then frozen death: a pattern of northland tragedy.

Club Members Rescue Snowmachiner from Crevasse

by Larry Kaniut

SUMMIT LAKE: Eielson group pulls Anchorage man, sled to safety.

The Associated Press, November 27, 2002

Fairbanks -- With savvy and muscle, eight members of the Northern Lights Snowmachine Club helped rescue a snowmachiner stuck for an hour in a crevasse near Summit Lake.

The eight were part of a group of about 14 people who pulled the man and his snowmachine out of the hole near the College Glacier.

"I really appreciate those guys," said Paul White of Anchorage. "I'm certainly grateful for them. It really makes you appreciate life much more."

White said he was able to ride his sled off of the glacier that day thanks to the experienced crew.

He said he was snowmachining about 15 miles from the Richardson Highway on Sunday and saw the hole a little too late. He hit his brakes, then fell headfirst down the shaft about 30 feet until he landed on a snow bridge.

"I managed to get turned around and get my feet under me," White said. "But there was no way I could climb up because the walls were all ice."

He had lost his helmet and one glove and quickly started to get cold.

"I didn't have a whole lot of hope," White said.

But luck was on his side. The area around Summit Lake was crawling with snowmachiners. Because of the lack of snow across the state, snowmachiners flocked to the area north of Paxson over the weekend.

"There's no place else to ride. That's forcing us to go further and further back," said Ron Lutrell, one of the rescuers. Lutrell said the eight of them -- Chuck Hess, Chris Nichols, Scott Strout, Matt Gladieux, Cliff Millard, Bill Paddock, Chuck "Zeke" Veitenheimer and himself -- were taking a lunch break nearby when a "frantic man rode up and says his buddy is in a crevasse."

The group consisted of six Air Force personnel and two civilian employees at Eielson Air Force Base. They had met on their off hours for a weekend of snowmachining.

When they got to the crevasse, they could see a sled wedged upside down about 10 feet down in the hole and they could hear a voice shouting up at them. White was about 20 feet below his sled.

"It was not like a great, big long crevasse like you'd think. It was more like a wind rift," Lutrell said.

The situation was more precarious because of another crevasse located a few feet behind the group.

"The concern was the whole thing that we were standing on could break free," Lutrell said.

Lutrell, vice president of the North Pole area snowmachine club and a civilian worker at the base, and Chuck Hess, a technical sergeant at the maintenance squadron on base, took charge of the rescue efforts.

Many in the snowmachining club have attended avalanche rescue training at the Alaska Mountain Safety Center. Lutrell said that ever since he attended the class, he has carried shovels, rope and beacons with him while snowmachining.

They were able to lower a radio down to White. From there, they determined the snowmachine was firmly wedged in the hole.

Next, they lowered a rope down to lift him up. They ran into problems when the rope tightened around White's chest and he cried out for a knife to cut him loose.

Lutrell was then lowered and stood on the snowmachine. He gave the man a knife to cut himself loose. Then he instructed him how to tie a better knot.

"I've never stood on the track of a snowmachine before and believe me I didn't jump up and down and check the suspension," Lutrell said.

If it gave way, Lutrell gave special instructions to other members of the group. "Before I went down I told those guys, 'No matter what, don't let go of that rope,' " he said.

Once they had Lutrell and White out, Hess went down after the man's sled.

"There's no sense in leaving it there. There were enough guys there that we could get it out," he said. With three of his friends and a snowmachine anchoring him, Hess was lowered down until he was able to tie a strap around the trailing arms and the machine was hoisted out.

The snowmachine started on the first pull and the rescued man was able to ride it out.

Gobbled up by the Inlet

by Larry Kaniut

"At one point a particularly strong wind gust snapped his aluminum boom at a joint, breaking it."

Wind surfing caught a wave in Anchorage in the 1980's. When the glaciers carved out the region's valleys, Turnagain Arm was born. The Arm stretches southeast of Anchorage 35miles to the Twenty Mile and Placer rivers. The Arm varies in width from five miles to over a dozen. The major windsurfing area encompasses over 75 square miles of water.

Big winds funneling through combined with the Arm's large body of water and easy accessibility to Anchorage launched wind surfing and sail boarders. The surf was up, and the rush was on. Those in the search prayed for a windy day and congregated at their Church of the Windy Waves. It was great sport.

Their playground was an easy thirty-minute drive from nearly anywhere in the Anchorage bowl. On windy days passing drivers enjoyed the multitude of wind surfers plying the waters. Multi-colored sails attached to masts and booms zipped over the gray-brown, wind-swept waves as a gaggle of dry suit clad surfers cavorted and played. It was common to see a sailboard and rider bust a wave and sky ten to fifteen feet off the sizzling surf.

In the late 1980's one of the leaders of the pack suffered an experience that affected the entire body of wind surfers.

It was Saturday, August 6, 1988, a decent day for wind surfing. A dozen miles southeast of Anchorage sailboarders bounced over Turnagain Arm's waters between Potter weigh station and Beluga Point. The gusty winds created the choppy water the participants loved.

Off Beluga Point a dozen sailboarders rode the waves. The tide was relatively weak and the water was at its normal 57-degree temperature in upper Cook Inlet according to U.S. Coast Guard.

Experienced sailor Patrick Hallin was among the group. The 29-year-old Anchorageite was one of the most experienced surfers present. He was well equipped and wore a neoprene dry suit and boots, hood and gloves.

Although he was further out than the other sailors, he rode his board within a few hundred yards of them. At one point a particularly strong wind gust snapped his aluminum boom at a joint, breaking it.

Hallin disconnected the boom, mast and sail and gave them to another boarder to tow to shore. Meanwhile he lay on his belly on his 8-foot Fiberglas sailboard and began paddling by hand the few miles to shore. He was a strong swimmer and anticipated no problems. Patrick had a reputation for competence and was the kind of guy you'd want along if you were in trouble.

At 6:00 PM he was a mile off shore. When he failed to appear, fellow sailors grew concerned. He was last seen headed for Beluga Point at 6:30 PM. Boarders spread out on their sailboards and skipped over the waves searching for him.

An hour of serious searching resulted in nothing. When they failed to find him, one went to shore to notify the Alaska State Troopers.

A rescue helicopter and small fire department boat were dispatched to the area and their personnel searched until dark (which would have been around 10 PM at that time of year). They found nothing.

Speculation was that the outgoing tide had sucked Patrick out into Cook Inlet.

Friends and searchers hoped he was on his board or had been able to reach shore somewhere along the Arm. They expected a greater search effort the next day.

On Sunday the U.S. Coast Guard cutter Sweetbriar joined the search. Two Coast Guard choppers and several private fixed wing aircraft crisscrossed the Inlet from Point MacKenzie west of Anchorage and the drilling rigs on the west side of the Inlet. They found no sign of the missing man.

Twenty-four hours later friends continued to hope that Patrick was alive on his board or stranded on shore. Some searched the shoreline along the highway. Other friends of Patrick's walked the roadless shoreline on the south side of the Arm from Hope to Gull Rock and beyond, over six miles.

The ground searchers found no footprints or any sign of Hallin. Later in the day his florescent hot pink, green and yellow board was found floating within 75 feet of the beach near Point Possession, 15 miles west of Hallin's last reported whereabouts. No other trace of him was found.

By the end of the evening Sunday the Coast Guard called off its search. The Troopers, on the other hand, decided to consult the Hallin family before they made their final decision to call off their search.

On Monday planes flown by the Alaska State Troopers, Civil Air Patrol and friends found no sign of Hallin. If he had been on shore near the location of his surfboard, searchers would have found him.

On Tuesday efforts to locate the missing man were concentrated on the mudflats. But all efforts ended in failure.

It wasn't until almost a month later, Thursday, September 1, that part of the mystery unraveled. An oil production worker, Mike Petrov, was working on the Dillon Platform ten miles north of Kenai. It was about 5:00 PM when Mike, working 80 feet above the water's surface on an Amoco Production Company oil platform, saw something floating north beneath the platform. He thought the incoming tide was carrying an airplane pilot wearing a flight suit. Mike tossed a life preserver to the body and radioed the ERA Aviation helicopter.

Marathon had a vessel in the area which motored to the site a mile north of the platform and seven miles off shore. The vessel's personnel picked up the body, clad in a blue-black drysuit.

Troopers later identified the body as that of the missing man. Patrick Hallin had been found

EPILOGUE

What happened to Patrick from the time he was last seen paddling offshore until his body was found? While Patrick paddled toward shore, did he become too physically exhausted to complete his task? Was he knocked off his board by the wind or a wave? Was the tide too strong to overcome? Did he suffer hypothermia? Is it possible he got sick or blacked out? Maybe he had cramps which incapacitated him? Or did something like a log hit him, knocking him off his board or knocking him out?

It doesn't appear we'll ever know the answers to these questions. But there is every reason to learn from this tragedy and to hope that Patrick's loss will not have been in vain.

People in the community expressed concern and suggested that stronger measures be put in place to enhance the safety of other sailboarders. Sgt. Bill Farber, spokesperson for the Alaska State

Troopers, said Hallin lacked a life jacket and a tether.

Gary King is a sailboard enthusiast and owner of Gary King's Sporting Goods. He came to the defense of sailors' choice when it comes to life preservers and tethers. He said that most sail boarders do not usually wear life jackets because they're bulky and retard movement. The neoprene float dry suits they wear provide flotation but not as much as a life vest. Tethering restricts the rider and can cause problems for the sailors.

However a growing number of boarders agreed that in a situation where one has only the board, tethering is a good safety precaution because a wave can wash a sailor off his board or turn it over and separate him from it. It is common then for the wind to push the lighter more buoyant board away from the pursuing sailor faster than he can swim to it (consequently a tether would keep the board within reach).

Perhaps one of the best pieces of advice is for people to use the buddy system and sail with a partner, constantly checking on each other and never leaving your partner.

One precautionary measure used for a while was strobe lights. But most sailboarders felt they were an unnecessary piece of equipment and abandoned them about the time the accident occurred. People theorized Patrick would have been rescued if he'd had a strobe. But what if he was too weak or sick to activate it or to keep it visible to searchers?

Hopefully local sailboarders will continue to expand their safety knowledge and use the buddy system to provide safe return for all.

SOURCE NOTES:

1. "Surfer Missing in Inlet," David Hulen, *Anchorage Daily News*, August 8, 1988, pages B-1 and B-4

2. "Turnagain Arm search comes to halt," *The Anchorage Times*, August 8, 1988, page A-9

3. "Sailer's fate haunts surfers on the wind," Patti Harper, *The Anchorage Times*, August 14, 1988, pages A-1 and A-8

4. "Troopers identify dead man," Jean Lamming, *The Anchorage Times*, September 2, 1988, page A-10

Death on the River

by Larry Kaniut

Tongues of boiling gray water licked out at the rafters and plagued the raft. The oarsmen attempted to steer a safe route. A huge boulder on the left and its hydraulics created a problem as the water roared over the top. On the right a monster hole waited to gobble up the raft. Vigilance demanded the rowers' attention. They rowed away from the boulder, waddled onto the brink of the hole and the raft rolled up onto its side. The inflatable walked the tightrope of balance then dropped back onto the surface and was sucked into and swallowed by the hole. The bow smashed into a wave, the boat buckled and four rafters shot from the craft.

Three men remained aboard scanning the water for their companions. Four heads bobbed above the water's surface, and the men anticipated pulling them aboard. They knew that to raft wild water is to get wet. But rafting wild water is not synonymous with death.

Of course, white water poses dangers. Deep holes, which are hydraulic reversals downstream from boulders, can overturn a raft or toss passengers from it. Sweepers can rake a passenger from the safety of the boat. Cold water, just above freezing temperature, sucks the heat and energy from anyone immersed in it. Powerful water can propel a person against solid objects, shattering bones. Or it can suck or push people under log jams depriving them of oxygen. And rocks—both unmovable and moving—can seriously injure a person.

Sure, there's danger rafting wild water. But this trip was a slam dunk. No problem. Until the raft hit the hole.

It started out innocently enough. Paul Claus, 28-year-old wilderness guide, had agreed to help obtain video footage for an upcoming episode of the television show Jay Hammond's Alaska.

Paul would be working closely with his father, a former counselor at Anchorage's East High School and a big game guide. They had a family business based at their lodge on Bear Island in the Chitina River, a tributary of the Copper in the Wrangell-St. Elias Mountains. Paul had cut his teeth on adventure. He'd begun flying in his father's Super Cub as a youngster, later getting his private pilot's license at age 17. Paul led wilderness outings, taught deep-sea diving in Hawaii, worked as a commercial fisherman in Bristol Bay during summers.

The group included Jay Hammond, 66. The producer was Jay's long-time friend and filmmaker, Larry Holmstrom, 44, of Fairbanks. Larry's daughter Maria, 21-years-old, would be his production assistant. The cameraman was 31-year-old Ron M. Eagle, of Wasilla. Paul's assistant guide was 47-year-old Daniel Kovacik. And Paul's wife Donna, age 33, rounded out the group.

They'd have a day and a half to gather footage.

They started the first afternoon hiking Maccoll Ridge. Next day Paul gave Hammond and his crew some options. They balked at visiting a glacier as the weather was poor. Riding horseback didn't ring their chimes, not exciting enough for them. Claus suggested rafting the Tana and that got their attention.

They wanted action footage for the show. They were in the right spot for action and beauty. In the heart of the Wrangell-St. Elias Mountains beauty and ruggedness surrounded them. It was sixty miles to the nearest road, the Wrangell-Saint Elias Mountains National Park and Preserve includes 13.2 million acres of pristine wilderness, six-times the size of Yellowstone National Park.

Bagley Glacier crowns the Wrangell-Saint Elias Mountains, birthing the Tana Glacier. Carving its path through the mountains, the Tana River roars through 8,000-plus foot peaks, the largest coastal mountains in the world, forty-five miles from the Gulf of Alaska. The Tana River dumps into the Chitina River.

The Tana embodies remoteness and huge water—fast, cold and wild. Nestled in its route are eight or ten rapids the size of the Grand Canyon, dropping as much as 20-feet. Many rapids are riddled with violent water.

Hammond's group was ready to tackle the challenge.

Paul's father John flew one of the planes to help get the party some silver salmon fishing footage of Hammond. Then they prepared to hit the Tana.

It was the morning on August 6, 1988. John Claus dropped the group onto the river and the wind began to blow. They loaded their gear into the 16-foot inflatable raft and prepared to push off.

Prior to filming the Hammond whitewater footage, Ron Eagle videoed Larry and Maria for one of her girlfriends. Maria posed at the river's edge, smiling in the wind and looking into the camera lens.

Her father introduced the "video postcard" by saying, "We're here in the wilds of Interior Alaska with Maria von Intrepid, the noted canoeist, kayaker and white-water river rafter. Now Marie, perhaps you could tell us a little about this river that we're about to raft. How are the waves?" 1

Maria responded...slowly, "Big." They carried on a brief conversation in which Larry asked her if she'd ever been on a white-water raft and if she was concerned. She responded in the negative. But when her father asked her if she was cold at all, her answer was a quick "yes."

Father and daughter laughed and cavorted before the camera for her girlfriend.

Having rafted the river previously, Paul chose to use one raft. He said that, "If you don't have a real experienced boatman to run (the Tana), you're better off using only one boat." Otherwise, "you have twice as many places go wrong." 1

Paul acknowledged that his raft was heavy. That's one reason he opted to have two men at the oars rather than a single oarsman. He also felt it would be safer and more prudent to have two oarsmen rather than two rafts. He contended that a backup boat under those circumstances was not an option.

Paul and his assistant guide Daniel Kovacik had rowed the Tana in tandem three times previously without experiencing problems.

Other precautions Claus took on the Hammond trip included a radio on board, and Paul had pre-arranged for John to stand by at the lodge only 15 miles distant, a Super Cub and De Havilland Beaver at his command. Paul also provided a safety lecture for the rafters before they began the float.

The raft rode well on the first few rapids and the group experienced no problems. Hammond was impressed with the performance of the raft and stated, "Man, I can't believe how good this boat makes this. It's easy." 1

Beyond the first few rapids they turned a bend, walls of the canyon rising vertically along the waterline. Just ahead lay the Gates of the Aurora, the river's most difficult rapid. Before them rose waves large enough to flip the largest of rafts. Dangerous white water holes dominated the gray, snarling water.

They rounded the bend. All eyes were downriver. Larry and Maria Holstrom sat in the bow with Donna Claus.

In the stern Hammond and Eagle prepared for the rapids. Eagle held the camera with one hand and grasped the raft with the other.

Claus had suggested that he store the camera until after this frothy hole, but Eagle said he wanted to film the action. Paul Claus and Dan Kovacik manned the oars.

Because it had been only a couple of days since they had rafted the river, Claus felt no need to scout the water they'd pass through.

He knew that a huge boulder on the left hand side could be problematic because of the water boiling over its top. He also knew that efforts to avoid it could put the raft into the huge hole on the right side of it. They needed to thread the needle between the two, and the worst would be behind them.

They overcompensated to avoid the boulder on the left. That put them squarely on course to drop into one of the largest whitewater holes in the Great Land. The raft shot into the hole they had so desperately hoped to avoid.

Later Jay Hammond declared, "It felt like it was going to flip over, but it didn't." 1 The raft pitched sharply before veering onto its side, took on water, then regained its balance.

Claus later remembered the incident, "We went down into it, and I saw it coming. The last thing I remember saying to everybody is, 'Hang on!' as loud as I could yell." 1

The bow slammed into a wave and veered to the side. Instantly the raft filled with water. A gear bag ripped away. The rafters in the bow—Larry and Maria Holstrom and Donna Claus—tumbled into the water on the left. Ron Eagle dropped off the stern into the water.

Apparently all four failed to hold onto the raft.

Claus commented, "It was just like instead of listening to what I said, they did just the opposite. The boat came up and they kinda threw out their arms...It didn't seem that violent. It wasn't a real buckaroo action or anything." 1

He believes that the Holstroms let go and that their combined momentum tumbling against Donna caused her to fall overboard.

Hammond theorized that Eagle fell out because he was trying to save his camera. They hit the water ahead of the raft. Their heads were above the water. Downstream diagonally crossing waves churned into treacherous water.

In the brief moments following the dumping those in the water floated downstream from the raft, their heads were above the water and they seemed to be alright.

Hammond said that "They were alert, and they didn't look

particularly panicked. Even then I wasn't particularly alarmed." 1

Claus was pleased to see that "They were doing what I told them. They had their...feet downstream and they were paddling backwards." 1

However huge waves awaited below.

Hammond concentrated on bailing water from the raft.

Claus was concerned about getting his pregnant wife into the raft and said, "I don't know if she was absolutely the closest...She was as close as anybody. She was my wife, and she was four months' pregnant. And the only thing I could think about was getting her back in right now." 1

He and Kovacik pulled Donna aboard as they entered the waves while water pummeled the raft for 30 seconds. Claus looked around for someone else to rescue. Moments later they emerged from the waves. They scanned the water for their floating companions. They were mystified at what they saw. They spotted them in the water, faces partially in the water. Claus spoke about it, "Then we went through some more rough water and by a wall and kind of lost track of them. The next time we saw them, rather than having that alert look, their heads were in the water." 3

"...I absolutely couldn't believe it...Instead of heads up and alert, they were just blobs in the water. None of them appeared to be conscious." 1

Ron Eagle was floating closest to the raft. Claus dived in and began administering CPR on him while they were in the water.

Hammond helped pull Eagle into the raft. Jay later stated, "He looked bad. Right from the moment we pulled him aboard." 1

Eagle had dropped his Betacam into the river. Still a 35-millimeter camera hung from his neck (wrapped around "about six times" according to Hammond).

Eagle did not respond to the CPR.

Two minutes later they pulled Maria into the raft. Blood oozed slightly from one of her ears. They thought she looked good. Claus said, "She was warm. Her color was not bad. I thought sure we were going to be able to save her." 1

Hammond and Donna Claus administered CPR on Ron and Maria as the raft continued downriver. But neither of them responded.

Meanwhile Larry Holmstrom had drifted downstream toward the next rapid. A water-tight, red gear bag floated next to him. Claus thought Holmstrom was alive and holding onto it. Faced with the decision of whether to retrieve Holmstrom or to beach the raft and more adequately perform CPR on the other two, Claus chose to go to shore.

They worked on Maria and Ron about an hour and 25 minutes. Claus said, "I had pretty much given up hope, but kept working. I hoped that Larry had made it out." 3

Ten minutes later Claus and Kovacik pushed off in the raft to continue downstream after Holmstrom and to get help. He left food and told his wife and Hammond that he didn't know when he'd be back.

In the meantime John Claus flew his DeHavilland Beaver over the pickup point but did not see the rafters. He spotted an emergency signal and returned to base camp at Bear Island. He then returned to the Tana in a Super Cub and picked up Paul at a gravel bar that served as a landing strip. John flew his son to the ranger station at May Creek 20 miles east of the canyon to report the incident.

The Chitina ranger station was notified and a helicopter was dispatched to the scene where Hammond and Donna Claus awaited with the bodies of Ron Eagle and Maria Holmstrom. Because of darkness the helicopter was unable to reach the scene.

During ranger preparations to launch the chopper, Paul Claus boarded his Super Cub and buzzed the home of his friend and neighbor Bob Jacobs in McCarthy. He flew over a second time and shouted for Jacobs to meet him at the airstrip. An emergency had arisen.

Jacobs recalled later, "He said that his wife and Jay Hammond were stuck on the river. That there were two people who were probably dead." 1

Jacobs tossed some things into a backpack and flew with Claus to a small sandbar five miles below the accident on the Tana River. Jacobs was to hike upstream to Hammond and Donna Claus' location while Claus planned to spend the night at the sandbar with Kovacik helping search for Larry Holmstrom.

Jacobs found Jay and Donna around 11 PM. He said, "They were in good spirits. As good spirits as you can be in with two dead bodies…Jay Hammond had already built a little wikiup out of alder brush. It was raining." 1

Jacobs set up a tent, laid out some sleeping bags and made dinner. He also helped Donna and Jay tie the drowning victims to a tree in case the river rose during the night.

Larry Holmstrom's body was found by park service rangers the next day floating in an eddy. The bodies of the three were flown to Glennallen.

Dr. Michael Propst, state medical examiner, concluded that all three died by drowning, but that hypothermia was listed as a contributing cause. "Since this was a glacial river and none of the victims were wearing wet- or dry suits, their body temperatures would have been lowered quickly. They would have rapidly lost the ability to save themselves," Propst said. 1

None had severe head injuries.

After word of the accident got out, the whitewater pros and the Monday morning quarterbacks jumped in to evaluate it. The bulk of the professional whitewater people questioned such things as the water level, Paul Claus' choice to raft the river without scouting, the use of only one raft—which many considered overloaded, the failure to provide all in the party dry suits, the absence of helmets and the use of two oarsmen.

It's much easier to speculate after the fact. Or from miles away when not on scene.

According to Vaughn Baker, a National Park Service ranger at Glennallen, following a week of warm days, the glacial water was running higher than normal and would be in the Class 4 category (on a scale of one to five, five being the most dangerous whitewater).

However Paul Claus, who lived in the neighborhood, stated, "The river was actually lover than normal, and there were almost no rocks exposed. It was almost an ideal river level. It was simply a freak accident." 3

Some expressed concern that the only one to survive the water was Donna Claus who wore a dry suit (both she and Paul were the only rafters wearing them).

Jay Hammond commented that their life jackets were adequate, "There was no problem...The life jackets were all Coast Guard approved and were very adequate from the standpoint of buoyancy." 1

A co-owner of Denali Raft Adventures commented about hypothermia, "You put somebody in sub-40 degree water and it doesn't take long at all to get hypothermic...And once that happens, you lose your strength, your will, your desire. You finally just stop fighting." 1

When questioned about leaving Larry Holmstrom and going to

the beach to provide better First Aid to Maria and Ron, Claus said, "That was a tough decision. But that's what I did."

In retrospect Jay Hammond said concerning the guides, their gear and the situation, "I never felt personally imperiled. Even when the people were in the water, I thought these guys were so expert at handling that thing—and so quickly snatched out the first two people, and even Marcie—that I was quite frankly impressed." 1 Jay noted that you can't make the wilderness risk free.

In retrospect Claus said, "Yeah, sure, there's a whole bunch of stuff I'd do differently. Everybody would have helmets. I wouldn't let them go down the river unless I had them now. I just flat wouldn't do it." 1

Claus has chosen to delete the Tana River from future commercial whitewater trips for safety, experience and insurance reasons.

He agreed that the Tana is a dangerous river, "The Tana is a powerful river. And even if you had everything absolutely ideal with your helmets and your dry suits and everything else, someone could still get killed there." 1

SOURCE NOTES:

1. "Return to the Tana," George Bryson, pp. N6-N17, We Alaskans, *Anchorage Daily News*, September 10, 1989

2. "TV crew killed filming raft trip with Hammond," pp. A1 &A8, *The Anchorage Times*, August 18, 1988

3. "Raft survivors: Safety measures were not omitted," Dean Fosdick, pp. A1 & A8, *The Anchorage Times,* August 9, 1988

4. "Return to the Tana," George Bryson, pp. N6-N17, We Alaskans, *Anchorage Daily News*, September 10, 1989

5. "TV crew killed filming raft trip with Hammond," pp. A1 &A8, *The Anchorage Times*, August 18, 1988

6. "Raft survivors: Safety measures were not omitted," Dean Fosdick, pp. A1 & A8, *The Anchorage Times*, August 9, 1988

Jeff's Last Run

by Larry Kaniut

On more than one occasion I've considered writing as a troublesome job. Usually it's because I dislike the implication that I get paid to write about people's travails. Sometimes it's because I have a close relationship with or know the victim. Like now.

When I looked at the front page of the *Anchorage Daily News* April 9, 1995, I saw the headline "Snowboarder dies at Valdez." Normally the only troubling part of a story like this is the fact that someone died. But this time it was more troubling because the story was about someone I knew.

The story chronicled Jeff Ambridge's experience snowboarding. Jeff wrestled for Dimond High School during my last tenure as the wrestling coach in the late 1980s. Now I'm reading about him in the paper. And I'm not pleased with the story.

Jeff was an avid snowboarder. His friend Scott Frost said, "Jeff lived to snowboard. If he had to die, that's where he would have wanted to do it—right there on the mountain." The previous month Jeff competed in the Alaska Extreme Ski and Snowboard Trials held at Alyeska Ski Resort. He finished 11th in the competition.

He worked hard during the summer months in the landscaping field with his friend Hans Bohlman. They had wrestled, hung out and graduated together from Dimond High School in 1989. They both loved the thrill of life and a good time. They were buds. Jeff saved his money so he could snowboard with friends like Hans during Alaska's long winter.

The thrill of snowboarding and the chance to watch the King of the Hill Extreme Snowboarding World Championship in April near Valdez, Alaska, was like an elixir that drew Jeff and his buddies. The Championship drew 30 world-class competitors who came from several states, Australia and Europe.

The trio of Ambridge, Bohlman and Frost, all in their 20s, had driven in Ambridge's camper with other friends Wednesday to snowboard in Thompson Pass thirty miles north of Valdez. All day Thursday and Friday they kicked up snow from their boards, slicing and dicing down-mountain.

Saturday Jeff and his pals headed out to Thompson Pass where some planned to board off Schoolbus Mountain, down Snatch Glacier. Among those friends were Scott Frost and Hans Bohlman.

At 23-years of age Jeff was known for his toughness, his hard work, ready smile and love of adventure. He looked forward to snowboarding, watching the competition and participating in the post-competition revelry

Recreational snowboarders swarmed the landscape, dark dots zipping downhill. They were eager to practice and enjoy their sport before capping off their day's boarding with the nighttime activity. Included in the group was the Jackson Hole Air Force, a nonmilitary mountain rescue team based in Wyoming which had come to heli-ski and observe the competition.

Once they arrived, Jeff and Hans rode on a snow machine with a friend to the top of the ridge, 4,500 feet up Schoolbus Mountain. They dismounted and carried their snowboards across the intervening snow on an old snow machine track to their take off point. They planned to follow the path of Anchorage snowboarder Mark Keith who had safely completed the run down Snatch Glacier earlier in the week. At the top of the steep run Hans and Jeff debated who should go first.

Hans said later that, "We had the usual 'Who's gonna go first' debate, and we were going back and forth...then I took another look and got a real bad feeling in my gut and told Jeff I didn't want to go. So he hopped on his board and took off. I put on my board, stood up and was getting ready to follow when I saw him go in."

Frost had remained 1,500 feet below his friends atop Ambridge's camper to capture the run on video tape. He watched the pair through the telephoto lens of the video camera as they ascended the slope on the snowmachine. He sat atop the camper, parked adjacent to the Richardson Highway on a muddy side road.

While Jeff and Hans strapped on their snowboards, Frost scanned their proposed route with the lens. That's when he spotted the crevasse. He said, "It was a big hole. The voice inside me was telling them 'NO, don't go down there,' but then I realized they couldn't see (the crevasse)."

Filled with horror and helpless to do a thing about the ensuing moments, Frost could only watch and hope that his pals would complete the run unscathed.

The last thing Hans saw of Jeff was his plunge into a crevasse and a puff of snow. The last thing he heard was a scream. "I have this horrid vision that I can't get to leave my head. It's like a loop of film that won't stop; I see Jeff go off the cornice, I see the little butt check (minor fall) he made, then he disappears. I see the poof of snow go up in the air, I hear the scream, and Jeff's gone."

For the most part, Jeff followed Mark Keith's snowboard track on the snow, varying slightly at the point of his fall. He was traveling five feet from Keith's tracks when the bottom fell out belowh his board.

Frost saw a cloud of snow billow up from the crevasse. He instantly yelled for his friend Tim Strike to seek help. Strike hustled to a commercial heli-ski operations landing zone and ran into several members of the Jackson Hole mountain rescue squad.

Meanwhile Bohlman was screaming for a response from Ambridge. Hans had soared down the slope on his board and inched his way to the opening of the crevasse. He said, "I yelled and yelled but Jeff never yelled back. I wanted to help him so bad."

While this was transpiring Frost feared Hans would end up in the crevasse with Ambridge and he'd lose two friends.

When Bohlman reached the site, he saw nothing but chunks of ice and the black, empty void below. After yelling a few more times and getting no response from Ambridge, Hans pointed the tip of his snowboard downhill and blasted toward the distant ribbon of asphalt.

He said, "I went as fast as I could, straight down. My sunglasses flew off my face, but I kept going. When I got down, I ripped off my board and started running. I was so terrified and tired....I had drool coming out both sides of my mouth, and I was gasping 'cause I just kept yelling 'Help!; over and over."

Bohlman's friends surrounded him and told him that a rescue attempt was underway.

Ambridge disappeared into the crevasse around 4 p.m. Strike approached the 8-member Jackson Hole crew five minutes later, and by 4:15 the team was in the air, choppering up slope to the site.

Setting up anchors above and to the sides of the chasm, the team prepared for someone to rappel into the depths. One member soloed into the hole to look for Ambridge.

What he found was far from encouraging. Ghastly would be a more accurate description. Thirty feet down the rope he found hair and blood on the side of the wall. Ten feet further down he encountered blocks of fallen ice spawned by the collapse of the snow bridge that had plunged Ambridge into the chasm. Much of that snow bridge caved in and onto Jeff.

For two hours he probed the ice debris with a pole. That's when he found Ambridge's body, beneath five feet of ice.

After two and a half hours of watching from below through the long lens of the video camera, Ambridge's friends knew that their pal was no longer with them. Dejected, they got into Ambridge's camper for the slow, sad drive to Valdez.

Strike said, "Driving that camper is the hardest thing I've ever done. There were no tunes, no laughs like usual when we rode in it."

Those gathered at the Totem Inn parking lot had learned earlier the name of the missing snowboarder. When word got out that it was Ambridge, Eric Kross, an Anchorage musician and snowboarder, said, "Jeff is tough. He'll make it."

Moments later, however, Kross learned that Jeff hadn't made it. A sad group tried to make sense of the news.

In the closing hours of the day the rescue group retrieved Ambridge's body, hoisting it out of its tomb. The rescuers believed that Ambridge died instantly, suffering severe head injuries while tumbling down the crevasse. After collapsing through the first snow bridge, he landed on the bridge 40-feet below and ice chunks from the initial bridge pummeled then buried him.

The awards banquet for the King of the Hill Extreme Snowboarding World Championship was interrupted around 9 p.m. with the announcement that a fellow snowboarder had dropped into a crevasse. The rumor was that he was alive and lodged on a ledge where rescuers had a problem with his rescue.

Two hours later, the banquet with its 250 attendees, was interrupted again by Steve Klassen who announced, "We had a fellow boarder die today. His name was Jeff. I don't know exactly what to say. Let's just hope he's in a really special place right now." He asked for a moment of silence before stating, "All right, Jeff, this night's for you, buddy." A loud cheer rose from the crowd as the band began to play.

Later Jeff's family said, "The joy of Jeff was felt by all who knew him and his attitude toward life could be seen in his smile and heard in his laughter, both of which will be missed by all."

His mother said, "Jeff was the kind of child every mother should have the chance to raise. He was so easy going, so pleasurable. He never had an angry word against the world. Knowing him for his lifetime has been one of the most pleasurable experiences of my life."

And his father spoke of him, "Jeff was always an optimist. He was always full of joy for life. Snowboarding was what he lived for. He and his friends would climb a mountain and stay up there all night just to snowboard down in the morning. He was a typical Alaskan— free-spirited, never one to sit around when he could be having fun outdoors. He loved this state. He loved fishing. He loved the summer and he loved the snow."

Jeff's fall into the crevasse marked the third such event in the same number of days during the competition for King of the Hill. Neither of the first two mishaps resulted in any serious injury.

Jeff Ambridge made his last run down the glacier. Although his friends mourned his loss, they felt he would think them soft if they gave up the sport he loved. Perhaps Scott Frost said it best, "We've got to keep riding for him...and when we ride, he'll always be with us."

SOURCE NOTES:

1.   "Snowboarder dies at Valdez," David Holthouse, April 9, 1995, pp. B1 & B2, *Anchorage Daily News*

2.   "Friends can only watch as snowboarder falls to death," David Holthouse, April 10, 1995, pp. A1 & A10, *Anchorage Daily News*

3.   "Obituaries," April 12, 1995, B6, *Anchorage Daily News*

Hike Turned Nightmare

by Larry Kaniut

"They were completely soaked...Lorna's hands were numb. Husband and wife shivered, and Lorna couldn't even speak."

The petite lady eagerly ascended the trail. Hadn't she and her husband Zeke been told it would be a leisurely three day hike of twenty-six miles? She outdistanced Zeke, Rod, Darcie and Chad as she rambled up through the scattered spruce and alder thickets towards timberline, knowing that the sooner she got up the steep part, the easier it would be going downhill.

Because she wasn't getting enough oxygen, Lorna realized that in her excitement to begin the hike she had started too fast and was hyperventilating. Her experience warned her of her need to slow down her breathing to normal. She knew that her protein breakfast was not as adequate in producing energy as carbohydrates and fruits would have been.

Chad and Zeke went on ahead while Rod and Darcie dropped back to accompany Lorna. The trailers dropped farther and farther behind as Lorna was forced to stop more frequently.

Lorna and her husband Zeke had left the parking lot near Girdwood, Alaska, at 11:00 AM. Friday, June 19, 1988. Their party included Rod, their host, and his two teen-aged children--Chad and Darcie.

As their group scampered for the skyline cabin, they were glad to be alive. Anticipating the mysteries of the twenty-six mile trail that lay ahead, their immediate objective was to have a good time enjoying the trail and the fellowship. Their goal for the day was a cabin at the 3,000-foot elevation where they would spend the night, just shy of Crow Creek Pass.

The further up the steep, mountain trail they progressed the fewer spruce trees they saw, and the more boulders they encountered. The trail became more vertical, evidenced by switchbacks and rougher rock formations. Old mining equipment lay derelict along the trail.

As the group climbed steadily upward, the warm sun caressed

them. They neared the halfway point to the cabin and stopped for lunch. It was 2:30 in the afternoon, and since Alaska's long summer days provided plenty of daylight, there was no urgency to reach the cabin.

While eating lunch and listening to her companions reveling in their outing, Lorna had a chance to review the morning's events. She had long since slowed her pace to reduce her heart rate. She knew the dangers of her diabetic condition and conscientiously chose to regulate her body's energy output.

The stop for lunch gave her added fuel and a chance to rest aching muscles. Before long the trail beckoned.

After a while however, Rod increased his stride, outdistancing the women, catching and passing Zeke and Chad. It wasn't long until Rod was out of sight. The many switchbacks gobbled up the leading hikers, taking them from view of the others within moments, even though only fifty to a hundred yards separated them.

In late afternoon and three miles from the parking lot trail head Rod reached the cabin, followed a short time later by Zeke and Chad. The cabin, an A-frame sixteen feet long and sixteen feet wide with a loft and room to sleep ten, was surrounded by snow patches a few inches deep. The cabin would provide shelter for the night. Although an outhouse was nearby, it was inaccessible because of the snow piled against its door.

Inside were a couple of bunks, a stove and an attic-loft. Although the Forest Service required users to reserve the facility, the hikers did not have reservations. They ate, visited a while and prepared for bed.

It was then that Zeke discovered that his double sleeping bag was a single. He had purchased it assuming it would be adequate for him and Lorna, but it wasn't.

As they fell asleep, they entertained thoughts of the morrow. Ahead of them lay the summit and a downhill hike into the visitors' center at the end of the road out of Eagle River. They should be there easily by Sunday evening, covering half the downhill distance each of the next two days.

Some time during the night a couple arrived at the cabin. Since Rod's group occupied the main floor, the newcomers took the loft. Along with the couple's arrival came the wind and rain. Rain fell steadily and the wind tattooed the cabin all night long.

By morning neither rain nor wind had slackened. Both groups arose and ate. Rod's group prepared to leave knowing they'd have some snow patches to cross before reaching the summit. Zeke wore a cheap rain suit consisting of pants and coat while Lorna donned a poncho. It would be but a short time before they realized their rain gear was woefully inadequate.

Although Rod's group started out first, it wasn't long before the experienced couple from the loft overtook and passed them.

When Rod's party had started out, everything was fine. They thought they were prepared for the hike and could handle it. What they hadn't realized was that this was more than a hike--it was to become a survival trek.

At the outset Zeke fell on the snow and ripped his rain pants, rendering them useless as a water-wind proof garment. Both Zeke and Lornas' packs became thoroughly wet. Because nothing inside was in water or airtight containers, everything therein also got wet— food, toilet paper, extra clothes.

A discernible difference existed between Zeke and Lorna and Rod and his children. It was obvious that Zeke and Lorna were not as experienced at hiking as Rod and his children. Only a week before Rod had taken Chad and Darcie on a hike, a trip that Lorna and Zeke felt would have given them a better feel for this trip had they been able to experience it. Even though they had been invited to go on this pre-hike trip, they had declined the offer.

As the morning wore on, the fatigue and frustration factor set in as both Lorna and Zeke realized that they were not prepared for this hike. They had a totally false impression of what they were getting into. They had never engaged in a hike of this nature and assumed from what they'd been told, that this was to be a leisurely hike, a few hours of steep, uphill travel to a cabin, then a rest of a few hours and after that all downhill. No problem.

Zeke's cold-clouded mind became increasingly concerned. In the days before this trip their longest hike had been across town, a distance of six miles or so. He'd had no fear of the hike. Zeke had feared only an encounter with a bear or an unhappy moose. The problems that they'd encountered so far hadn't even registered with him until now. His attitude was that they would walk up the pass, walk right down and walk right out within three days, a few miles a day and Bingo, they'd be done. His philosophy was "all you have to do is put one foot in front of the other. What else is there to it? It's simple." But the wind, the rain and their condition called up another scenario.

Zeke wondered how far the group would get in the bad weather. He recognized his wife's trouble. By the time they got to the pass, they thought they could get through this part. But he had no idea how much further they had to go. He was getting tired, and he deduced if he was, Lorna surely was.

They were not used to carrying packs. Their thirty-five pound packs seemed heavy to them. They trudged along in the blowing wind and falling rain.

Zeke found himself wishing they'd never come, and hoping for a way that they could get out of the weather. Lorna entertained similar thoughts. She was angry.

She was having a problem just standing up. She was generally miserable in the rain, cold, wet, gravel, rocky, dark and cloudy terrain.

They lurched along for a while, stumbled, fell into the snow patches, arose and stopped every little bit. For Lorna the hike had become predictable—walk a little way, fall down, someone would help her back to her feet only to stumble on and fall again.

After so much of this activity Lorna realized she could go no further. They were in the fury of the wind at the summit of the pass, and getting out of the weather was imperative to Lorna's health. They began setting up their tent.

The wind was blowing very strongly; and they had a hard time with the tent. Rod sent his son and daughter ahead to the other side of the summit; and he stayed and helped set up the tent. The tent was set up as far as it had a frame. There was no way to peg it, to hold it down. The only way to hold it down was to be in it. Lorna and Zeke entered the tent as Rod left them to join his children.

Lorna was physically exhausted and knew that Zeke wasn't too far behind. They were completely soaked. Although their feet weren't in too bad of shape, Lorna's hands were numb. Husband and wife shivered, and Lorna couldn't even speak.

Being cold, wet and sleepy Zeke decided to take a nap, thinking everything would be alright after that. Lorna fought sleep. She thought if Zeke fell asleep, they wouldn't survive. Thinking that this was the end, she told herself, "It's over."

Meanwhile Rod had rejoined Darcie and Chad. Thinking he'd finish preparing their camp then return for Zeke and Lorna, his thoughts were interrupted by the approach of some other hikers.

The newcomers consisted of Dick Griffith, 62-year-old renowned Alaskan hiker, his son Barney and Doug Hubar. Rod told them about his friends and asked the newcomers to stop to help them. Only moments after Lorna and Zeke got inside their tent Griffith's group showed up.

Griffith called out, "Hello. How you doing?" and looked inside. What he saw, Lorna and Zeke sitting lethargically in their soaked clothes and staring toward the opening listlessly, alerted Griffith that this was an emergency. Griffith, a veteran of outdoor survival scrapes, knew he had to get the couple to safety. Griffith told them, "We've got to get you off the mountain."

Zeke told him they were cold and wet. They were unable to walk, and the quickest means of getting them to safety was to slide them down a snowfield.

Barney took one of them while Doug took the other, sliding with them down a snow chute. Dick followed with their gear. The rescuers got the couple out of their clothes and into dry sleeping bags. After that Lorna and Zeke were given hot soup.

Griffith's group continued on their round trip journey.

During the next three hours Zeke and Lorna slept. After that time the couple roused themselves to continue the journey. Lots of daylight remained. They decided they could complete the hike on schedule if they gained another three or four miles before camping.

They got into some dry clothing and got going that evening. They hiked to a stream and discovered the bridge was out. They had to find a shallow place to cross the stream to the trail on the other side.

Lorna was able to go only about a mile before the group decided to stop for the night. Even though Lorna wore two pair of socks (wool socks w. cotton socks on the outside), she still managed to get blisters while wearing work boots.

On Sunday morning when they got ready to go, Lorna had made up her mind to keep up with the group. Zeke was carrying the sleeping bag and the tent and all the wet clothes in a plastic bag. He kept having trouble with it, kept dropping it or having it fall from one side or another in his pack. As it turned out everybody else got out ahead of him. As they walked towards the river, he kept wondering if he was ever going to see the rest of the people.

After a time he stopped and rested a bit. Darcie and Lorna walked up behind him. He didn't know how he'd passed them. Rod and his son were up ahead. After eating they continued, and before long Darcie moved ahead of the couple.

Lorna and Zeke got used to bringing up the rear. They were at a disadvantage because they had no idea how far ahead the others were.

The couple wondered about Rod and Chad when Chad appeared.

He had returned to lead them to the river. It was supposed to be just around the corner, but Lorna didn't think they'd ever make it. They'd find a place to stop and then come back to get the stragglers. It became routine for one of Rod's children to return to Lorna or Zeke and hike with them.

One of the blessings of Saturday is that the group had managed to stay dry. Even though there was a constant mist or occasional rain and their outers were damp the entire time, they were able to keep dry.

Eventually they reached the river. They prepared to cross the first branch knowing the rocks beneath the surface were smooth, round and slippery and that the water was running pretty fast. Then they crossed the second one. Just before they reached the shore Lorna fell to her knees. At the same time Zeke fell into the knee deep water. For some reason they couldn't get up. Rod's son returned and extended his hand. He helped them regain their feet, took Zeke's pack and they made it across okay.

After the group crossed the river, they stopped and made lunch... had some soup. After lunch they headed out again and that night they stopped for the evening on a little sand bar on the river, where they saw a bear high above them on the mountain.

They got up in the morning Monday and headed out again. They were going along the cliff stepping cautiously because the river had eroded the bank away. As had become the custom, Rod and his children were ahead of Lorna and Zeke. Always out of sight. Zeke and Lorna kept stopping to catch their breath or take the pack off for a little bit.

Zeke couldn't get enough water. He constantly stopped for water breaks.

Lorna labored along in a state of exhaustion, and it didn't take much to discourage her. She would come up against an obstacle and stop right there and say, "This is it. I can't go on any further." After a while she'd decide she had to go on, so they'd continue on.

At one point that morning Lorna had a spell of blindness. They had eaten a hurried and inadequate breakfast. Lorna's sugar level dropped. Zeke had a whistle which he blew. The others heard the whistle and came back. Zeke told them what was wrong.

Everyone was pretty alarmed. Lorna needed something to eat quick. They got some little snack bars. Zeke and Lorna stayed until she came out her temporary blindness while the others continued. She popped out of it a short time later.

As the group neared the end of their journey, Rod hustled his family along since Darcie had to get back into town. That would permit Lorna and Zeke to continue at their own pace while not slowing down the leaders. Figuring Lorna and Zeke would get out that night or early the next morning the plan was to have somebody return to check on them.

Still uncertain as to the distance to the end of their journey, Lorna and Zeke continued to plod along at an easy pace. They followed the trail, stopped for lunch and pressed on. By now they'd reached the area called the burn. Not long after that they saw a man and a woman coming in their direction. They were the park people, Chugach State Park rangers. They asked Lorna and Zeke if they'd be able to go on out if the rangers relieved them of their packs.

After being told it was about four miles, the couple decided they could make it.

They walked through a boulder strewn area about as fast as they could until they finally got to the visitors' center on the Eagle River side at 6:30 PM, taking longer than they'd thought it would. They had walked eleven difficult miles to complete their journey. It wasn't until the last day that their clothes completely dried out.

They reached their car and drove home. By the time they reached their home in east Anchorage around 8 o'clock they felt pretty good. Lorna gave herself a foot bath to take care of her blisters. Later Zeke developed problems with toe nails. After three nights in a tent, it was good to be home to a soft, dry bed and under a leak proof roof.

Looking back Zeke and Lorna acknowledged their lack of experience and conditioning in the kind of hiking involved hampered their hike. Their physical condition developed a negative mental outlook which was very stressful. In addition to Lorna's concern for her diabetic condition and resultant needs, Zeke expended mental energy with his concern for Lorna. Before they go out again, they will be better prepared and in better condition.

Man Survives Waterfall

by Larry Kaniut

SITKA: Gallant clung to rock for 2 1/2 hours until help arrived

Peter Porco, *Anchorage Daily News*, August 29, 2002

I re-wrote Peter's article June 2021

Three men working with the U.S. Forest Service camped at Pavlof Lake, a narrow mile-long lake on the east side of Chichagof Island, roughly 55 miles north of Sitka. Employees of the Hoonah Indian Association, their job was to determine whether sockeye salmon in the area can meet subsistence needs. While William Sanders cooked breakfast in their platform camp—a tent on a float in the lake—Fred Gallant and Jerome Abbott, both from Hoonah, headed out in the flat-bottom fifteen-foot skiff.

With heavy rains Tuesday night, water coming down the hills from Pavlof River poured into the lake.

About 10:30 AM, the two found themselves pushed by the wind and current into shallow water where their outboard motor was useless. They were closing fast on the falls, when Gallant yelled to Abbott that he was going to jump out of the craft. The Pavlof Lake falls, roughly 50 feet wide, slope down at first at a low angle. Then they drop quickly, to about 45 degrees and steeper, dumping into Pavlof Bay. The tremendous volume of water made them more treacherous than usual.

Gallant tried to jump free before the crest, but his foot snagged on a corner of the skiff. He wore a flotation vest but also chest waders and when he fell into the water, his waders filled and he went under. The water pressure took him under for over a minute and he had to fight for his next breath. Abbott had also jumped from the boat and clung to it, trying to keep it from slipping downstream. He managed to make his way to shore.

Gallant ended up going down the falls another 10 feet, right behind the boat and he clung to it, standing thigh-deep in the water. Felt lined the soles of his boots and gave him purchase on slippery rocks. He knew that if he placed his total weight on the boat, it would go over the falls with him. All he could do was hold on.

Meanwhile tourists on the lake trail summoned help. Rescuers headed that way from nearby Tenakee Springs and from Hoonah. State Troopers, the Coast Guard and forest rangers were mobilized. Gallant's feet eventually went numb, not from cold but from the strained position he held. He thought of his two beautiful children at home and a community that supported him.

Two and a half hours later the Coast Guard helicopter arrived and plucked him from the swollen waterfall, dropping a line and a rescuer. Gallant was uninjured.

Jerry Austin to the Rescue

by Larry Kaniut

Sometimes tragedy strikes and things work out okay/people survive without the help of others. Sometimes the survival of participants requires a cast of heroes. This is one of those times/ stories. During the 1988 Iditarod, known as The Last Great Race, which covers 1000-plus miles from Anchorage to Nome, Alaska, a dog musher came down with a serious illness. Although he might have made it alone, the likelihood was slim. Fortunately for him he shared the trail with a bunch of good people who put his safety above their personal gain.

Surrounded by miles of snow covered wilderness, the dog musher clung to his sled. Delirious and weak, Mike Madden wondered what was wrong. Could the cut in McGrath have gotten infected? What was causing the waves of faintness? Things were fuzzy. His muscles felt like jelly.

Although he'd cut his right leg with an ax while preparing dog food in McGrath and he had received three stitches, Mike had hit the trail without losing much time.

Now his right knee throbbed with pain.

That evening he stopped to feed his dogs at 6:30. But he didn't have the energy. His trail partner and fellow racer, Jamie Nelson, helped him.

Wearing a vest and a wool shirt, very light clothing for the weather, she commented on "how beautiful it was." 3

Mike Madden said, "I had on parkas, goose down, pile. I was just chattering my teeth and my head was real rummy." 3 He told Jamie that he was having trouble thinking. They were preparing to enter one of the longest, and, perhaps, one of the most barren, stretches of the race, 90-miles between Ophir and Iditarod.

Before he left Ophir Jerry Austin had given him some pointers on the stretch of trail ahead. He knew he had to remain conscious and on the sled until he could get help in Iditarod. Got to keep going. Jamie was somewhere behind him. Maybe she could help.

Flat land punctuated by stunted spruce trees covered the ground.

Stars filled the sky and cold chewed on him.

Mike was alone.

He charged his dogs to mush on. But within a short time his energy and strength left him. He slumped forward over his sled's handlebars. Concentrating on his every action, he held his snow hook. His last action before collapsing onto the snow was plunging the snow hook into the snow to anchor the sled.

Twenty minutes later musher Jamie Nelson happened onto Mike. She was amply qualified to be on the trail as witnessed by her victory in the John Beargrease Sled dog Marathon the previous year in her home state.

Thirty miles out of Iditarod Nelson suggested building a fire, but Madden wanted to get to a checkpoint. She told him she'd follow him.

Madden left but within a short time he was overcome.

When Jamie found him, she quickly got him into layers of clothes and a sleeping bag. She said later, "It was something anybody would do. But I'd never dealt with that. I realized there was something wrong, but I didn't realize how bad it was." 3

Before long Mitch Brazin, Kathy Halverson, Linwood Fiedler and Jerry Austin showed up.

Halverson and Brazin arrived first, followed by Austin and Fiedler

Austin said, "I was traveling with my buddy Mitch Brazin and our teams were slowly getting over a sickness that had plagued us since the start. Kathy Halverson was also in and out of our group.

"The next day we went through large caribou herds being chased by wolves and split up. We came upon Mike and Jamie Nelson stopped off the trail just a few miles from Don's Cabin, and the old Iditarod checkpoint named after Don Montgomery who ran the race. We passed Mike and Jamie and went to the cabin and stopped for several hours resting the dogs, feeding them, and getting about an hour's sleep ourselves before getting ready to head out again."

While they rested, Mike and Jamie passed them. Jerry said, "... they looked fine. We headed out not too long after they passed but never caught them. The weather was beautiful, few clouds in the sky and little wind. The temperatures were hovering just a little below zero, perfect traveling.

"After several hours I began looking for a familiar place to stop and snack the dogs. Kathy was a short ways ahead of me and Mitch a short ways behind. I'd guess it was about 9 p.m. when I came around a corner in the trail and Kathy was stopped right in the middle of the trail. Race rules demand that you snack, camp and feed off the trail, and this was the place I was looking for, so I asked Kathy if she was going to stop or clear the trail or what. She said, 'Well, Jerry, we kinda have a problem up here with Mike.'

"I looked over by the side of the trail and there he was partially into his sleeping bag and not looking good at all. Jamie was by him fussing with his sleeping bag. Kathy helped me get my team off the trail and I helped with hers and we snacked them so they would be still. Mitch pulled up, saw the problem, and did the same." 4

The three mushers retrieved their foam pads and sleeping bags in order to get Mike off the ground and away from the cold it would conduct into his body. Jerry noticed that Mike was "acting chilled even though he did not feel cold to the touch." 4

Austin, in his tenth Iditarod, took control (rookies not familiar with country and/or needs of Madden). Normally Austin would be among the leaders 170 miles ahead, but this year his dog's diet was out of kilter and he was chugging along with the thought of taking care of his dogs and getting to Nome.

Jerry said, "The first thing we suspected was a infection from the cut on his knee." 4 He and Mitch tried to raise Mike's pants' leg in order to evaluate his wound.

"Mike was fairly delirious and thirsty. I always carry prescription drugs in case myself or a friend or client suffers from a bad appendicitis, be we were all leery of using anything since he had no other symptoms of that or any pain there." 4

Even though another possibility was the flu, they felt that hypothermia was the most likely culprit and treated Mike for that, attempting to get as much liquid into him as possible. And from the beginning they treated Mike for shock.

In a short time another musher, Bernie Willis, a 727 pilot for Alaska Airlines, stopped. He recognized the gravity of the situation immediately and offered his help.

Madden vacillated between shivering and sweating. The mushers didn't know what was wrong nor how to treat him. They expected hypothermia which would cause dehydration, so they built a fire, layered Madden with clothes and sleeping bags, boiled water and forced warm liquid into him.

Madden shouted things like "god, take me inside" and "What about the three gallons of coffee?" 3

Next Linwood Fiedler came along and stopped.

After discussing Madden's need for emergency medical attention, the group chose to send someone to Iditarod rather than trying to transport Madden on a dog sled. Austin said, "We agreed that the risk of moving him 35 miles in rough side hill terrain was not worth it in lieu of the fact that something was obviously wrong with him internally.

"We agreed that Linwood and I would dash for Iditarod, the old ghost town checkpoint, Linwood for his speed and me because I had flown and driven the trail many times." 4

Brazin, Halverson and Nelson remained to assist Madden and to await his rescue.

Lightening their sleds, both men dropped equipment and pushed off. It was an uneventful trip of four hours, Austin got a little ahead of Linwood who had to stop to put a dog in the basket.

As they mushed away, Fiedler felt that his group was carrying out the original intent of the event—mushers assisting others in serious medical need. Fiedler said later, "It really kind of put the fear of God in us. It makes you realize how quickly things can happen. It was definitely serious. It wasn't a matter of someone just feeling weak." 3

When they arrived in Iditarod, it took some time to reach someone on the radio. The men woke up officials. Austin said, "I told the checkers and the HAM operator the trouble and that I'd promised Mitch and the others we'd get a helicopter there ASAP...all these rookies were losing valuable time.

"John Wood was the race official at Iditarod and all of us started trying to make contact. It was only through some other Ham out in the Aleutians that we finally got the message through." 4

At that point all they could do was wait for the chopper which was having some difficulty coming through Rainy Pass because of fog in Rainy Pass and McGrath.

Austin volunteered to return with the chopper as guide and musher of Madden's dogs, which would need to be brought to Iditarod.

Austin continued, "When the helicopter finally arrived, they didn't even shut down and were really in a hurry. We learned that they were unable to land for fuel in McGrath and wanted me to take them the most direct route to the site rather than just follow the trail, that winds around a lot. We jumped in, put our helmets on and sat down for takeoff.

"I was in the jump seat with the two pilots and even though I've flown smaller helicopters, this was a really big one with a large crew. We were all connected by radios in our helmets and someone kept asking, 'Sir, are you ready for takeoff?' After several repeats a guy grabbed me and asked if I could hear him. It was only than that I realized they were talking to me. I told him nobody had called me sir for a good number of years and yes, I was ready.

"We took off and had no trouble going direct to the site. There then commenced a lot of talk about if the helicopter could land since the trees were so close. The Captain asked the doc if he was rappel trained and he said yes, he was. Next question was, 'Sir, are you rappel trained?'

"I took one look at how close the trees were and answered 'You bet!' I had actually had the training on previous assignments. This looked tight. We were running critically low on fuel and kept looking for a suitable place and finally settled on one.

"The crew took over and for the first time I realized why there were so many of them. The co-pilot flew strictly on instruments while the pilot 'called-out' the visual from up front and other crew members from both sides and the tail. When we finally settled down, there were only a few feet between the ends of the rotors and the spruce trees. The snow was too soft to put the full weight of the aircraft down so the pilot semil-hovered while the doc and a crew member and I carried the litter over to where the girls and guys were taking care of Mike."

Even though the mushers had been pouring liquid into Mike for several hours, a brief exam showed him to be suffering a fever and severe dehydration. The doctor told them of the urgency of getting an IV into Mike for fear of losing him. The men got Mike on a stretcher then struggled through the snow, falling through in places, before managing to reach the helicopter and load Mike aboard.

On the way to Mike Madden the chopper stopped in Grayling to pick up Iditarod volunteer Dr. Dan Stevenson, an Air Force doctor from Fairbanks. They picked up Austin to direct them to Madden. He left his dogs with Fiedler.

The chopper crew was hopeful that Austin knew where he was going as they had only about ten minutes of spare fuel.

Stevenson commended the mushers for the medical attention they'd provided Madden and let them know that had he remained in his current condition a couple of more hours, he would likely have died.

Brazin said, "When the doctor came and said that another two hours and they might have taken him out in a body bag, that kind of hit home. We were pretty quiet there for a while." 3

Stevenson's thermometer showed Madden's temperature to be 103.4. He had trouble getting Madden to understand. When the doc asked Madden where he was, Madden responded with his place in the race, 21st. Madden was finally able to tell Stevenson that he was on the Iditarod trail.

The mushers assisted the chopper crew loading Madden then it left.

Austin then prepared to mush Madden's team over the trail he had just completed.

While en route to the hospital Madden began crying because he was no longer in the race. He said, "I had such a nice team." 3

Mike Madden:

Sturdy 6-footer

Carpenter from Billings, Montana, put his life on hold to train for 8 months for the Iditarod

Moved to Alaska in 1983 and began mushing dogs in 1984

Dreamed of running the Iditaod, encourged by his brother-in-law, veteran Iditarod musher, he entered in 1989 from North Pole, Alaska

Without other mushers' help, he might have become first fatal casualty of Iditarod

Jerry Austin:

Has the ability of making friends. Pudgy and roundish in form, other mushers like Jerry and often say he's too nice to win the Iditarod—too friendly, nice, helpful, quick to enjoy life, doesn't have the killer instinct necessary to win the grueling race.

Thinning hair

Bearded or fu-manchu mustachioed, depending on the year

Constant smile, friendly disposition, sense of humor

Loves life

Carried rifle for moose protection; wrote me once re: running into two polar bears on the trail on the sea coast of Alaska.

Jerry is quick to admit that he doesn't have the time to making winning his priority because, "Mushing is important to me, but on the list of priorities it's way down from my family." 1

He grew up in Seattle, now lives in St. Michael—wildlife contrasts are pigeons and grizzlies.

He and his family live in the home he built from three sided logs which is the tallest building in town. One wall is covered with trophies from dog races in Alaska and Europe. He's won the Kuskokwim 300 twice. An Alaskan's Alaskan. He hunts, fishes, traps, uses the resources of the land for his family's edification. A polar bear hide covers his living room floor and a mounted grizzly lies on the polar bear rug—the griz tried to eat Austin. Book shelves include fiction and anthropological and historical studies of Alaska and St. Michael.

Single-sideband radios for use in his Yutana Barge Line summer business. They have running water, one of few homes

Left college at 21-years of age and a degree from University of Washington (poly sci, English and anthropology). Poet with works published in national anthology

Hungry for knowledge/to learn—won awards for reading most books in grade school (expertise varies: carpenter, barge captain, dog musher, big-game guide).

Went to work in Stebbins for VISTA (Volunteers in Service to America) at the urging of former president of Alaska Pacific University, Glenn Olds. Later left to work as the Chevron fuel distributor in St. Michael 7 miles away.

Austin Arms and Exploration includes guiding, property and building rentals, Chevron products, commercial fishing, freight, firearm sales, Native handicrafts, non-fiction works and champion racing kennels.

Jerry is a problem solver.

Came to Alaska looking for new-big adventure. Has always had the love of the woods. Every weekend growing up he was in the woods.

Background:

Years before Jerry Austin broke his hand when his sled crashed a few hundred miles into the race. He merely taped it up and kept going. Although it didn't heal properly, it doesn't bother him. He said, "It's crooked, but it's all right. I can still play basketball." 1

- Mike Madden on the Iditarod Friday, March 10, 1989
- Unidentified intestinal infection leaving him dehydrated, disoriented, cold
- 27-year-old rookie at death's door
- other mushers who helped: they turned their backs on the race/abandoned the race effort in place of providing their colleague support
- rookie racers led by veteran Austin
- Mitch Brazin, a friend of Austin's from St. Michael
- Jamie Nelson of Togo, Minnesota
- Lynwood Fiedler of Canyon Creek, Montana; insurance salesman
- Kathy Halverson of Trapper Creek, Alaska
- Tended campfire and Mike's needs

Between Ophir and Iditarod at 10:30 p.m. Friday

Race Manager Jack Niggemyer said, "They could see he was having trouble staying on the trail and staying on the sled. They stopped and he was obviously hypothermic." 2 Later discovered by Anchorage doctors that Mike was hyperthermic rather than hypothermic—overheated, not underheated.

Treatment provided by the mushers—keeping Mike warm with fluids—was effective

Event:

Jerry Austin put Madden in a sleeping bag, built a fire and drove his dog team toward Iditarod t a radio

He reached the Iditarod checkpoint around 1:30 a.m. Saturday

Rescue via Elmendorf Air Force Base in Anchorage would not be able to respond until daylight with an HH-3 (Jolly Green Giant) helicopter

It was 9:30 a.m. before the chopper arrived to assist Madden, having stopped at the Grayling checkpoint to pick up a doctor and then in Iditarod to pick up Austin

Mike given intravenously on flight to Anchorage (which continued at the hospital)

Madden was saddened by his experience but glad to be alive and thankful to those who assisted him

Still had a temperature of 103 degrees Saturday, doctors working-conducting tests to determine the cause of the illness. No idea whether infection is form bacteria in food, water or it was a virus. Eventually discovered that salmonella was the culprit. Some suspect it was transferred from his hands after handling his dog food.

Jerry Austin mushed into Iditarod checkpoint to report Mike's need of emergency medical attention, suffering from severe hypothermia 25 miles east of Iditarod

During Austin's absence, Madden had been sweating, and those attending him thought he might be dehydrated. Temperatures were around 10 degrees.

Flown to Anchorage Saturday March 11, 1989 Humana Hospital-Alaska, stable condition

Aftermath:

Race Manager Jack Niggemyer said, "They were fortunate to have had someone there like Jerry Austin. He knows how to deal with things when things get tough." 2

Austin's actions gave him a leg up on the competition for the Sportsmanship Trophy, an honor that he has captured in the past. Austin's actions included caring for Madden, mushing Madden's team to Iditarod, going for help and guiding rescuers.

Austin's action also took him out of the running for a top 20 finish in the race and race board member Tom Busch said Austin's selfless act "will probably make him one of the last teams to come into Nome. But Austin wouldn't think twice about sacrificing trail position to help someone" 2

Busch also indicated that the three rookie mushers who stayed with Madden probably gave up their chances for the $1,500 Rookie of the Year award.

Madden's memories of his circumstance are few...just a vague. His conscious thoughts fluctuated between nothingness and wishing the helicopter would arrive soon. He did not fear for his life, "I was hurting too much to think that."

Brazin and Halverson took turns watching him. One slept while the other kept an eye on Mike. Every ten minutes one asked him how he was.

At one point Anchorage rookie Bernie Willis stopped to help briefly. A number of mushers passed without stopping or asking if there was a problem. The rescuers weren't impressed. Brazin stated, "We were all sitting around a camp fire shivering to death. A guy's lying there in three feet of sleeping bags." 3

Mike spent a day in the hospital before being flown to Nome. He wanted to welcome his rescuers when they crossed the finish line in Nome (under the spruce burl). And he was. Although weak, he was well, happy to be alive and ready to buy his friends a drink.

They began arriving on Friday night. When Austin crossed the line, Madden's mile wide grin met the St. Michael's musher.

The rescuers finished some 18 hours behind the leaders and way down the list of finishers. Had they ignored Mike Madden's needs and mushed for the money, all would have been much higher than their final placing. Brazin was nine minutes behind the top rookie Richard Self. Before Madden's incident, he led all mushers.

Regardless of their loss in finish placement, they gained a great deal more when you consider the value of a human life over that of money and fame. Madden said, "I feel real fortunate to have people on the trail like that. Whether I would have died, I don't know. If I was by myself, maybe yeah." 3

SOURCE NOTES:

1. "At Work to Win," Craig Medred, *We Alaskans* (supplement *Anchorage Daily News*), February 28, 1988, pp. D8-D13

2. "Musher survives a close call," Craig Medred, *Anchorage Daily News*, Sunday, March 12, 1989, pp. A1& A12

3. "Iditarod rescue is sweeter than victory," Lew Freedman, *Anchorage Daily News*, Monday, March 20, 1989, pp. E1 & E2

4. Personal correspondence from Jerry Austin, February 14, 1990

Sunny Day of Kayaking

by Larry Kaniut

HOMER: As Gabriel Kehn clung to cliff, his girlfriend, Bethany Lynn, slipped away.

Tom Kizzia, *Anchorage Daily News*, January 22, 2002

I re-wrote Tom's article June 2021

Steve Ebbert of Anchor Point still isn't sure why he headed through Tutka on Saturday for a recreational run. He spotted an unfamiliar aid to navigation on Casey Island and turned. How was he to know his decision would label him a hero?

Tutka Bay was calm Wednesday morning, enticing the couple into their blue-and-white kayak for a rare winter's day trip. They were experienced, having kayaked as far as Homer, about nine miles away, the previous summer.

Bethany Lynn and Gabriel Kehn, both 26-years-old, were in the midst of their second winter caretaking the Tutka Bay Lodge on the south shore of Kachemak Bay. The couple from Idaho had been together five years and had come to Alaska in 1999. Kehn was writing a book about the lodge while Lynn was learning to paint. In an effort to escape the mundane, they had decided to kayak the waters.

Their voyage was interrupted when the wind came up suddenly Wednesday. They turned back hoping to cross the mouth of the bay to the lodge, several miles away. Strong wind gusts forced them to point instead toward the head of the bay. Tiring, they decided to turn around and let the wind push them ashore on Casey Island, which lay just behind them.

However as they turned broadside to the wind, a wave rolled their kayak upside down. They slid into 40-degree water. They kicked off their boots to keep from sinking. The 175-pound Kehn helped his 115-pound girlfriend into the half-submerged kayak, but it rolled over again. Holding onto the sides of the kayak, they drifted toward the rocky island.

Drifting passed the island, they let go and swam for the rocks.

The swim was tougher than he expected; Kehn gulped salt water, waves crashed over his head and Lynn splashed wildly, frightened. He yelled for her to keep moving.

At length they reached an exposed rock and with bodies still dangling in the water, they clung to the rocks with their fingers. Perhaps thirty minutes had passed when they finally pulled themselves up and passed out.

They spied a rib of jagged rocks sticking up from the receding tide, barely submerged. The rocks led to safety on the main island. They stumbled across, their socks ripped to shreds, and found a nook in the rocks at the base of a 20-foot cliff.

Confused by hypothermia, they slept, awakening in the dark. Kehn had a dry bag from which he pulled a headlamp and a lighter. Stumbling and falling several times, he managed to reach the top of the cliff where he collapsed. His numb fingers disallowed his fire building efforts with the wet grass and sticks.

He climbed back to Lynn and she stared blankly into the light of the headlamp. He wrestled with her, slipping and falling, pushing her up the cliff, until she grabbed onto a dead tree about halfway up. She clung to it, then let go. They both slipped to the bottom. After that, she was limp and couldn't be budged.

Kehn climbed up again, trying again to light a fire, thinking it would entice her up. Again he failed. When he came back down, his headlamp was growing dim and Lynn was asleep. He shook her and yelled at her but couldn't get a reaction. Finally he stopped. The light from his lamp faded out. He sat beside her in the darkness until the tide reached their perch. Then he climbed back up the cliff and gave up. He awoke in daylight and couldn't stand. He peered over the edge of the cliff. The rocks below were bare.

He stumbled, sometimes walking on his knees, toward a small cabin he'd seen on the island the previous summer. Once inside he found a little water and a plastic bottle of Ginger Ale. His feet were starting to bleed and burn with pain.

For three days, sometimes with frozen feet wrapped in towels and duct tape, he stumbled out to rocky points where he waved a red curtain from a cabin cupboard. Though several boats passed, no one saw him waving.

With changing weather and lowered temperatures, his situation turned desperate. Saturday he saw a speck on the horizon. Could rescue be at hand? He grabbed the curtain and hobbled out to the nearest rocky point.

When Kehn realized the skiff from Homer kept approaching, he said, "He kept coming...that was the first time I started bawling and my emotions came out, because I knew I was going to make it, and if Bethany had been with me, she'd have made it too. She kept asking me if we going to die?' I didn't think we were. I thought we were going to make it. The island was so close.

"She kept saying, 'Let's stick together.' I didn't want to let her down."

Kehn was rescued and taken to South Peninsula Hospital in Homer. He was listed in stable condition Monday. Doctors said he might have to remain a month because of frostbite.

On Monday, Kehn lay in his hospital bed with black swollen feet and wiped away tears as he described how his girlfriend fell irretrievably asleep on the rocks. He remained with her until the incoming tide lapped at their bare feet.

"There was a part of me that felt like she was dead. I kind of gave her a kiss. I knew that would be it. I didn't know what to do. I was so confused and disoriented myself...I keep going through it now in my brain, wondering what I could have done."

Alaska State Troopers called off a brief helicopter search for Lynn's body Saturday because three days had passed since the accident.

"Her family was OK with that," trooper Rick Roberts said. "They understand that's the way it works up in Alaska sometimes."

Friends have searched since Saturday with skiffs and a diver, said Tom Hopkins, who runs the Jakolof Ferry Service. He said Lynn was well-loved, a "vivacious young gal in the prime of her life."

The trooper said Kehn's account of the accident checked out — both the physical details and the emotional timbre of his retelling.

SWALLOWED ALIVE

The Bottom Fell Out

by Larry Kaniut

"He lived life to the fullest and always had time for his friends."

It was around 4:30 PM Wednesday, April 8, 1992. Thirty miles northeast of Summit Lake 46-year-old Steve Keiner and some friends rode their snowmachines across a glacier near Paxson. Cruising over the snow and ice they rode along the edge of a crevasse that spanned twenty feet of space.

Without warning the snow at the edge of the crevasse beneath Keiner collapsed, plunging both him and his machine into the gaping hole.

Keiner's friends stopped. They could not see him and called out to him. There was no response. Some of his friends traveled to Summit Lake to alert authorities and to instigate his rescue.

The Arctic Man Ski and Sno Classic Eight was in progress and eight people rode their machines to the crevasse. When they arrived, they attempted to lower a rope to Keiner.

It appeared the crevasse was at least eighty feet deep.

A team of rescuers worked until 8:30 PM and then a second team took over.

Wednesday night Alaska State Troopers from Glennallen and an Anchorage-based helicopter with the troopers Mountain Rescue Group responded. Alaska Air National Guard also took part.

Thursday rescuers descended 140 feet into the maw of the crevasse but melting snow and ice began falling on them. They were forced to give up the search, knowing that hope for Keiner's survival was futile.

"He lived life to the fullest and always had time for his friends. He loved helping others and will be dearly missed by all who knew and loved him." 3

Letter to the editor: "Rescuers showed true selves"

I would like to express my thanks to the many people who helped in the attempted rescue of my dear friend, Steve Keiner.

Steve died on April 8 when he fell into a crevasse on the Cantwell Glacier.

During the search, many people, almost all complete strangers, came to our aid with support and encouragement.

To the approximately 30 skiers and snowmobilers who came to help, thank you. Thanks, to the couple who snowmobiled out at midnight with hot coffee and sandwiches, your company and the food made a terrible situation easier. A special thanks to Jeff Babcock and pilot Bob Larson of the Alaska State Troopers, Capt. Ernest of the Rescue Coordination Center, The National Guard, and Doug Fesler, who headed the volunteer Alaska Mountain Rescue Group. The troopers, Mr. Fesler and rescue team Mark Williams, Kenich Kibe and Will Renden showed a lot of courage and professionalism. To all of you, my sincere thanks and admiration.

Steve's death is a tremendous loss to his family and his many friends. However, there is something positive I witnessed as a result of this tragedy. I saw that during a crisis, people show their true self. The courage and selflessness shown on the glacier that day proved to me the basic goodness and decency in people, the true spirit of Alaskans.

--George Branche

SOURCE NOTES:

1. "Rescuers try to reach snowmobiler who tumbled into glacier crevasse," *The Anchorage Times*, April 9, 1992, page B-3

2. "Hunt for snowmobiler who fell in hole ends," *Anchorage Daily News*, Friday April 10, 1992, page B-2

3. "Rescuers showed true selves," *Anchorage Daily News*, April 26, 1992, page H-4

Know Your Playground

by Larry Kaniut

Canoers Nanette Campbell and Thom Hieronymus canoed Eagle River July 13, 1986. Both were Kentucky natives and had previously canoed Westchester Lagoon in Anchorage, a small pond covering a dozen acres or so and the Kenai River. They had no canoeing whitewater experience. Their story has a tragic ending. Their canoe ran into a rock in the river above Eagle River Campground. I read about them in the newspaper and wanted to warn others about the need to know their surroundings.

They reached the river in the evening around 7 PM. The couple had a friend who'd floated Eagle River successfully. Their friend's level of expertise encouraged them and they felt they'd have no problems. Their plan was to add to their experience and to enhance their skills. They worked well together in a canoe.

Thom had canoed since he was 13-years-old in southeast United States primarily on flat water in both streams and lakes.

They thought that they could handle Class II that existed outside the Class III water of the Campground Rapids. A friend of Nanette's had been an instructor in a class she'd taken and he felt by taking out their canoe before entering Campground Rapids, they'd be okay.

They felt that they were prepared to meet the challenge. Dressed in polypropylene and wool clothes they wore standard life jackets when they set out in their canoe eight miles up Eagle River road.

Encountering flat, easy water in the initial going was a comfort as they began their float. In faster stretches they practiced turns and avoiding obstacles.

When they encountered white water, they slowed down, back watered and evaluated their route. The right side looked the best so they paddled that way. Almost immediately they struck a submerged rock, got straightened out and hung up on the bottom again.

Because they were losing control and couldn't see the rocks underwater, they considered getting out. But there was no place to take out. Then they attempted to switch sides to the left side of the river. The bow hung up on a rock, lifted out of the water and the pressure of the water swung the craft around stern first.

They rearranged themselves and got off the rock. They continued downstream and hit some bushes on the bank. After that little episode, they took a deep breath and continued downstream, trying to get back to the right bank.

Part way across at midstream the curl of a hydraulic crabbed the canoe and they took on water. The added water weight and characteristics decreased the canoe's maneuverability. They then hit another hydraulic and the canoe filled to near three-quarters with water. They hung up on yet another rock and the canoe tipped over soon after. They lost both paddles at that point.

They righted the canoe and got back into it. The water in the craft and lack of paddles caused them to swim. Just as they started for the bank 15-yards away, the canoe dragged bottom again.

Thom was tossed out and toward the middle of the stream. He put his feet downstream and turned onto his belly in order to look back for Nanette. He didn't see her.

He floated and swam to a cable spool near the bank. At that point a commercial rafter showed up. Thom was okay and yelled to tell the rafter that someone was with the canoe. Then he lunged across the intervening water to shore.

The rafter was Eugene Buchanon from Alaska Travel Adventures and he waded toward the canoe.

Then Thom went back into the water and started to wade across. He lost his footing and was swept downstream before he was able to get to shore again.

By then a second raft came onto the scene and the guide threw Buchanon a safety line and hollered for him to check the canoe in case someone was trapped in it.

That's when Thom saw a life jacket floating downstream. It had popped to the surface. Then he was terrified. He caught a glimpse of a leg stationary in the current and pumping up and down with the motion of the water ten feet from the canoe. Thom shouted to Buchanon to apprise him but before he could respond Nanette disappeared.

It was obvious that the current was taking her downstream. If the men had gotten to Nanette, it may have been too late to save her. They waited a few moments scanning the water to locate her and trying to determine where the current was taking her.

Then the guides got Thom to one of their rafts. They took out at the campground.

Thom went to the car hoping to find Nanette there. But no such luck.

They called the Anchorage Police Department while Thom warmed up in a van. His right foot was totally numb and he was chilled and cold.

For two days men searched for Nanette, even putting a net across the river. But Thom had given up hope of their finding his canoeing companion.

Thom thought that Nanette's previous experience on organized rafting trips gave her the experience to know what to do in their situation. She knew basic water safety and was in control during their trip, talking conversationally. Not overreacting.

She had been convinced all along that they were going to have a problem and dump the canoe.

Thom said, "I don't feel like we went unprepared. We didn't do anything foolish. Other people have lost canoes in the river. Our case was just a fluke. The people I've talked to felt we made the right decisions. The only question I have, is why didn't we stop and check out the rapids from ashore. From the canoe, the power of the river was not evident.

"Alaska is not as forgiving as the Southeast where I'm from. It's tolerant up to a point. Then it extracts a price. " 1

Knowing the water or running it with an expert before attempting a float may have saved a life and grief.

Many who float Eagle River put in at a spot called the canoe landing, about 8 ½ miles up Eagle River road. The water is actually a slough and very calm. Many people are lulled into a false sense of security by the water's mellowness, floating along for several miles. Then they hit whitewater, and a whole new set of circumstances envelops them.

There's a 1 to 1 ½ mile stretch of water upstream from the Campground Rapids. Anyone who has no whitewater experience needs to take out of the river before entering Class II rapids.

Jim Ramey, vice president of Knik Kanoers and Kayakers said, "There are crunched canoes everywhere along the river. Each year, there are probably hundreds of people who get in trouble on the river. It was no real surprise to hear someone had died. But I personally felt real bad. I use the river a lot; it's like if somebody dies in your backyard. Nobody should drown in that river." 2

"People hear that the rapids are Class II and they think 'No problem.' Well, it is a problem if you have no whitewater experience. You shouldn't be running Class II rapids in a canoe if you've never been on whitewater before." 2

"It's one thing to run Class II rapids in the Lower 48, where the water is warm. But up here, it's a different story. Without a wetsuit, you have about five or ten minutes of functional time. Then you're basically a cork, floating down the river, out of control." 2

Considerations for floating Class II water in Alaska and other cold water climates includes:

Acquaint yourself with all relevant information about the stream— especially check on the river's surface based on varying water levels,

Assess your abilities,

On unfamiliar rivers, stay on the inside curves where water is slower and shallower,

Have whitewater experience,

Wear a wet- or dry suit and a coast-guard life jacket (PFD-personal flotation device),

If dunked into the water, get to shore as soon as possible— abandon your gear and do whatever necessary to survive,

Constantly assess of the weather, especially the temperature and how it affects you/your party (be able to take out and build a fire/warm up—having warm liquid would be a plus), and

Use the "weakest" person in your party as a gauge—if you keep him safe, you will likely save the party.

SOURCE NOTES:

1. "Canoeist; 'We didn't do anything foolish,'" *The Anchorage Times*, Sunday, July 27, 1986, pp. E9 & E11

2. "Eagle River can be a dangerous playground," Bill Sherwonit, *The Anchorage Times*, pp. E9 & E11, Sunday, July 27, 1986

What If?

by Larry Kaniut

You can read more about this story in APPENDIX 1.

Thousands of stampeders headed for the Throndiuk River in Canada's

YukonTerritory in the late 1890s. That was its geographic name before the newsmen got hold of it, changing the Indian word meaning "hammer water" into Klondike. The locale was a place of trapping salmon by way of hammering wood posts into the streambed. The Klondike discovery was made and the rush was on.

Some years later Harry Boyden followed his predecessors to the gold fields near Dawson City, arriving in 1908. Four years after that he joined gold stampeders flocking to Chisana in the Wrangel-St. Elias country, a couple of hundred miles south of Dawson City. Harry prospected and freighted cargo in the White River-Nabesna area before moving to McCarthy in 1936.

He later returned to the Chisana area where he ran a trading post at Nabesna until 1957. He then built a cabin at Chistochina Flats and resided there until his death in March 1968. During the last thirty years of his life Harry gained fame as a guide. The same legendary Alaska guide tells this story.

It didn't look good. It never does when a man goes solo into the wilderness and is caught out, back of beyond with little food and gear, especially when the weather is well below zero. It was 1925, and the trekker was in a pickle. He was deep in the White River country near the Alaska-Yukon border, a savage and unforgiving land. Only by piecing together the evidence he left—scrawled notes, equipment, clothing, tracks and his own remains would the survivors be able to guess at what happened on his journey.

He was in the Wrangell Mountains. Thoughts of *what if* plagued him. *What if I'd brought more gear? More food? An extra horse? What if I'd come two weeks earlier?* Looking off into the black of night, his tiny fire brought some solace. He sipped weak tea and planned the next 24-hours.

While wet snow pelted his rain pants and slicker, he cursed the white stuff which was already a foot deep. He'd been in more jams than he cared to remember and knew he'd find a way out of this one. His journey had been compounded by the dead horse, lack of food and now the snow.

He'd ridden horseback into the mountains, but the horse had wandered off one night. For several days he'd searched for it, finding no sign of the animal. Then he saw a flock of ravens circling down river a couple of miles. He went to investigate and found his horse at the base of a cut bank. It looked like the horse had dropped from the 50-foot bluff and broken its neck. The discovery was disappointing, but it was not a cause for great concern. Just one that demanded a change in strategy.

The man turned and headed for camp, noticing the southern sky beyond blotted out by gray snow clouds. It was only October 10 and somewhat early for snow. *It probably won't stay*, he thought.

He pressed on, tried not to think about the necessity of getting out and the problem it posed. He was some fifty miles from his cabin. To reach it he'd have to climb to higher elevation in order to cross the mountain pass which would have at least twice the snow on the ground as his river camp.

He knew that crossing two to three feet of snow would be extremely difficult without snowshoes—without webs he'd be nearly helpless.

Another factor to consider was the probable temperature drop of 30 to 40-below. Momentarily he thought about staying, hoping that someone would come looking for him in this desolate country. But he knew better. *Who would come out here this time of year? There is absolutely no reason for anyone to come here now.*

He was positive that no man lived in the valley. He'd seen no one in his recent search nor any signs of human activity, and he knew no Indians resided here. Trapping season was three weeks away. He knew he had to make a move soon or it might be too late.

His situation demanded a survival strategy. He knew the necessity of remaining calm and assessing his situation.

I'm a gamer. I can do it. I've been in other jams and worked my way out. More food, warm clothes and snowshoes would make it easier, but I'll have to make do with what I've got.

He knew the first ten miles through timber would be the easiest and that the next thirty in the barren plateaus east of him would be the toughest to negotiate. *Those rolling hills will be covered with two to three feet of snow. There won't even be a twig for building a fire.*

He also knew that the wind following the storm would come howling out of the north, cutting through clothing like a sandblaster. To be caught out poorly clothed in below-zero weather in screeching winds would be like committing suicide... slowly.

He turned in, knowing that the trip was unavoidable. He lay cozy in his sleeping bag. And he cursed himself for making an impulsive decision and preparing so poorly. At home he'd be snug and warm and his sixteen horses would be feeding near his cabin in the meadows. He was angry that he hadn't brought a spare cayuse.

He hadn't intended his trip to turn out the way it had. Originally he'd planned to scout new game country for four, maybe five days, push ahead for new territory. But it seemed that every new valley and distant ridge was more tantalizing than the last, and he kept traveling deeper into the mountains...eventually losing his horse.

When he awakened the next morning, he roused out of his sleeping bag. Eighteen inches of snow had accumulated overnight. He prepared some of the last of the tea he'd hoarded, boiled a few strips of dried moose meat and chomped a piece of pilot bread. It wasn't much but it was better than nothing.

He dug into a saddle bag and extracted seventeen shells for his .22 single-shot rifle, thinking he might get a crack at the moose which had left the tracks he'd seen while searching for his horse.

Leaving camp with his rifle and skinning knife, he headed for the horse carcass, planning to extract what he could for his sustenance over the next several days. During the night the stomach had been torn open and part of the entrails eaten by a wolverine. Ravens had picked a large hole in one ham.

The frozen flesh compounded the use of the sharp knife, however he carved off fifteen pounds. The horse had put in a long season in the mountains and was lacking fat, but the man sliced off as much as he thought he'd need, knowing it was necessary to provide body heat in the days ahead.

When he returned to camp, he prepared a cup of tea, ate from his dwindling supply of moose meat then cut four 8-foot green willows from which to fashion snowshoes.

He spent the next morning finalizing his snowshoes with rawhide strips of horse hide. Then he placed them near the fire to shrink-dry them. Next he took the saddle blanket and constructed a backpack.

Then he made a sling for the .22 rifle.

The following morning he placed his saddle in a tree where it would be safe from rodents and rabbits. *Better carry the snowshoes through the timber so they won't get damaged. I can put them on when I leave timberline.* He shouldered his pack, grabbed his rifle and set out on his journey over the mountains.

Exhausted near dark, he reached the edge of the timber. *Not as good as I'd hoped, but it'll have to do.* He selected a large spruce, dropped his gear at its foot and broke off dry branches below its overhanging limbs. He scrounged enough dry firewood in the area to build a large fire. *This will be the last heat I feel till I get through the pass and over the barrens. Might as well enjoy it as much as possible.*

The temperature plummeted during the day, and he knew he'd feel its effect this night.

When the northern lights twinkled and hissed overhead, it was laughter-like, mocking and leering down at him. *Almost a live thing making fun of my stupidity.* He was angry with his situation. Again, it caused him to question his lack of preparation.

He shivered through the night, rebuilding the fire before daylight. It hit 25-below overnight, all the reason to cherish his last piece of moose meat that he boiled with a hunk of horse fat. He savored the meat with his last piece of pilot bread.

Finishing his meal, he gathered up his pack, rifle and webs and struck out for the open country beyond. He struggled onward through the crotch deep snow, fighting exhaustion and the tangled alder thickets. With two hours to go until nightfall, exhaustion again embraced him as he topped the last ridge and looked out across the bleak, snow filled land known as the barrens. Snow three feet deep leered at him over thirty miles of rolling hills on the plateau. The white stuff, untracked by another human, lay before him, both beckoning and mocking.

He guessed it was 35 to 40-below as his nose hairs and beard frosted over. But he had chosen his path. He tied on his snowshoes and trudged onward.

As he labored along, the webs lacking the usual upturned front caught a lot of snow. It was a grueling trek, each step sinking nose-ward on a snowshoe and exacting a tremendous amount of energy to bring the tip above the snow for the next step.

He guessed that he'd covered two miles in the final two hours before darkness engulfed him. He selected a gully to get out of any potential wind and scraped out a depression with his snowshoe. He spread his sleeping bag in the dip and covered it with the piece of canvas then placed a foot of snow on it for insulation. The canvas would keep any melted snow from him.

Planning ahead, he carried a hunk of horse meat into his bag with him, hoping it would thaw during the night next to his body. But such was not the case. When he awoke the meat was still half frozen.

He gnawed on the meat a while before setting out into the waist deep snow. He traveled this way for two days. Then he repeated the mundane process: right foot step, sink, lift the front of the left web from the snow and step with it while the right snowshoe sank; lift the front from the snow on the right snowshoe and shake it off before stepping again. Onward without end.

Two days and two nights witnessed the same activity...stop for the night, scrape snow to form a depression on the ground, spread his sleeping bag and canvas, cover them with snow, arise in the morning, gnaw more raw frozen horse meat and attack the day.

By nightfall of the second day he knew the frost was penetrating his extremities. *Can't keep my hands warm. Think they're freezing along with my face. Must be about 45-below.* Adding to his troubles, a frigid wind out of the north cut like a knife.

The rifle was extra weight. That night he thought about jettisoning it but he reasoned that it could bag ptarmigan or a caribou should he get the chance. It was a tough decision. The weapon could save his life.

The wind woke him the third night. Wind driven snow scoured the landscape. Like a high powered sand blaster, ice particles blistered the barrens and everything in their path. There was no let up. His situation gripped him with fear. *What if I'm buried by the drifting snow?* All night he listened. And the snow in his depression built up.

At daylight he dug his way out, hearing the howling wind the whole while. Once clear of the snow, the icy hand of death pummeled him from every side. Visibility limited him to a handful of yards. The bitter wind and blowing snow, combined with the 45-below temperature, drove him back to his nest. Gripped by fear and hopelessness, he knew that he was hamstrung by the elements. *No land marks. Will have to stay here till I can see. Maybe the wind will let up soon.*

He lay in his nest gnawing on the frozen meat and wondering and hoping. *How long will the 10-pounds of meat last? How much longer will the wind pin me down? If I stay warm and conserve my strength, I may get out.*

One day turned interminably into the next until a week had

passed. He left his cocoon only to grab another hunk of frozen meat or to relieve himself.

For seven days the wind prevailed. She played a cruel joke on him.

When he awoke on the morning of the eighth day, he arose to silence. *The wind stopped.* He struggled from his sleeping bag and gazed upon the sun. For as far as he could see a frigid, white world loomed to the horizon. Ridges poked up all around, but the gullies were choked with snow drifts, some as deep as 20-feet.

At that point he cooked his goose.

Though reasoning may have been beyond his capabilities, he thought of a solution. *My meat supply is nearly gone. If the wind starts again, I'm dead. Back at the river I can have wood, a fire and heat. I can get more horse meat. I might find that moose or get some rabbits. Maybe I can make a better pair of snowshoes and walk out.*

This proved by far his most trying wilderness test. A tough customer, he hated to admit defeat but the cold, the wind and the snow had whipped him. He accepted it and chose to re-group and to try again. He turned back.

After three grueling days he reached his river campsite. He immediately made for the horse carcass expecting to find meat. But a wolverine and a pack of wolves had beaten him to it. They'd left nothing but some bone fragments, hooves with the shoes on, the skull plate and strips of hide. Not even enough here for a thick broth.

Over the next week he hunted hard for the moose, but failed to find it...or any other creature.

Although protected from the wind by the forest, the cold and hunger brought him closer to death's door each day. Starvation sapped his strength.

Late November found him checking rabbit snares. That's when tragedy struck. Thin ice and the cold teamed up to destroy him. While crossing ice he plunged through into the water below and got drenched to his crotch. From the time he freed himself from the frigid water and reached his camp, his hands and feet were frozen.

Death stalked him now as never before. He shivered the night away trying to get warm in his sleeping bag next to the dying fire. Camp bound because he could not walk, he watched his hands blacken then turn gangrenous. *I can't walk, hunt, collect wood or eat. How long till the Grim Reaper calls my number?*

By day he watched the gangrene get worse. He wasted away,

becoming weaker with each sunrise. By night he languished in his sleeping bag, shivering and agonizing because of the physical pain. Who could know the depths of his despair?

Slowly but surely, starvation pinched his spine. December witnessed his helplessness. And Old Man Death knocked on his door, welcoming him with open arms.

And surely the "if onlys" must have plagued him to the bitter end.

SOURCE NOTE:

"Man Alone," as told to John Porter by Harry Boyden, *ALASKA Magazine*, pp. 24-26, September 1981

A Brother is Lost

by Larry Kaniut

Twin brothers Marty and Michael Phelps flew off into the Wrangel-St. Elias Mountains the second week in August 1993 in search of Dall sheep. These guys were the quintessential outdoorsmen having hunted, hiked and camped throughout the state of Alaska since their arrival in 1989.

Both were Anchorage residents. Marty was a self-employed builder and part-time guide. Michael worked in the North Slope's oil patch.

A few months before in May the brothers assisted their visually impaired mother to the top of Mt. McKinley. The 54-year old Joni Phelps, is believed to be the first visually impaired person to climb the 20,320-foot peak.

Because of the twins' love of the outdoors, they had had their share of close calls in the arms of Mother Nature. Once they were snowed in on top of a mountain without additional food or clothes for a night. But up to now they had escaped serious injury.

Planning to hunt the Barnard Glacier area 200 miles east of Anchorage, they flew up the Chitina River past Hawkins Glacier some half dozen miles, landed, gathered their gear and headed east up the Barnard Glacier valley.

Their final experience together became the nightmare of all nightmares. And the worst part of it was that one did not wake up.

As they worked their way along a tongue of Barnard Glacier Monday, August 16, 1993, their love affair with the wilderness turned ugly and tumbled down around them, quite literally. Near the face of the glacier, car-sized chunks of ice slipped from the river of ice without warning. Tons of ice cascaded onto the brothers, trapping them.

When the ice movement stopped, 29-year old Michael managed to dig his way out of the snow and ice in spite of the injury he sustained to his ankle. Perhaps his smashed backpack provided him some protection. Frantic that he couldn't see Marty, he called and dug for an hour. Frustrated with his failure and knowing that rescuing his brother was, regrettably, beyond him, Michael immediately began hiking to the airstrip 12-miles away. He hoped to acquire help and equipment to save his brother.

Who can imagine the agony Michael suffered on his journey, the extent of his sorrow at not being able to help his brother and the untold questions that bounced around in his brain?

Word went out to the Rescue Coordination Center at Elmendorf Air Force Base in Anchorage. The RCC's spokesman, Mike Haller, said, "He was able to reach the airstrip by morning, so he must have walked all night. That would put the accident sometime Monday evening." 1

Michael Phelps was flown to Providence Hospital about the time an Air National Guard helicopter and a refueling plane were dispatched to the accident scene. The chopper departed Anchorage at 10 AM Tuesday with four para-rescuers on board.

The National Park Service also sent personnel on Tuesday to search.

While the rescue was underway, Michael was treated for his ankle injury and released.

The guardsmen reached the glacier at noon. Spokesman Haller said, "They got out there and surveyed the area and spent a chunk of the day searching for the other individual. They looked at, climbed around and dug into the glacier but couldn't locate him." 1

They spent four hours searching before departing Barnard Glacier after 4 p.m. Because of the glacier's unstable condition and the inability of rescuers to find Marty, no plans to resume the search were anticipated.

The parents of the boys were reached by phone and Stanley Phelps said, "We're sure he's dead. The Park Service gave up. He's buried in the ice. It was a freak thing." One great consolation for the family was that both brothers were Christians and "right with God," said Stanley.

Joni Phelps said that she wasn't sorry that her sons moved to Alaska. Even though they had a fatal accident, she admitted they had many uneventful and unforgettable outdoor adventures. "They took every precaution they could. I have no regrets." 2

A mountaineering ranger for Denali National Park, Daryl Miller, said, "The area itself is not dangerous. They just happened to be there when that ice fell. They weren't doing anything so terribly wrong. They were just in the wrong place at the wrong time." 2

What began as an outing couched in brotherly love and camaraderie, ended so very differently, changing the lives of the key players forever.

SOURCE NOTES:

1. "1 man hurt, 1 missing after piece of Barnard Glacier collapses," Hugh Curran, *Anchorage Daily News*, pp. B1 & B2, August 18, 1993

2. "After ice fall, a twin goes home alone," Pamela Doto, *Anchorage Daily News*, pp. A1 & A8, August 19, 1993

Muskox and Matador

by Randy Bailey

A family friend stopped by our home one November and told us about a close call he had while hunting. Randy Bailey, a native Alaskan who graduated from Bartlett High School, worked mostly construction—such as house building (including a log home in Eagle River, Alaska, for his parents Coy and Ruth)—and heavy equipment operation. He has hunted big game nearly since childhood.

Randy told us that his experience earned him a nickname... and spun his tale... The guys I work with call me Randy Dundee now. They ask me, "How'd you get that muskox?" They can't understand how I got in position to take that picture. They thought that something wasn't right.

In June or July I got a job opportunity to work out in the Bush. I went and was interviewed by a representative from Neland Company and he told me the possibilities for employment were good that they'd send me to Mekoryuk on Nunivak Island to be a superintendent over a housing project. Since I love to hunt, I immediately started callin' Fish and Game and some other people that I knew that had been out there to find out what kind of game was on the island and if there was a season open for duck hunting, caribou hunting or even musk ox hunting. During one of the conversations I had with a Fish and Game agent located in Bethel, he told me that they did give out five cow tags for musk ox seeing as how the drawing was already over; but you had to be in Mekoryuk by 8:00 in the morning on August 3lst. Since natives prefer hunting from showmachines, I knew I'd have a musk ox tag.

Although I ended up in Napakiak, I stated to the general superintendent that I'd like to go to Mekoryuk for the drawing. He assured me he'd allot me time to fly over and show the crews how to do this and maybe I could get a the permit.

When it came down to the last day, August 3lst, I was flown over and I showed the guys there how to frame these houses and how they were supposed to be put together. The next morning I was able to go down and get a permit. Since I was needed back in Napakiak to run the crews, I couldn't stay there to go on a hunt the next day or the day after that.

At Napakiak I had to get several days ahead of the crew with my layouts for me to leave. Soon as I did that, I flew on the plane back to Mekoryuk.

That evening project manager Chris Mc Claine flew my friend L.C. Fann and me out. We had both gotten permits. He flew me out first and dropped me off then he came back and got L.C. During the flight we did see several musk ox, but not in big herds like I anticipated (where they surround each other and all you see is heads and horns showin')—just scattered musk ox, just two or three here, several miles apart.

We found a dried pond and threw a pop can out to see if it would dent the ground or how hard the ground was before we set down... because you can't tell, it looked like mud. We saw the can bounce several times so we knew it was safe to land.

We dropped down and after he brought L.C. back, we set up camp and all we had was a pup tent. Neither of us had a back pack because we'd come up to work not really to hunt. I thought the musk ox deal would be real slim so I didn't bring my normal hunting paraphernalia.

The next morning we got out—we weren't in a hurry because we knew there were musk ox around. Later in the day we decided on a couple of cows that we had been watchin' for quite a while. We had to try to get close to these...in fact we figured they were two hundred yards away. There are no trees there to judge distances. The only rifle I'd brought up was a .375 H and H which was quite a bit more gun than was needed.

Deciding to simultaneously take two musk ox, we sat down. I figured at two hundred yards with the way that gun was sighted in I'd just hold on the back. I had three shells in that rifle. I clicked off one shot and nothin' happened. They milled around a little bit and then L.C. shot. Nothin' happened on his first shot either.

We had a discussion. "Well, how far are they?"

"Geez, I thought they were two hundred yards." This conversation flashed back and forth between us, and I said, "Well, maybe they're further."

Anyhow I fired another round. I'm sure I never cut a hair on one of those animals. But L.C. was shootin' a 7 millimeter magnum which is a little more flat shootin'. I'm not sure if I was droppin' way low, I got that idea because when we paced it off, it was darn near 500 yards—it was just a long ways. L.C. told me later that he ended up holdin' a foot and a half high, and his was sighted in at a hundred and fifty yards. That 7 mag could make a shot like that.

What had happened, he'd hit one in the leg, but we never saw that one flinch. And he'd shot again...I'm not sure of the sequence which one he'd hit first but we did see one jump straight up into the air. I told L.C. to quit shootin' because I thought there were two hits. The one that jumped up went down and jumped straight back up again, so we knew one was hit really well. The other one, though, as soon as they broke off and started trottin' away, we could see one gimpin'.

I had never stuck any extra shells in the pocket of my coat. Because I figured this was gonna be too easy in the beginning, we should have walked closer, 'cause it was no big deal.

But it was a big deal. We'd made a mistake. When I asked L.C. to look around, he had one shell left. I didn't have any shells left and we had two wounded musk ox.

Camp was at least two miles away. To go back and get more shells and to return to the wounded musk ox, it would have been right at dusk, towards the end of the day to even get back, and if we let 'em go completely out of sight for me and L.C. both since we are both color blind, the chances of finding blood in that moss and being able to see it especially at dusk would have been kind of stupid.

So I told L.C. to go up around the knoll where the musk ox headed. The one that was hit in the lower left front leg gimped around the hill another way. I told L.C. I'd go after that one and maybe I could kill it with a knife or somethin'. It was just kind of a joke at the time, but I knew we had to do something and that we couldn't let a wounded animal wander off and I didn't want to lose it.

L.C. went around one side of the hill. I kind of ended up herdin' the broken legged animal up through this little saddle of the hill it went through.

Beyong the saddle it was like an empty volcano arena—it was probably the only place on the island where there were rocks that were sixty, seventy rocks...like miniature boulders. The musk ox walked to the center of the arena, turned around and squared off. It didn't feel like it was goin' anywhere; it was just watchin' me.

By that time L.C. had shot his and came up over from the back side of the knoll. It almost looked like the days of the gladiators. I was already into it with the musk ox. Since I walked towards it, I'd taken my knife out. It was a bigger than average hunting knife, an Old Timer with a 6 1/2 to 7- inch blade sheath knife. I thought it might do the job if I could work on the musk ox without gettin' hurt myself.

The first time I walked up on it, I found out I wasn't out pickin' daisies. It made a run right at me. Even with that broken left front leg, I couldn't believe how fast it got to me, that quick. I turned to sidestep it but it got a horn on one of my legs and hooked me. It spun me around and flipped me. I landed on my hands and knees and it wheeled again to come back on me.

Things happened so fast that I was down and up immediately and out of the way. By that time my blood pressure and adrenalin soared. I realized that I couldn't match this animal with strength.

I had previously gone to a few bull doggin' practices and twisted steers' heads, and for some reason, I was under the impression that I'd bulldog this 500 pound musk ox like the rodeo steer that's used for bulldoggin'. There was obviously a big difference. The musk ox knew that I wasn't just gonna bend its neck. It knew that I was tryin' to kill it, therefore it wasn't in the shape where it wanted to run over the mountain and down the next side. It was a standoff.

I tried to get a knife in it on a couple of occasions and I think I did poke it once in the ribs. But I never did quite get the angle—it was too fast, and usually I found myself trying to get away from it more than it was tryin' to get away from me.

L. C. was on the top, saw what was goin' on and was yellin' and laughin' at the same time, thinking it was kind of hilarious. Every time he yelled, there was an echo because of the huge bowl back in there, like a canyon. He suggested that I throw a coat over its head. He was on one of the top pinnacles lookin' down when he yelled, "Throw the coat over its head...head...head...ead...ad."

I said, "Good idea...dea...dea...a." And the musk ox charged again. It only charged when it perceived me advancing on it...it was defensive right off the bat. Soon as it did, I threw my coat over its head and jumped out of the way. That animal whirled back on me, tossed the coat off its head, pinned it to the ground with its hoof, shredded it with its horns and stomped it with its good front leg

L.C. yelled back down, "Bad idea...dea...dea...a." I knew he was up there laughing at me.

I yelled up to L.C., "If this is so hilarious, why don't you come down and get a picture."

While he was comin' down, I'd already been thinkin' that there's no way I'm gonna be able to get a knife in this musk ox without totally gettin' hold of it. I know the chances of gettin' a hold of it without gettin' a horn in me and without really gettin' hurt were slim. I started lookin' around and decided, "Maybe I can slow this thing down with a rock if I can hit it right on top of the head." I decided it was worth a try, it was a better idea than throwin' a coat over its head.

Everything's moss and rollin' hills and every once in a while you'll see a cone shape like an anthill that's huge, and inside there's rocks—otherwise you don't see any rocks on the island.

I grabbed one of the bigger rocks lyin' on the ground. I know it weighed at least sixty to seventy pounds because it was heavy getting it above my head. I also knew I could get momentum coming down with both hands on it. I took a few steps towards the musk ox, and as usual, as soon as I did, the darn thing came right after me. Right before the musk ox would have hit me, I came down with both hands on that boulder. I drove its head right to the ground as I heard this whop. The rock was slate like and was brittle. When I hit the musk ox's head, the rock broke in half. I heard L.C. roar. It was hilarious because I'd hit it with a huge rock with everything I had, and the musk ox went down and then jumped up almost as quick as it went down.

I had debated, "Instead of dodgin', what's gonna happen if I stay in there?" (kinda like knowing you don't have enough gun to kill something this size unless you wait until the absolute last second... the hardest part was keepin' my nerve, stayin' in there)

It growled...it didn't sound like a cow, not a bellow or moo. It came from deep down in the chest. It came right back after me again. Of course, I had to sidestep it. You can't go back from a musk ox. They're a straight forward charger. It's kind of like boxin'...your chances of gettin' away from 'em by backing up are not very good... you go from side to side from the left to the right, which makes the animal have to rebound and hook back around.

I picked up rocks at least fourteen times. And I'd hit this thing every charge. My hands would end up within a foot of the musk ox's head when I released the boulder.

After the musk ox took several shots at me, it was sad because when I'd walk towards it, it knew it had to charge me, that that was its only defense. It knew it was gonna get hit again, for some reason you could see it in her eyes. All I wanted to do was get it over with.

I felt bad for the musk ox. I was wore out. So finally I figured out the only way I was gonna kill this musk ox was if I stack up more than one rock. The skull is to thick. (When I skinned it out later, there wasn't one crack over the skull. There was a little blood over the fatty tissue over the skull, like a bruise.) I ended stackin' two rocks up. I figured if I knocked it down and was quick enough to grab the other rock and hit it before it could recover, I could then jump on it and cut its throat.

Right when it was gettin' up, I hit it with a second boulder. Right when its front legs almost got fully extended, I drilled it again. It went down this time to the side which was the first time it ever went down to its side. It was off balance. That's when I jumped on it, held onto one horn and got my arm around its neck.

The darn musk ox had so much will to live even when I had hold of it and was stunned at that point I had to cut its throat before it revived to full strength again. When I stuck its throat, it was still slingin' its head back and forth tryin' to get me off it.

I knew the knife went all the way in and I'd ripped a big hole... I looped my arm around it to make sure I hit high on the neck on the other side and I pulled all the way around; and the strength went from it within thirty seconds. I was still on top of it.

I felt like it could have killed me, I felt like I was torturin' the animal unintentionally. We were both glad that it was over so L.C. and I never talked about it, wondering if the pictures would turn out or any hand shakin'. We were both relieved and upset.

It didn't seem like it was gonna get personal, but it did become personal with the musk ox because you could see how it tried to fight for its life. At the same time I didn't know if I was doin' justice to it at all, killin' it that way. Even though it was more fair play than shootin' it with a high powered rifle, it was cruel.

We had good weather. When I killed the musk ox it was 45-48 degrees. I was wearin' a T-shirt since my coat had gotten torn up. I was workin' so hard that I didn't need a coat. I told L.C. to head back to camp about 2 ½ miles. I skinned the musk ox just before dark. I knew L.C. had been caught by the dark.

I'd look east through this valley that ran right to the ocean. We had to head exactly west. I could see the fog. It was weird, like a spooky movie. The fog came rollin' up that valley at such a rate that my pace picked right up because I knew we could be in some big trouble if that fog beat us to camp. About the time I got halfway to camp, it was jet black, and the fog was so thick I could only see my footstep in front of me.

I'd stopped for my first rest—I had the cape and the whole hide down to the hooves along with the head. We had planned to come back after the meat in the morning. Actually I got real lucky. Right where I'd stopped, I heard L.C. yell for me where he was restin' a quarter of a mile from me. I yelled and told him to stop and let me come to him. We found each other and then I tried to convince him that we'd better stop right there to spend the night. I never saw L.C. until I was within five feet of him.

L.C. had left camp without a coat. He had a heavy wool shirt and a sweater, but not a jacket. I told him we'd never find camp in the fog 'cause I'd been in the thick fog before; and it's foolish to stagger around in the dark and fog even when you think you know where you're goin'. In that area you'd never find your camp unless you walked right over it. He didn't want to stop, so we walked another twenty-five minutes before he realized camp could be anywhere. I told him, "We'd better just get tough, put these hides over us and curl up and wait out the fog. It might clear up during the night, and it might not. It might clear up tomorrow. But it'd be a lot smarter to stay put because we knew we were close.

We curled up in the hides with the hair side in. The grossest part of mine was that I had to lie down in that hide covered all over with blood from its throat. The fur was touching my face and it was a wet, damp, gooey sensation—almost like snot. But it was either that or freeze to death. The hide wasn't really large to comfortably cover a six foot man, but when my feet got cold, it felt great getting the boots under the hide.

The fog never did clear up that night. I could hear L.C. every once in a while cussing. I'd say, "Are you gonna make it?"

He'd say, "Yeah, I'm gonna make it, but I don't like it." He was freezin'. The temperature was down in the twenties. We had crossed little puddles with ice on 'em. It's a different type of cold on those bare islands with the wind travelin' over 'em. The wind just bites through your clothes. Now I know why those musk ox have that much fur.

We spent a good six or six and a half hours inside the hides, during the coldest part of the night.

We did wait it out and the first thing in the morning the fog had lifted within a half hour after daylight. A half hour later we reached camp. It was a shame that we had to suffer the whole night when we were less than a quarter of a mile from our tent.

Chris came in the next day as planned and shuttled us out. He came in to check on us, and we still had to return for the meat. L.C. wasn't in the kind of shape I was, and I ended up packing three-fourths of L.C.'s out and then had to return for mine and pack it out. We each had three hundred pounds of meat by the time it was over.

Since neither of us had a back pack, I had to carry all the meat in a duffel bag, sometimes a hundred pounds or more to the pack (my last load weighed 148 pounds).

When I got back to Mekyoruk, I was just exhausted, I felt like I'd been hit by a train. There was just one place in the entire village to take a shower and that was the high school. I walked into the high school in my Carhart pants and jacket that were soaked in blood. I went into the shower without taking my clothes off, and from the top of my head all the way to my shoes it run blood off me. I stayed in there forty minutes.

Nightmare in Progress

by Larry Kaniut

The frail, young woman skidded and bounced down the icy glacier. She saw the looming crevasse ahead of her. What were her chances of stopping before she reached the edge and plummeted over the brink? She gained speed, her body twisting. She wanted to grab anything to stop her momentum. But there was nothing to grab.

How could her hike and photo-taking effort turn into this nightmare? Was it possible that she was dreaming?

It was Sunday afternoon October 26, 1986. Virginia Renfro and her friend Joel Kenison were going skiing. An outdoor enthusiast, Virginia had experience ice climbing, traversing and skiing glaciers including Matanuska Glacier and Mt. McKinley.

These friends had skied every month at least once, usually in a different area. But on this occasion they chose to invite others. Virginia stated, "This was the first time we had invited MaryAnn and my family to join us on one of our ski trips during the summer."

Virginia's family included her husband Chuck and their children Brie, almost 2, Chad, 4 and Rob, 6. MaryAnn Smith was 24-years-old, and Virginia knew her as the girlfriend of 26-year-old Joel.

The group arrived at the glacier at 3:30 p.m. It was a beautiful day for a hike up Byron Glacier. The Portage area they hiked is within Chugach National Forest and 48 miles southeast of downtown Anchorage.

Most people have never seen, much less travelled on a glacier, so their knowledge of them is lacking. A glacier is a river of ice that is affected by snowfall and gravity. Snow accumulates over centuries and layers add to the mass with every snowfall. Because of the moving, shifting nature of glaciers and the pressure from tons of ice and gravity, it is common for them to split in different areas. Crevasses, huge cracks in the ice, develop throughout the glacier's surface. These can increase or decrease in size within hours or days, and they vary from inches to yards in width and up to hundreds of feet in depth.

The hanging Byron Glacier clung to the valley walls. Like a badly wrinkled blanket piled on a bed, it covered the valley, sloping up the sides, a mile wide and nearly twice as long. A large hump at the head, a thousand feet higher than the toe, sloped 20-45 degrees downhill.

The smooth, white head, dusted by brown-gray scree, cradled a few large wrinkles while the surface at the toe was dissected by dozens of small, blue-green creases running perpendicular to the glacier. Fighting invincible gravity and the weight of centuries of snow accumulation, Byron Glacier's monstrous ice mass gradually lost the struggle and snailed into the valley below.

Before long, winter would blanket the area with snow and the summer-fall hiking season would end.

Virginia said, "The weather was warm. Joel and I were concentrating on climbing up the glacier and not paying any attention to those who were below us." 2

As the group climbed up the twenty-degree slope of the glacier, traction was no problem on the glacier's surface, even for MaryAnn who wore sneakers.

MaryAnn wanted to photograph nature and scenes above her position. She worked her way up the ice a hundred yards or so, then sat down to enjoy the panoramic view of the surrounding mountain peaks, the toe of the glacier and the valley below. As she sat taking pictures, she noticed a crevasse 40 yards below. It ran crossways across the surface, opening 6-10 feet in width from the uphill opening to the downhill side.

Completing her picture taking, she determined to return to her group below. She thought that the surface felt slicker than it had on her ascent. Choosing prudence in her descent, she remained seated and decided to slide down the glacier.

Almost instantly she was sliding faster. She noticed the gaping hole almost reaching out to her. As she bounced over the surface, she screamed "Help!"

A young man standing near the edge of the crevasse saw the panic in her eyes and on her face. He froze in his tracks.

"Stop me!" she cried. But it was too late. She soared off the surface and shot into space, the gaping mouth below ready to gobble her up. Descending into the blackness below, MaryAnn ricocheted from wall to wall.

Virginia Renfro stated, "I'm guessing it had taken us about 15 minutes of climbing before we heard someone frantically yelling to us.

I thought the voice said, 'Brie Ann fell into the crevasse.' In my heart I felt my daughter had just died. Joel yelled a couple of times to those below before we were clear on what was actually said was that it was Mary Ann who fell in.

"Joel put his skis on right there. I remember it was extremely steep where we were and it was difficult to get into the bindings. He took off right down the icy slope. As I recall we had marked crevasses with rocks on our climb up so we'd have a clear and safe route down.

"I thought it too steep where I was to put my skis on. I took my boots off and walked back down the incline in my wool socks. They provided fairly good traction." 2

Standing on the downhill side of the crevasse, Chuck Renfro had seen MaryAnn's turbulent slide and fall. He rushed to the edge to see what he could do to assist her. At the precipice he lay on his stomach and slowly eased his frame forward. As he peered into the hole, he saw her thirty feet below. She was wedged in the hole. Her body was jackknifed face down, legs and feet higher than her head and her arms dangling lifelessly. An unconscious "Oh, my God!" escaped Chuck's lips.

He feared the worst and wondered if she'd broken her neck. Or worse yet, if she were dead.

Eric Sachs, off duty para-rescue man assigned to Elmendorf Air Force Base in Anchorage, rushed to the scene, reaching it simultaneously with Renfro. In his five years as a para-rescuer Eric had helped 42 people in life and death situations. Earlier in the afternoon he'd heard the creaking and groaning of the glacier. Glaciers were an incredibly beautiful phenomenon but a dangerous adversary under the wrong conditions. This was one of those.

As he observed MaryAnn, he realized that this was probably his worst rescue situation ever. This was a bad one.

One of his immediate concerns was that MaryAnn's body heat would melt the ice around her and that she would slip further into the huge crack, possibly from site. He also knew that a glacial crevasse can close in moments, depending on the pressure exerted upon it by gravity, the weight of the ice above and the differential pressures between.

While discussing MaryAnn's plight, Eric indicated to Chuck that he was trained in rescue, that they needed the right equipment and that every minute counted. Then he told him, "If she comes to, keep her spirits up. I'm going for help." 1

MaryAnn's boyfriend Joel had arrived with Virginia.

Virginia said, "I could hear MaryAnn calling to Joel and talking to whomever would talk to her. We could not see her, and were aware at times that she was slipping down a bit further. Chuck, Joel and I kept talking to her to keep her awake and alert as possible. My strongest emotion was relief that it was not my daughter, Brie, who was in the crevasse. I realized that with MaryAnn we could communicate and we could rationalize with her and give her instructions. Brie was too young to have been able to do this." 2

Joel did not want to stand idly by and chose to join Eric in an effort to find help. They sped off down the mountain for the parking lot a mile away.

Completing their day of ice climbing Marko and Vicki Radonich and Mike Miller heard shouts for help, "Come quick! A woman fell into the crevasse. We need somebody with climbing gear."

The three rushed toward the gap in the glacier which held MaryAnn in its jaws.

After falling into the crevasse and bouncing to a stop, MaryAnn was out of commission. After a while she stirred. She had no clue as to her circumstance. She felt wet and slippery. Her head pounded. Gradually she regained her senses and realized she had fallen. She ran her fingers around her. She blinked her eyes. She wondered how she was going to escape her tomb.

Then she heard Chuck's voice above.

She called out, "Chuck, where are you?"

He called back, "I'm right here, MaryAnn. Are you hurt?"

She indicated that her head hurt and that she was bleeding.

"It's okay. Help is on the way. Everything will be alright."

Panicked, she screamed, "Oh, God! I'm slipping." The pressure of the ice that pinned her head and shoulders loosened slightly. Fearing further slippage and hoping to secure herself, she thrust her legs against the icy walls.

Wanting to divert her attention, Chuck called out to her as he looked into the chasm, "You haven't slipped far. Talk to me about Joel."

There was no response.

He tried again, "How long have you known Joel?"

"Seven…seven years."

They'd met at a ski lodge. She flashed back to Christmas Day.

I was 17. But she couldn't shut out her fear of her situation. I want to live. I don't want to die. Claustrophobic because she could not turn her head and only able to stare down into the abyss, she felt desperate.

Chuck's voice reached her again, "How did you meet Joel? MaryAnn, talk to me."

In time she responded, "My head hurts so. Can't hold on much longer."

Chuck glanced toward the lowering sun. At that time of year Anchorage daylight disappeared around 5 p.m. Chuck became somewhat frantic and wondered if they'd be able to extract her before darkness fell. And he wondered what problems darkness would bring.

Meanwhile the ice climbers had arrived and engaged a plan of action. Miller was an oil-drilling foreman and had recently completed an emergency-trauma treatment course. He immediately volunteered to drop into the hole to assess MaryAnn's predicament. He looped a 165-foot rope into a seat harness and secured the rope with ice screws, anchoring it to the rim. Then he lowered himself over the side.

Within fifteen feet his body wedged into the tight fissure. The 6-foot-one, 178 pound man could descend no farther. Realizing that MaryAnn wore light clothing, he knew she was in danger of becoming hypothermic. The melting ice dampened her clothes, and the jaws that clamped her in their grasp poked frigid fingers of heat-sucking cold. Before long her body would lose more heat than it could produce, plummeting her core temperature and increasing her chances of death.

Mindful that something must be done, Miller called to MaryAnn, "I'm going to lower a rope." He then attached a clip onto the end, hoping that she could fasten it to her jeans or jacket. But she could not grasp the rope in her stiff fingers.

Just then Joel reappeared. Eric had phoned for a rescue team and equipment. Joel sprawled onto the ice next to Chuck and called out, "MaryAnn! Honey, I'm here."

Eric now arrived at the edge of the crevasse. Knowing that he was smaller than Mike (at 5-foot-8 and weighing 150 pounds) and realizing that Mike could go no further into the depths, Eric volunteered to swap places with him.

Moments ticked into minutes. Time was slipping away as the danger of sliding deeper into the chasm or its closing faced MaryAnn and the group of rescuers. Eric called out to MaryAnn, "I'm coming down headfirst, and I'll try to lasso you around the ankles. Stick your feet up as high as you can."

Mike was hauled up to get more rope as Eric crawled downward in his head down attitude. He realized that the fissure was tight.

Moving ever so slowly, Eric crawled deeper. His ribs hurt from the crevasse walls' cramping jaws. He took tiny-short breaths to keep his chest from expanding. He was aware that any second the crevasse could increase or decrease in size. It was a struggle of giant proportions to keep focused on the lady below rather than the danger of shifting ice. There was no way a tiny human spec could keep those massive jaws from grinding together.

Like a game of 5-card stud poker, the glacier held the winning hand while the man inched his way down. Would Eric pull a wild card from the deck and win? Or did the glacier have a stacked deck?

Eric held his head sideways. Then he heard a faint sound. A ringing sound. And he wondered, Are the ice layers shifting? Will the crevasse close, entombing both of us?

Inch led to inch. Then the inches equaled a foot. He pushed downward.

When he spoke next, his voice was but a whisper, "MaryAnn."

She asked, "Where are you? How close?"

"Ten feet. Point your toes."

Eric felt his ears and face going numb. Struggling against claustrophobia which could halt the entire effort, he focused on the white sneaker just below him. He worked the rope into a loop and dangled it downward with his right hand, constantly reminding himself that he needed to get closer.

Although Eric wanted to lasso both legs, he saw only the one shoe. He encouraged her to hold on. Then he jiggled the rope over her ankle, telling her that those above would pull him out of the way to keep from hampering her ascent, "Then we'll get you."

Sunlight was fading. It had been more than an hour since MaryAnn had dropped into the crevasse. Likewise the temperature had dropped below freezing.

MaryAnn could hear voices of contention above. She wondered what they were waiting for.

"We might pull her leg out of joint," someone said.

"No, we have to go ahead," spoke another.

Nerves stretched to their limit and unable to take any more,

MaryAnn shouted to her rescuers, "Get your act together!"

Then she heard Joel, "We're tightening the tension, MaryAnn... ready."

A strong tug shook her body and she screamed, "Stop! My head! You're hurting me!"

The tension relaxed.

Then she closed her eyes tightly and tried to ignore the unbelievable cold. She recalled an auto accident she'd had as a college student. She and her passenger had been tossed from the vehicle onto the roadway. As she lay near the vehicle, she'd told herself, "I'll make it."

Later her father had told her, "You're a survivor."

Recalling her attitude after the accident and her father's words, she steeled herself against her ice cold hell, "You're alive. You made it then. You'll make it again. Just hold on!"

The rescuers hatched another plan. A second rope. Perhaps by looping it around her wrists as well as the one on her leg, they could extract her.

Five minutes later she heard Eric's voice again, "MaryAnn...listen very carefully. I'm coming back down. I'll drop another rope. You've got to grab it and slip the loop over your wrists."

Eric swung into the hole. He monitored his breathing and his knowledge of claustrophobia's paralyzing effect. He willed himself onward then coached himself to fulfill his effort. He reached the extent of his space and, scarcely breathing, summoned MaryAnn to "grab the rope."

Meanwhile the trapped woman struggled to stay awake. She fought off drowsiness and cajoled herself. She knew if she didn't stay alert, she'd die. With cold, stiff fingers she fumbled with the rope, clutching it to herself. Then she slid the loop over one hand and clasped it with the other.

Eric called to the rescuers above to see if they were ready.

MaryAnn reminded herself to be tough. To refuse to quit. To face and to embrace pain if necessary in order to get out.

The rescuers tugged. Once. Twice. Again. And again.

She was wedged and wouldn't budge.

Eric called up reminding the others that "She went in at an angle. We'll have to move her back and forth like a key in a lock."

That they did.

Over and over Eric commanded, "Go." He addressed one team then the other.

At length Eric counseled MaryAnn to let out all the air in her lungs.

With ropes straining, seesawing back and forth, cork like, MaryAnn suddenly popped from her trap. Ice chunks tumbled from the walls around her.

Eric yelled to those above, "Pull! Pull! She's moving now."

Her strength nearly gone, MaryAnn clung to the rope. She felt herself rising. Up. Up. She heard those above shouting encouragement. Excitement reigned.

Then she was out of the hole.

Loving, tender hands reached out to her, cradling her onto a stretcher. She savored the evening. Fresh, clean air never tasted so good. She was out of the hole!

Joel pulled a blanket up to her chin and kissed her while telling her, "Honey, you're going to be all right. Thank God."

A helicopter rumbled off toward Providence Hospital in Anchorage. She remained in post-intensive care for four days. Her injuries included a concussion, multiple lacerations, bruises and hypothermia.

One day a deep male voice and a squeeze of her hand awakened MaryAnn. It was Eric Sachs who told her, "You were brave. I wanted you to know that."

She responded, "If I was, it was because you and all the others helped me be that way. We did what we did together."

And so, a lady slipped literally into the belly of a glacier. Almost miraculously she lived. And even as incredibly her rescuers retrieved her from the depths. Her story could have ended very differently. Fortunately she was not alone on her hike. Fortunately there were others nearby with ice climbing gear. Fortunately a rescue man with years of experience in the wild was present.

MaryAnn Smith was a very fortunate lady. Indeed. Very fortunate.

SOURCE NOTES:

1. "Trapped in a Glacier!," Marguerite Reiss, *Reader's Digest*, April 1988

2. Personal correspondence from Virgina Renfro, January 25, 1999

Five Men

Condensed by Larry Kaniut

Straining to see through the smoking sleet slicing his visor, flight engineer Fred Kalt, tries to make out a crouching figure in the chopper's rescue basket. He can't move the basket. Then he hears over his headset, "Someone's hanging on the basket!"

Moments, as in nano-seconds, later the basket clinger is gone. Down, down, down. One hundred and three feet into the smoking surf.

Meanwhile the sound of steel on the deck reminds the rescuers that a man lies in the basket—his beard festooned with icicles...his cheeks look like ice. The rescuers strip Bob Doyle of his survival suit and wrap him in a thermal bag. He's been in the 38-degree water nearly eight hours...with four others who'd hit the water when their ship sank.

*   *   *

Mission minded, two groups of men set out...one for fish, the other for men. Five men ended up in the water; five men flew in search of them. The Coast Guard men were trained to save lives.

If ever man met mountain, it was on the Fairweather Grounds in the Gulf of Alaska. The date was Friday, January 30, 1998. Five men aboard the La Conte launched from Sitka to long line 150 miles to the north. The 77-foot long, 66 ton ship, built in 1919, was outfitted with the latest in electronic gear. Mark Morley, skipper, deckhand Mike Decapua, Robert Doyle, William Mork and Hanlon pushed into the Gulf of Alaska aboard the La Conte.

Who would have guessed they'd be blasted by a storm of immense proportions? Who would have known those five would abandon ship and struggle in the frigid water, a cataclysmic struggle for survival? Who would have guessed that five other men met the "mountain" and scaled the "rescue peak"?

*   *   *

La Conte wallowed through the water, grunting up a wave, falling off and slamming into a trough. Often, unable to climb the hundred-foot wave—twice as high as the vessel, she merely punched her way through the wall of water. The wind chill registered 18 degrees below zero and spray froze the moment airborne. The ship crawled toward safety, the nearest landfall 80 miles east. Severe wind gusts pummeled the ship, riddling mixed hail or sleet, hamstringing her progress. In six hours she managed a mere three miles.

Fighting to maintain his footing at the wheel, Mark Morley struggled to see through the half inch Lexan window, sheeted with ice. The pounding seas and temperature turned the rigging and the mast ghostly white. The ship took a shellacking. The darkness of night embraced the ship. It didn't look good.

Both sump pumps had shorted out. Water flowed both outside and inside the vessel. Previously the bilge had pumped twenty-two hundred gallons an hour. Now...ZERO.

A rogue wave slammed into the ship. The La Conte floundered. From the doorway deckhand Decapua warned skipper Morley that they were taking on water. Below deck Bob Doyle was tossed about in shin deep frigid water before being slammed into a bulkhead.

Joined by Mork and Hanon, Decapua arrived and began bailing water with Doyle. Their bucket brigade was futile. Water was thigh deep. Then chest deep. The engine was silent. The La Conte lay dead in the water.

Morley appeared at the hatch, saw the men neck deep in water and shouted, "Get outta there. We're going down!"

Men pulled on survival suits and prepared to abandon ship. Morley called a MAYDAY on his VHF radio. He heard nothing but static. He grabbed his EPIRB—a transmitter that emits a satellite signal—and scrambled onto deck. A mountain of water rose above the stern, momentarily hung there, then smashed the wheelhouse, blowing out the windows...shotgun loud.

Amidst the screaming bedlam and with plates and canned food falling onto the men below, Morley instructed them to rope their waists and to connect themselves together onto a three-quarter inch rope. The raft they desperately needed was NOT onboard. The human chain clawed its way up the deck and each man crawled over the railing.

Above…the roar of the wind, blowing hail like mini-guided missiles, blasting their bodies. Below…a seething ocean, disguised as a dark hole. They didn't know if they'd drop fifteen feet… or a hundred. If they'd be swallowed by the sea by drowning or by hypothermia. They had no choice.

In spite of the fact that they could be smashed against the ship's hull or drop a hundred feet, Morely shouted, "We go in together. On three!" At Morley's "three!" they hurled themselves into the frothing, black void.

Their hope of rescue was on par with Mighty Casey after three strikes in Mudville. Or you might say, similar to Larry Bird's missing a game winning hoop at the buzzer of a crucial game…not so good.

*　　　　　　　*　　　　　　　*

William Monk felt the cold, tightening like pliers on his temples. Thump, thump, thump…he heard the rhythmic sound of his heartbeat. Falling forever into the darkness. Then he rose from the water depths, bursting through the surface, gasping air…and then…down again.

The second time he reached the surface. He kicked his legs before realizing his survival suit was inflating. He knew he wouldn't drown.

The first thing he noticed was the red and white strobe light on the EPIRB. Then he recognized swirling ice, floating bird carcasses, pieces of wood, a buoy and…several hundred yards in the distance, the La Conte. He saw only the hull, pummeled by the sea. It disappeared behind a swell. When the wave passed, the ship was gone.

Within moments, his shipmates popped to the surface, heads only a few feet away: Hanlon, Morley, then Decapua and Doyle. Seemed like ice and hail replaced the air, challenging their ability to breathe. A thundering, rumbling wind compounded their efforts to communicate, forcing them to shout to be heard.

A man's chances of surviving five hours in those waters were about 50/50.

*　　　　　　　*　　　　　　　*

Two U. S. Coast Guard Jay Hawk helicopters responded to the EPIRB and headed for the five men in the water. The first chopper flew into the maw of horrendous winds. They suffered mechanical problems; their co-pilot was dizzy and vomiting; the flight mechanic shook from exhaustion and vertigo; they had lost communication and with dwindling fuel on board, aborted their mission. The chopper returned to base.

The second chopper cruised to the Fairweather Grounds and searched for the five fishermen. Fighting winds that allowed the bird to travel a half mile in twenty-five minutes, they continued. At length the rescuers spotted the EPIRB and five survivors clinging to a fishing float around the EPIRB. Five flares jettisoned from the chopper toward the water. The rescue basket slammed around in the wind, unable to reach the water. The flares died out. Nearly five hours earlier the La Conte vanished. The chopper must return to base. They left the men in the water.

Even though the Coast Guard classified this as a high risk mission — survivors are close to perishing in desperate straits and rescuers flying into a life threatening situation, a third chopper launched to attempt rescue. Pilot Lt. Stephen Torpey, co-pilot Lt. Cmdr. Theodore La Feuvre, rescue swimmer Michael Fish, flight mechanic Harold Lee Honnold and flight engineer Fred Kalt forged into the night and the totally wailing weather. They did their jobs, never dreaming that their mission would become a classic story heralding heroism and talked about forever throughout academy classes and airbases. It could be a game changer for each man involved, whether in the air or in the water.

In addition to their training, they carried an extra flight mechanic, chemical glow sticks enabling the survivors to see the rescue basket in the dark, 26 special flares that burn for 50 minutes and an additional 700 pounds of extra fuel.

They reached the scene. Torpey and Le Feuvre fought headwinds, blurred dials and nausea while approaching the area of the missing men. Crouching by the jump door and shouting altitudes Kalt and Honnold assessed their roller coaster ride as nightmarish.

Kalt spotted what appeared to be reflective tape on waving arms. He dropped nine flares which hit the water and burst into white light. He lowered the rescue basket which landed in a trough several hundred yards downwind from the men. He continued to hoist and the basket, failing to get it closer to the survivors. Meantime Honnold shouted directions to the pilots.

Even though rescue jumper Fish volunteered to jump into the ocean, Torpey refused to allow him to do so.

As Kalt dropped more flares, the craft was hammered by a severe blast of wind and blown a quarter mile backward and into a trough. Honnold, Kalt and Fish screamed "UP!" to apprise the pilot of the danger of being hit by a wave which would likely be fatal for the crew. A rising wave rolled up to meet them...and they barely out climbed it. It took twenty minutes to return to the survivors as Torpey dragged the basket within five yards, close enough for them to reach it.

Honnold spotted a man swimming for the basket and flopping into it. He shouted "Survivor in the basket" and Kraft hit the hoist lever to bring it up. Spinning and bouncing for ten seconds the basket reached the door and a William Mork rolled out, curling into a fetal position on the floor. Fish slid a thermal sack around him while the basket dropped for another man. When the basket hit the water and a man climbed into it, Kalt raised it. It bounced like a Yo-Yo and seemed to be stuck. Then the chopper guys realized there's a man in the basket and another hanging from it. Before they pulled the one in the basket into the chopper, the other man dropped from sight.

The helicopter crew has been airborne three hours. They're dehydrated and dizzy with vertigo. The three rescued men are hypothermic. With serious fuel problems added to the stress of the past three hours the chopper heads for Yakutat, closer than their base in Sitka. Two men from the sunken La Conte are still in the water. Awaiting rescue. Hoping.

Next morning two Coast Guard C-130 planes based in Kodiak and a chopper from Sitka criss-cross the water of Fairweather Grounds. At 3:30 PM the chopper wrests a body from the water. It's Mark Morley, skipper of the La Conte.

The assumption is that the missing David Hanlon will be found within a week. The search cost $678,545 before being called off February 4th. Six months crawled by before David Hanlon's remains were found.

The crewmen from the La Conte—William Mork, Mike Decapua and Robert Doyle recovered. They still fish the high seas. The chopper crew—Lt. Stephen Torpey, Lt. Cmdr. Theodore La Feuvre, rescue swimmer Michael Fish, flight mechanic Harold Lee Honnold and flight engineer Fred Kalt—were awarded the Distinguished Flying Cross, highest aviation honor given in peacetime.

SOURCE NOTES:

1. Rescue: Crew members had no life raft aboard by Todd Lewan, *The Associated Press* (via *Anchorage Daily News*),

December 27, 1998

2. Rescue in sight, just out of reach, By Todd Lewan, *The Associated Press*, December 29, 1998

3. 'Survivor in the basket,' By Todd Lewan, *The Associated Press* (via *Anchorage Daily News*), December 30, 1998

4. Wrenching rescue; puzzle solved By Todd Lewan, *The Associated Press*, December 31, 1998

Not a Good Decision

by Larry Kaniut

While enjoying the outing and soaking up the beauty surrounding them, the couple approached Blackstone Glacier. The tidewater glacier, like hundreds of others, periodically calved slabs of ice into the salt water below its face...slabs of ice that ranged in size from a few cubic feet and hundreds of pounds to thousands of cubic feet and hundreds of tons. Immense slabs with nothing between them and the ocean save air.

Blackstone Glacier calved a slab of ice Thursday June 17, 1993. Under normal circumstances that would not have been a noteworthy event, but these were not normal circumstances. On that day Sue Putt of San Diego and her boyfriend floated on the blue-green waters of Blackstone Bay beneath the glacier.

With their two kayaks tied together at the west side of the glacier eight miles south of Whittier, Alaska, the couple rode the surface. Without warning, the white sheet of ice slipped from the face and silently ghosted seaward onto the man and his kayak.

The weight and momentum of the ice and rock debris crushed the man and hammered the kayak, breaking it in two. Miraculously, the ice missed Sue, and perhaps more miraculously, she managed to wrestle him into the portion of his kayak that still floated.

The couple had separated from a group of three others who had set up a camp earlier in the day a mile away at Mile 17 Beach. Sue paddled for that camp hoping for help from the others.

When she reached the campsite, they stripped off her boyfriend's wet clothes to counter his hypothermic condition. They tried to warm him while James Rustamier, a Seattle physician's assistant in the group, attended his injuries.

They were limited in their ability to help him and they had no way to communicate their emergency. Even though they were only a half dozen air miles from Whittier, rescue required paddling a dozen miles to the mouth of Blackstone Bay and around Decision Point, a peninsula separating them from Whittier, another nine miles away.

The group chose not to hazard the trip at night to alert officials, but when the injured man slipped into a coma, Rustamier set out at 3 AM the next morning aboard his kayak to muster help. Seven hours later still laboring in Blackstone Bay, he encountered the tour boat Mystic Seas. Her crew called the U.S. Coast Guard and Officer Dan Jewell, head of a volunteer search and rescue team in Whittier, was contacted.

Jewell departed aboard a rescue boat for the camp just after 1 PM that day. The ride took the normal one and a half-hours in time. But it was too late for Jewll and his team to offer any aid. The 36-year old man had died after Rustamier had left the camp.

Officer Jewell said, "He got too close to the glacier and some rocks and ice came off. He was hit pretty hard." Jewell was impressed by Sue Putt's incredible efforts to get her boyfriend into the smashed kayak and hasten him to rescue, "That was a pretty amazing feat in that ice water. They were both soaking wet." Apparently Putt's previous survival training enabled her to maneuver her boyfriend aboard his broken kayak and transport him to the camp.

Troopers did not release his name since his family had not been notified.

SOURCE NOTE:

"Calving glacier crushes man kayaking in Sound," Pamela Doto, *Anchorage Daily News*, June 19, 1993, pp. B1 & B3

Pieces of the Puzzle

by Larry Kaniut

On Monday July 24, 2000, I walked to our Anchorage mail box. It was a beautiful day, cotton ball clouds polka-dotting the azure sky, temperature around 65-degrees.

I was delighted to find an envelope marked Mail Tribune, P.O. Box 1108, Medford, OR 97501-0229. It was post marked July 20, 2000. Within was a dot matrix print out (2 pages on a long sheet of paper) delineating the information: "ACCESS NUMBER 33126," "DATE 05/30/95," and "HEADLINE Snowbound man survived 9 weeks before he died." I reviewed the information and added it to the story below.

I was incredulous when I read about the man who sat in his camper awaiting rescue. He was some eighteen miles from succor. What started as a scenic drive ended very tragically for him, his family and his friends.

When a man turns up missing, what can be done?

The following anecdote is a classic example of the negative results of non-communication, lack of geographic knowledge and inexperience. And, even though we can only speculate about many of the events, and as painful as it may be, there is a message about a man's faith and his works.

The known facts are that DeWitt Allan Finley was on a sales trip through Oregon. He worked for Mic Sieler, owner of S&S Campers of Kalispell, Montana. DeWitt had worked for S&S several months as a salesman. He was hauling a brand-new demo camper on the back of a four-wheel-drive diesel pickup. Before leaving Kalispell, he'd gone over the route on a map with his sales manager Bob Perzinski.

The details after this get hazy. DeWitt's most recent stop was in Coos Bay, Oregon. He decided to take the back roads through the Siskiyou National Forest to Grants Pass over the scenic Klamath Mountains while driving east over the pass.

Names of geographic locations that he would drive through, near or toward seem almost prophetic: Humbug Mountain State Park,

Powers, Drowned Out Creek, Remote and Grave Creek.

On November 14, 1994, DeWitt left highway 101 along the coast. He turned onto highway 42, the connection between the coast and I-5, the super highway paralleling the Pacific Ocean and running north and south 50 to 60 miles east and linking Mexico and Canada. Later he went through Powers and ended up on Road 33. He passed three signs on Bear Camp Road which warned that the road was not maintained during the winter.

DeWitt did not know that within a few short miles he'd have reason to regret his decision. Bear Camp Road hums with traffic during the summer—white-water rafters clog the asphalt ribbon shuttling people and gear back and forth from Agness to Galice in their pursuit of pleasure on the Rogue River. Part of the highway is subject to snow accumulation throughout the winter and the Forest Service does not plow it. Therefore once the snow comes, the road remains impassable to normal road traffic until spring.

This was November, the beginning of the cold, snowy months in the higher elevations of Oregon's Cascade Mountain range.

DeWitt had left no message with anyone as to his intended route. Nor did he inquire about the conditions of the roadway.

The locals were privy to the road's situation. But strangers, such as DeWitt, would have no such knowledge without inquiring.

Although hunting season was still open in the area, Road 33 is popular with neither hunters or nor snowmobilers. Therefore the likelihood of anyone's finding Finley was greatly reduced.

Officials did not know that anyone was on the road and had no reason to expect or to inspect it. As it turns out, the day after Finley drove up the mountain road, rangers posted a sign at the bottom reading: "Road may be blocked by snowdrifts six miles ahead."

And it was. The single-lane, paved road was coated with ice. While grinding uphill, DeWitt slid off the roadway high atop the Coast Range. The truck tires rested on gravel beneath the snow on the side of the roadway closer to the mountain. He was in the section of snow build up just around the corner from pavement that is clear year around.

The pickup was equipped with a camper. Although there was no propane for the furnace and DeWitt had no food, the unit contained a kitchen stove, bed and bathroom. Because it was getting dark and the temperature was frigid, DeWitt chose to sleep for the night.

Mic Sieler later commented that he thought Finley carried tire chains and anticipated waiting out the night, putting them on the next day and driving from there.

Had officials covered the middle section of highway on foot, snow machine or from the air, they would have known a passenger vehicle was stuck in that expanse.

When no one in Finley's family heard from him, his sale's manager and friend Bob Perzinski became concerned. He hadn't heard from Finley in four days and said, "I started to get a real eerie feeling." 5 "The next day he contacted every major sheriff, hospital, morgue and highway department along the route Finley had planned to take. He kept in daily contact with Finley's two sons and his fiancee." 5

Perzinski went to Oregon to look for DeWitt. He found out that his friend had checked out of the Coos Bay Best Western Holiday motel on his way to visit distributors at a Grants Pass RV center. Perzinski had gone over the proposed route on the map with DeWitt and was bewildered that his friend would deviate from it. DeWitt was a stickler for detail, and Perzinski said, "I mean, this just wasn't like DeWitt, to take a different route. He never, I mean never, deviated from the plan." 5

Suspecting foul play or an accident in southwestern Oregon, he put up posters offering a reward of $5,000 for information leading to Finley's whereabouts. He also hired a pilot to fly the rugged, timber country over DeWitt's proposed route, but the pilot never got within 30 miles of the stranded man.

On the seventh day of Finley's disappearance, detective Dan Loony of the Cos Bay County Sheriff's office was handed the case. No one suspected that Finley had taken an alternate route.

Deputies also sent up a helicopter to search.

If DeWitt had known more about the area or the weather, the results would likely have been very different. Since DeWitt had spent most of his life in California's Los Angeles area, Sheriff's Detective Allen Boice figured Finley was unfamiliar with snow conditions. Later Finley's boss agreed that DeWitt lacked survival skills such as those his Kalispell neighbors would have acquired after having spent time in snow country.

It appears that DeWitt's unfamiliarity with the country coupled with his faith in God and man, lulled him into thinking rescue would come at someone else's hand. Therefore he made no attempt to save himself beyond melting snow and drinking the water.

Had DeWitt abandoned his vehicle the night he became stuck, he could have followed his tracks in the snow and in a short distance found himself on snow free pavement. At the very least he would have encountered a few hundred yards of snow. The maximum distance through snow would have been 3 miles. DeWitt could have walked in his tire tracks to pavement then hiked 16 miles down the mountain to Frank Sandlin's Cougar Lane Store and safety.

Evidence at the scene indicated that Finley never left his vehicle. Meanwhile, he accepted his fate. He sat in his camper checking off the passing days on his day planner and wrote a stack of letters in neat handwriting on a legal pad—letters to his sons, other relatives, his fiancee Mary Soop and his boss. Stamped, sealed envelopes bore missives to those he loved and to whom he felt responsible. Mic Sieler explained later that DeWitt always carried writing materials with which to write clients when he was on sales trips.

In the letter he left for his boss DeWitt described part of his journey from the coast to the mountains. He explained his predicament, "Everything was fine until the top of the mountain...A patch of ice was my downfall...Even in four wheel drive the truck's tires did not hold... That night, the first major winter storm hit southern Oregon. For the next three days it snowed." 5

During his two months in the camper while awaiting someone to find him, DeWitt found solace in his faith and felt he grew in fellowship with God, making peace with the Creator and those to whom he wrote.

In the letter to Mary, DeWitt wrote, "This road has little or no traffic at all. This could be the end." 5

At one point DeWitt wrote, "Day Seven. Well, time for breakfast, a block of snow. At 9:30 this morning, after seven days of being inside the truck cab, I crawled out a window onto the hood. The snow is still about three feet deep with a crust of ice on top. No way, even if I were in good shape, could anyone get very far. If someone doesn't find me, I'm going to meet the Lord." 5

Who can know the anguish DeWitt experienced alone during those two months on the mountain? With no food to eat and no connection to his world he spent his time thinking, praying and writing.

His letters reflected some of the same messages thousands have sent from the Beaver State over the years, "Typical Oregon weather clear for a few days and storms for the next few days has left me in a tomb for the [past] 30 days."

The brown-eyed, shy smiling Finley, 56, had lots of time to reflect upon his life up to this point. He'd been a fund-raiser in the San Diego area for the Christian charity World Vision before moving the previous summer to Montana. It was in Kalispell that he had learned to love fishing on Flathead Lake. He'd begun building his dream house on a golf course and made plans to get married.

He stayed in the camper's cab, a roomy cabin with cloth seats. Among the few items he had were his Levi's fur-lined jacket and a road map. He used cushions and bedspread to make a bed on the bench seat.

Daily he waited, worshipped God and continued writing.

One letter stated, "Death here in another month or so, or he sends someone to save me. Yet knowing His will I'm at peace and His grace will prevail. If I'm save[d] to finish my life here, please know I'll alway[s] be thankful to you and remain your servant. If not—I'll see you in Glory."

On January 17, sixty-four days after starting up Bear Camp Road DeWitt wrote, "Sight a real problem today…Focusing doesn't work. Get very dazzy (sic). In fact, writing also hard. Will try tomorrow, Bye for now." 5

At one point snowmobilers rode within a mile of Finley's truck before they got stuck. They extricated the machine and rode back down the mountain.

The final day Finley crossed off on his calendar was Jan. 19, 1995.

Four months later, almost to the day, on May 20, 1995 two teenagers, who'd become stuck in the snow below Finley's truck, spotted his rig and hiked up to it to investigate. The winter's accumulation of snow had melted around the truck and camper enough to expose the rig. The 17-year old reported the find to the U.S. Forest Service.

Forest Service law enforcement officer Ray Sunblad peered through the truck's window and saw Finley lying on the front seat, face up, his head on the passenger side of the truck against the dashboard. The keys were in the ignition and the doors were locked.

Enclosed in one letter was $100 and the key to Finley's Chevrolet. In another letter he left a hat to a friend, "If I don't make it and if it fits, I would like you to have" it." 5

The tall, burly Finley had survived for weeks only on melted snow water.

Officials prepared to remove the truck from the mountain.

That same weekend "America's Most Wanted" television series had planned to air the story of the missing man's disappearance.

Glenn Carpenter of Gold Beach drove a front-end loader preparatory to digging out the highway May 22. He would remove the 5-foot snow blockage on the roadway and open the highway for summer travel. While engaged in his road clearing Carpenter dug out Finley's pickup. Indicating the truck's position Carpenter said the snow "never stays on that road but right there."

Another local, tow-truck driver Everett Amos, gets calls every winter to haul people from the snow. Sometimes they call on a cellular phone or a CB radio. Otherwise they walk out. Finley had neither a cell phone nor CB radio. Nor did he choose to hike out as had the teenagers who found him when their vehicle became stuck in the vicinity of DeWitt's truck.

With the patience of Job DeWitt had scribed, "I have no control over my life. It's all in His hands. 'His will be done,' "

Detective Allen Boice said, "He just laid there until he starved. It's real tragic. You just wonder why." 3

Forest Service spokesman Jim Kelley said, "It was a senseless death. That's what's so sad about it."

As a competent pilot reviews aeronautical maps of the route he's to fly in order to familiarize himself with the route, so it would be wise for man to study his land route with the use of maps or checking with a local citizen about the roadways in the area.

In one of his letters DeWitt wrote, "The most wonderful thing out of this ordeal has been the never-ending fellowship with the Lord. I've not eaten since noon of Nov. 14th yet I feel great and I'm in good spirits. I've never known such fellowship nor how His plan for man can be a love for us beyond all things."

It seems that had DeWitt asked more questions before leaving the main highway, taken a cell phone, extra food and water or walked out after a reasonable time of awaiting rescue, he would have enjoyed life with his family and friends for many more years.

Perhaps he could have eaten some vegetation or tree parts from the area—boiled pine needles or scrounged for pine cone nuts. It is bewildering that after weeks of searching and wondering, the answers are still not known.

The pain of this tragic loss to him and his loved ones was somewhat eased by the knowledge that DeWitt Finley died peacefully and at one with God.

SOURCE NOTES:

1. "Faith kept man stuck in snow," AP, Jeff Barnard, pp. A1 & A10, *Anchorage Daily News*, June 3, 1995

2. "Fatal Faith: Snowbound Driver Dies Waiting for God to Save Him," The Salt Lake City Tribune, June 3, 1995 Jeff Barnard, *The Associated Press*

3. "Montana man chronicled his last days," Bryan Smith, *The Oregonian*, May 31, 1995, pg. D01

4. "Trapped in Snow in Oregon, Salesman died After 9 Weeks," *The New York Times* NATIONAL, Wednesday, May 31, 1995

5. "In Search of a Friend," Melinda Jensen Ligos, *Sales & Marketing Management*, January 1997, Vol. 149 Issue 1, pg. 28

Acknowledgments: Julie Drengson and Betsy Brubaker, Jackson County Library, Medford, Oregon

Doctor, Father Tell of Struggle for Life

by Larry Kaniut

Doctor, father tell of struggle for life beneath Koyukuk River ice

'I THOUGHT I WAS ONE OR TWO SECONDS FROM DEATH'

RACHEL D'ORO, *The Associated Press*, June 14, 2003

I re-wrote Rachel's article June 2021, titling it *River Ice Can Mess You Up*.

The certainty of death prevailed...looming on the river.

Flashes of bone-chilling water, smacking their heads against the bottom of the ice, gasping wildly for breath in a thin pocket of air. What seemed pleasant and harmless turned ugly...in a heartbeat.

Blake Stanfield and his 65-year-old father Neil of Oklahoma City floated the Koyukuk River in a cataraft. Rounding a bend on the river, Blake saw a solid sheet of ice ahead. There was no way to turn the craft around in the rushing current which thrust the Seward doctor and his father toward the 2-foot-high white wall. The right pontoon slammed against the ice, flipping the raft upside down and under the slab.

The doctor said, "It was sheer panic. All you see is that you're going under this sheet of ice, and you have no idea where it ends. We were sucked under immediately."

Stanfield, a family practitioner at Providence Seward Medical Center, is known as an avid mountain climber and outdoor enthusiast. The trip was to have been Stanfield's birthday gift to his father, a real estate consultant. It would be just the two of them as Stanfield's pregnant wife, Shelly, stayed home with their 14-month-old son, Heath.

The plan was to be dropped off at the north fork of the Koyukuk, about 200 miles northwest of Fairbanks in Alaska's Interior. They would spend a week floating 90 miles of winding river, eventually taking the middle fork to the town of Bettles.

The Stanfields set off that Friday under clear skies and

165

temperatures in the 70s. It was so warm that Blake wore only shorts and a T-shirt, no shoes. His father wore a T-shirt, long johns, waist-high waders and boots. Both wore life jackets.

A few hours after launching, they encountered the ice, which stretched about 30 yards. After being plunged below, they resurfaced through a break in the ice, gulping air, before the swift current swept them under again at least 100 yards, by Stanfield's estimation.

This time there was no air space between ice and water. Stanfield stated, "I thought I was one or two seconds from death. I was thinking, 'Boy, this is it. What an awful way to go.' I thought of my family and how sad it would be for them. Then I popped out into open air and open water."

Blake quickly made his way to the bank of the 50-foot-wide river…while his father, clutching an oar, was carried downstream.

The younger Stanfield sprinted barefoot along the bank passing his father who had stopped on an icy ridge in the river. Blake grabbed a dead spruce branch and held it for his father to catch. By the time he reached shore, Neil Stanfield was shivering uncontrollably from the cold. His son urged him to keep moving and led him to drier ground where Blake used his water-resistant lighter to build a fire.

As his father warmed himself, Stanfield hiked up a hill looking for the raft. It was across the river and upside down… surrounded by icy patches and a raging current.

Blake told his father there was no way they could reach it and they'd have to spend the night, forming a survival plan. They found a large gravel drainage and left the oar along their path, pointing downriver as a sign for searchers.

Incorporating spruce branches, rocks and moss, Stanfield built a wall against a V-shaped gully to create a small shelter. He cut tall, dry grasses to line the floor. Dry wood was plentiful for their fire.

All their food was lost, with no other options in sight.

The following morning Stanfield told his father he was going for help before weakness overcame him. He wore his father's long johns and boots, leaving his father with the waders and neoprene socks.

Blake planned to hike to Bettles, getting a good start and passing a grizzly and the biggest black bear he'd ever seen. After hiking some twenty miles, he encountered an insurmountable hurdle in the form the confluence of the Koyukuk and Tinayguk rivers.

A few days passed with Blake waiting and worrying about his father. He chose not to waste energy building a shelter but focused on building fires for warmth and as a smoke signal for any passing plane pilots. With tons of fruitless cranberry bushes and nothing to eat, he subsisted on an occasional ant or spider. He was surprised that he had no hunger.

In Blake's absence Blake's father kept the embers going and caught brief naps before collecting more firewood. The elder Stanfield admitted, "There was no food, but I had a lot of water and, of course, I ate a lot of smoke. Then you spend a lot of time trying to figure different ways to study your navel."

Tuesday evening while flying sightseers in the area, bush pilot Dirk Nikisch spotted the younger Stanfield. He returned with a neighbor, Bernie Hicker, who helped drop a radio and food to Stanfield, who radioed back.

"He sounded very happy he had someone to talk to," Hicker said. "Then he told us about his father. We looked for him for quite a long time before we found him."

The men dropped food, a tent and a sleeping bag to the elder Stanfield. Nikisch also supplied the coordinates that enabled the Army helicopter to retrieve the Stanfields early the next morning.

Father and son were rescued early Wednesday by an Army helicopter. They were bruised and scratched, exhausted and famished, but otherwise in good condition.   Relaxing Friday at his Seward home with his wife, son and father, Blake Stanfield said he would now plan differently for such a trip. For example, he would enlist a pilot to make a flyover safety check midway through a trip.

"I wouldn't hesitate to do it again," he said. "Only probably not this summer."

From Safety to Statistic

by Larry Kaniut

Cornice break tumbles woman into fight to live

OUTING: Accident on glacier killed two, left husband with desperate task of saving wife.

By Nicole Tsong, *Anchorage Daily News*, April 29, 2002

I re-wrote Nicole's piece June 2021.

Who would have guessed that the group's enthusiasm and expectations would meet with tragic consequences? Wesley Rice, 39, his wife, Susan, 38; his 35-year-old brother, Donnie and his 14-year-old daughter Jessica; and Uncle Tony Baca; anticipated an enjoyable weekend in the mountains.

It was common for the experienced outdoorsmen brothers to take time off from their jobs at Fairbanks Gold Mining in order to enjoy hunting, fishing or camping. Wes' wife and Baca, a close relative, frequently took part in their family snow machine trips. Refusing to miss being with her father, Jessica had come along despite a cold.

It was a clear January morning with single digit temperatures when the group started a weekend motor home trip from Fairbanks. Their destination was twelve miles north of Paxson and a gravel turnout by the Richardson monument, where they'd park and have easy access to some of their favorite trails.

The plan was to finish with a snow machine jaunt up Gulkana Glacier in the area of the annual Arctic Man Ski & Sno Go Classic. Because it was to be a two-hour joyride, they didn't take the usual backpack crammed with blankets, flashlights and emergency food.

Once on their way, they steered their sleds through rugged, rocky terrain before climbing up the glacier's gentle slope toward an adjacent ridge that afternoon. The group momentarily parted when Wes stopped to change his sputtering machine's spark plugs. While the others rode on expecting to view Canwell Glacier, he and Baca stayed back to fix it. In less than five minutes he and Baca had changed the plugs on the Yamaha. Wesley mounted his machine and rode ahead of Baca toward the ridge.

When Wesley arrived at the top of the ridge, he found a deserted snow machine and no one in sight. He yelled for his wife and brother. Then he heard Susan. He approached the edge of the ridge which showed a crack, indicating a sheared off cornice. He dropped to his knees and peered down the nearly vertical drop.

Susan saw Wesley and asked whether Donnie and Jessica were with him...knowing if they were not with Wesley, they were elsewhere. He threw himself from the ridge, tumbled fifty yards over snow, rocks and ice, and then slid another hundred and fifty yards before stopping spread-eagle. Bruised and bleeding and with an injured shoulder, he pulled himself to his feet and ran to Susan.

One snow machine and silence met him.

Then he heard someone.

"Donnie, help me!" Susan called for her brother-in-law.

While Wesley was sliding down the treacherous slope, Baca had made his way to the edge of the broken cornice. Wesley yelled at him to get help. Baca jumped on his snow machine and raced down the glacier.

On the mountainside below, Wesley had reached Susan and begun a frantic dig to free her. Susan remembered she still had the cell phone in her pocket. After freeing her, Wesley retrieved the phone and made a quick 911 call. They learned that Baca was on the other line with dispatchers and that state troopers from Delta and an Air National Guard helicopter were on the way.

Susan lay facing the steep, rocky slope she'd just tumbled down, buried to her neck in snow and helmetless. Her snow machine and her helmet, lay close by. Her battered head throbbed from the bumps and bruises covering it. She told Wesley her legs hurt too. She had last seen her husband tinkering with his disabled machine but went ahead with Donnie. She had the cell phone which Donnie wanted to use from the ridge top, where he could get a signal. He planned to talk to Fairbanks relatives, requesting needed snow machine parts and a replacement sled for Jessica. Her snow machine sustained mechanical problems earlier in the day, forcing her to ride double with her father.

Even with the addition of his daughter, Donnie was a faster rider than Susan, who followed their tracks to the ridge. As Susan approached she saw Donnie and Jessica, standing several feet from their snow machine and taking in the view of Canwell Glacier to the north.

Susan pulled alongside. She saw the snow cracking between the two machines. "I thought, no, this can't be," she said. "Then poof. It was." Susan saw only white and felt herself free-falling. She passed out.

Daylight was fading fast, and the couple had no light sources. Since Susan couldn't walk, Wesley used the snow machine's hood to build a shelter to protect her from the wind. He lay down on her to warm her when she got too cold.

Wesley could think only about finding his brother and niece and he scrambled around the steep slope looking for them, telling Susan to sing songs in order to ward off sleep.

Help arrived an hour and a half after the cornice dropped down the slope. By then, it was black on the mountain and the wind howled. The helicopter's search lights couldn't locate them. Although Wesley tried guiding the rescuers with his cell phone, the beams came within 100 feet of the Rice's before passing by.

On the other end of the phone line, trooper Lt. Chuck Lamica, the state search-and-rescue coordinator, knew that time was a factor and necessitated finding the injured, stating, "We were convinced that my dispatcher might have been the last one to ever hear this guy talk... His last messages were that he was getting very cold; he and his wife were getting hypothermic."

The cell phone battery died and the chopper was low on fuel, necessitating their departure. Even though Susan told Wesley to leave her and to save himself, he told her he's stay.

Although the chopper left, Troopers and state rescue workers formed a different plan. By 7:30 p.m., about three hours after the avalanche, troopers gathered near the Richardson monument decided the only choice left was to take snow machines to Gulkana's broken cornice. If they could find the Rice's, they would wave in the helicopter, which had refueled and returned, from the top.

The temperature was near zero and the wind raged on the ridge. Perilous rescue conditions meant it was too risky to look for and bring out anyone other than the survivors.

Riding slowly and picking through rocks at the bottom, Trooper Tim Tuckwood and another trooper took a little more than an hour to make it to the ridge. At the edge of the broken cornice, Tuckwood could barely hear shouts, but Wesley's reflective clothing showed when the trooper aimed the spotlight at the voice. Tuckwood quickly signaled the helicopter in.

It landed on a precarious ridge only a couple hundred feet from another drop-off. Rescue workers rushed across the treacherous slope toward Susan with a stretcher and loaded her into it. Even though they dropped the stretcher several times, fumbling over chunks of snow and rocks, they successfully boarded and reached Fairbanks Memorial Hospital an hour later about 11:30 PM.

Knowing his brother and niece were still on the mountain, Wesley confirmed Susan's well being at the hospital and that he had no severe injuries of his own, then left Fairbanks by car at 3 AM returning to the Richardson monument where he joined troopers and rescue workers in a desperate search.

Hours later Alaska Search and Rescue found the bodies of Donnie and Jessica. Troopers decided a recovery was impossible because of the high avalanche risk. Rescue workers were lowered from a helicopter only long enough to touch the two and confirm they were dead. "This is a very hostile environment," Lamica said. "They basically fell from the top of one glacier down onto another glacier."

The Rice family arranged a Fairbanks organization called Alaska Alpine Rescue Group. AARG climbers went in and with the assistance of a state trooper helicopter recovered Jessica's body on Feb. 3, then Donnie's two days later. A memorial service a week later at Door of Hope Church in Fairbanks helped bring closure to the family. Wesley said, "You had to come to reality that they were gone forever."

Donnie left behind his wife Connie and daughter Melissa, 12. He often played guitar or sat at the piano singing, coached his daughters' softball teams and led Jessica's fast-pitch squad to the state championship the previous year.

Connie said their daughter Jessica has been a fiercely competitive West Valley High School sophomore who would likely be a drill sergeant or manager who was always first in line at school or the first one to return from a scavenger hunt.

Susan, whose pelvis was broken in three places, spent a week in the hospital. She returned to work and doctors said her physical recovery will be complete. The Rice family plans to erect a monument near the broken cornice where Donnie and Jessica fell. They want to define the edge of the ridge and warn other people about the danger of avalanches.

Broken Bones, Legal Trouble Mar Sheep Hunt

by Larry Kaniut

NIGHTMARE: Father breaks ankle, leg; son loses first-kill memento.

Tim Mowry, *Fairbanks Daily News-Miner*, August 31, 2001

Fairbanks -- The first thing Kevin Ewing wanted to do was cry.

He had just broken his ankle and leg trying to hop across some boulders in a glacial stream with a backpack full of sheep meat. He was out in the boonies with his 13-year-old son, Lowen, there was bear sign everywhere, it was 5 p.m. and they were still two miles from camp.

"I think if I had been by myself I would have fallen apart right there," Kevin said. "I just bit the bullet."

Up to that point, it had been a dream hunt in the Alaska Range.

Father and son had flown in to a remote airstrip on the Robertson River, 150 miles southeast of Fairbanks, two days before the season. They hiked seven miles to set up their camp, and Lowen had shot his first Dall sheep, a full-curl ram, on Aug. 10, the opening day of the season.

"We were both so excited," Kevin said. "I got it all on videotape."

It was late when Lowen shot his ram, so they eviscerated the sheep, boned the meat out, put it in game bags and hiked five miles back to their spike camp. They retrieved the meat and horns the next day.

It was on their way back to camp that the dream hunt turned into a nightmare.

"We always cross this stream at the exact same spot," Ewing said.

The stream, about 6 feet wide, is too swift and deep to ford. Instead, the hunters jumped from a rock at one edge of the stream, onto a rock in the middle of the stream and then on to another rock at the other edge of the stream.

Ewing was carrying about 90 pounds of sheep meat on his back, while Lowen carried the horns and the rest of their gear.

"When I jumped from the first rock to the middle rock, I hit it with my left foot and it slipped just enough that I thought I was going to fall in the water," Ewing said. "I tried to push off with my foot and hit the last rock, but I hit kind of sideways and my foot buckled under."

His ankle rolled, breaking the tibia and tearing most of the ligaments that held the ankle in place. He also broke his fibula below his knee when he landed on his leg.

Like most serious Alaska sheep hunters, the 44-year-old Ewing is no wimp. His wiry 6-foot, 170-pound frame does not harbor much in the way of fat. He's an accomplished hunter and veteran of the 2,000-mile Tesoro Iron Dog Snowmachine Race. He knew he was in a bad situation.

"I was pretty sure it was broken," Ewing said.

Lowen cut some willows to help his father construct a makeshift splint with sticks and an Ace bandage. Then they headed back to camp, leaving the meat lying there. Ewing used his rifle as a walking stick for support.

It took them two and a half hours to travel two miles through brush and rocky terrain.

"To this day I don't know how I did that," Ewing said. "I think it was the adrenaline. I knew if I got to spike camp everything would be OK."

Once in camp, the pain began to set in, keeping Ewing up most of the night. The next day, his leg was swollen to about twice its normal size and purple from the knee down.

They spent three hot, sunny days at spike camp, hoping a plane would fly over. Lowen cut the white coveralls they used to stalk sheep into 8-inch wide strips and spelled out the word "HELP" on the hillside. But not a single plane passed over.

Down to three days of food, Ewing decided to head for the airstrip they had flown into back on the Robertson River.

"It was going to be seven days before the plane was even going to come looking for us, and the rest of our food was at the airstrip," he said.

Ewing told his son they would leave the gear and sheep horns and come back for it next summer. He explained the game laws to the boy, telling him the meat must be brought out before the horns -- and the meat had been left behind.

Wearing only the clothes on their backs, they packed up their food, tent and sleeping bags. At the last second, Lowen asked his father if he could drag the horns out with him. Ewing said yes, figuring if he'd deal with the matter if his son actually got the horns to the airstrip seven miles away. The trip required climbing up and down the side of a 5,000-foot mountain and then hiking down the Robertson River for three miles.

It took two days.

The day after they reached the airstrip, a plane from Forty Mile Air in Tok arrived. The pilot took one look at Ewing's leg and almost gagged before he radioed for Ewing's pilot, who arrived two hours later.

Ewing underwent surgery on Saturday.

While the story had a happy ending, it is not without a sour twist.

On Monday Ewing reported the incident to Fish and Wildlife Protection Troopers in Delta Junction. Lowen had managed to drag and carry the horns the seven miles to the airstrip. Under the circumstances, Ewing expected a sympathetic ear.

Instead, he got two choices: Donate the sheep horns to be put up somewhere of their choosing or go to court on charges of failure to retrieve game meat and removing horns from the field before meat.

That he probably won't get to keep the horns from his first sheep is a bummer for Lowen.

"We can have them put up somewhere and go look at them but it's just not the same as having them," he said.

Interestingly, you can't keep people from danger. You can talk all around the subject, but their own (stubborn) attitude nearly always wins in the argument of danger vs. common sense as the following story (which I read from the internet this morning—4/15/2002) indicates.

174

Sledders vs. Glacier Traps

by Larry Kaniut

One snowmachiner dies, two hurt in ice field accidents

SPENCER GLACIER: Machines fall into cracks.

Elizabeth Manning, *Anchorage Daily News*, April 15, 2002

I re-wrote this article June 2021 and titled it, *Sledders vs. Glacier Traps*.

Three men slugged their way up Spencer Glacier roughly fifty miles southeast of Anchorage, Alaska. Sled heads yearn for good snow machine riding from fall till spring. Alaska sledders are no different. Taylor Gramkow, 35, and Bruce Stingley, both of Eagle River, Alaska, and Taylor's cousin Craig Leonard of Kuna, Idaho, parked at Ingram Creek along the Seward Highway, rode up Placer River Valley, then up Bartlett Glacier. They cut over to Spencer Glacier, where they started practicing turns and playing in a big, open snowfield some 3,500 feet above the valley floor.

Although Stingley felt safer on a glacier than on an avalanche prone mountainside, he knew the dangers of glacier riding and had warned his buddies to look around and to be careful.

As Taylor rode a few hundred yards uphill from his cousin and Stingley, he and his snow machine silently plunged into a yawning crevasse on the glacier.

When Stingley noticed Gramkow had been missing for several minutes, he followed Taylor's tracks to the crevasse and spotted the sled 35 feet below. Apparently Gramkow didn't see the 10-foot-wide gap until he topped a hill. Stingley said he's turned his back and his friend was gone, "It just sucked him in...He must have been going slow enough that he couldn't get over to the other side but fast enough he couldn't brake... It was every sledder's worst nightmare... He was an excellent rider, but if you disrespect things for a moment, you can really get into trouble." Stingley indicated that his friend "just happened to be in the wrong place at the wrong time, and it cost him his life."

Rescuers from the 210th Rescue Squadron of the Alaska Air National Guard retrieved Gramkow's body around 8:15 p.m. Saturday. He is survived by his wife, Adriana.

Within twenty-four hours of Gramkow's incident rescuers again combed the snow-covered glaciers near Portage. Not far from the crevasse where Gramkow lost his life, two snow machiners fell into another crevasse.

Girdwood Trooper Bill Welch heard about these two gentlemen and assumed the worst. When he learned that the men were being rescued and had only minor injuries, he said, "Them two gentlemen better say their prayers tonight…They are very lucky. I really thought we had another body recovery."

Major Dave Looney of Anchorage's Air National Guard, Gordon Woodard fell into a crevasse first while riding high up on Trail Glacier when a snow bridge gave way beneath him. Woodard had been making a turn and jumped off his snow machine as he fell 45 feet down into the crack. With a banged up ankle he crawled three-quarters of the way back out on his own before rescuers arrived.

One of Woodard's riding buddies, Mike Gribbon, also of Anchorage, parked and walked over to check on Woodard. The snow gave way and he fell 75 feet, most likely into a separate crevasse. He suffered a head injury. The third rider, Wendell Tipton, rode down the glacier to call for help.

Pulled from the crevasses that evening by the Air National Guard pararescuers, they were taken to Alaska Regional Hospital.

In an unrelated incident earlier Sunday, Larry Astrup of Eagle River lost his snow machine into a crevasse on Spencer Glacier. He jumped off before his machine tumbled in. He had gone back to try to retrieve his machine.

Within the Chugach National Forest, the Portage-area glaciers and the snowfields above them are known for spectacular, if somewhat risky, riding. Normally snow covers the crevasses to a depth—25 to 30 feet—that provides safety to the riders. After that rescue Alaska State Troopers recommended that all snow machiners leave Spencer Glacier and avoid the area.

Solo Trek

by Larry Kaniut

Plagued by hordes of flying insects, distraught with the loss of her boyfriend and near panic with the prospects of her survival, Lydia Marie Barragan plodded on. The exhilaration she'd felt a month previous vanished in light of her predicament. What should have been a pleasant sojourn in the wilds of Canada, turned into a survival trek which would try her very being, physically, emotionally and spiritually.

In a surreal world she sat upon the beach, immobile. Shock reigned as she gazed across the lake at the haze surrounding the forest fire. Thoughts came slowly, almost lethargically to her. How could this have happened? My life has ended. And even if it hasn't, my life will never be the same.

Through the haze of the growing smoke cloud she saw the arctic sun, a red-orange orb. So close but yet so far. It shone almost as a leering face in the void. Laughing at her predicament. Her sole companion, it tortured her.

The sun had the face of a menacing gargoyle, threatening her very life... challenging her to either suck it up and survive or surrender to the environment and die.

But paradoxically, the sun also provided heat and light. Lydia could either capitalize on those aspects and seek sustenance in her journey or accept the tragic odds of her solo situation.

She chose to live.

Lydia Marie Barragan, 24, and Jean-Jecques LeFranc, 28, of Montpellier, France, planned to spend a year studying caribou seventy-five miles north of the Arctic Circle. They'd spent time canoeing the arctic two years previous and had some wilderness survival training and skills. They had established their campsite 75 miles from the town of Colville Lake in the Northwest Territories of Canada. Their camp at Lake 766, so named on the Canadian maps, was an isolated 8-mile-long body of water two miles wide.

The couple had not left word with Canadian authorities of their plans nor their proposed whereabouts. Any tragedy they faced would be endured by them alone.

As midnight July 14, 1987, approached, the sun hung slightly above the horizon while the angry skies flashed fingers of lightning. Thunder filled the air as a powerful electric storm raged.

Before long a forest fire flamed to life and scoured the earth, hungering for fuel.

At first because the wind blew the flames in the opposite direction, the fire did not concern them. However when they awoke the next morning, they discovered that there had been a shift in the wind direction overnight. A growing swath of fire marched unchecked and steadily toward their campsite.

They were faced with the universal question of what to do in their deteriorating situation. An experienced outdoorsman, Jean-Jacques outlined an evacuation plan. Their only means of escape lay across the lake and they packed their food and gear into their canoe for transfer to a site on the far shore. They hoped to save as much of their equipment and food as possible in order to salvage their project.

In order to survive any emergency the key was to remain calm, and to have a controlled attitude. Should the fire threaten them, they would rely on their experience, their map, compass and knife. Hopefully they would encounter no animal which could pose danger, such as a bear, wolf or cantankerous moose.

Moving camp required two trips. Lydia explained, "It took 45 minutes to one hour to make the first crossing with our clothes and sleeping bags and some equipment." By 1 p.m. they had completed their first trip, ferrying their tent, clothes, sled and snowshoes where they cached them on the south shore.

They returned to camp the second time to retrieve sleeping bags, a knife, photographic equipment and food.

Having loaded the canoe, they launched out into the lake, observing smoke filling the air. They stroked onward assuming all would be well on the other side. A strong wind gust sprang up, sweeping over the lake without warning. Waves pummeled the 16-foot canoe and the couple paddled frantically to stay afloat and to keep from rolling the light water craft. They'd reached the halfway point when a large swell overtook them and tipped the canoe onto its side. Instantly it filled with water.

The slightly built physical education teacher and biology student Lydia Barragan, said, "We were moving our belongings three kilometers (two miles) across the lake to escape the fire when the wind picked up, the canoe was swamped and it capsized."

They tried unsuccessfully to right the canoe in the wave tossed water. Each time they turned the craft over, it instantly capsized. Because they were being carried toward the widest part of the lake, the couple chose to abandon the canoe and swim for shore. They were a half mile from the beach and Jean-Jacques felt it was their best hope for surviving.

He shouted to Lydia, "Swim!"

Frigid water met their effort, smashing into their faces and washing into their mouths, seriously affecting their breathing. Meanwhile the acrid air and falling ash from the fire bombarded them. Lydia experienced stabbing pains in her lungs and sides. Coupled with the water's numbing cold, a euphoric-like hypothermia swathed her pain and enabled her to struggle on, one stroke at a time. Got to keep my mouth clear of the water to breathe. She could not escape the thought that she was drowning.

Instinct took over. She rolled into a floating position and stroked numbly with short strokes. She kept reminding herself, stay in control. Don't panic.

She swam ahead of Jean-Jacques. "We swam together for 45 minutes. He got very cold. He grew tired before I did. I tried to pull him along but could not."

With the beach still some distance away, Jean-Jacques struggled, thrashing behind her in a wild fashion, gagging and sputtering. His efforts failed him.

Lydia swam to his side, reached her arm around his neck and stroked backwards. She could not hold his limp body. Again, with numbness embracing her she attempted to support him and to swim. Her efforts were in vain.

Le Franc drowned.

Lydia summoned her strength and energy and stroked onward toward the beach.

She swam out of the frigid water, effectively beaching herself on the pebbles of the shore. Exhausted and cold, she could not think. She lay sprawled face down on the gravel trying to recall her final moments and wondering. Gradually reality returned. How did I get here? Am I alive? At length she sat up and coughed water from her lungs. That was when she remembered where she was. And she remembered Jean-Jacques. She looked out onto the wind tossed waves of the lake but no one was there. She involuntarily shouted, "Jean-Jacques!" He was gone.

Dejected, alone and crushed by his loss, she said, "I wanted to go back into the lake and join him. I wasn't scared. I was sad to be alive."

Shivering, she awakened the next morning at six. As she rose unsteadily to her feet, she was dizzy from hunger. She considered her chances of surviving without food and the likelihood of overcoming an encounter with a bear or wolf. She clung to the memories of her boyfriend, allowing his spirit and his love of adventure and life to sustain her.

After facing her abysmal situation and resolving to live, Lydia set out for Our Lady of the Snows Mission which lay on the far side of Colville Lake, ninety miles south. Tundra punctuated with swamps and dense forest lay in her pathway. Her wristwatch, compass and butane lighter had survived the swim and would prove valuable to her in her journey.

A mile after starting she found their first cache. The discovery elevated her hope for survival and fortified with some items. She said, "I took a compass, a winter jacket, winter boots, winter pants, a sweatshirt, matches, a cigarette lighter, bug repellent, two packages of dry rice, a small pan for water, a map, our two passports and two photographs of my family."

She carried her equipment in the nylon bag which had held a sleeping bag. "I didn't take the sleeping bag because my jacket would keep me warm, but I took the nylon bag to protect myself from the mosquitoes. It would have been a horror without that bag."

She followed oil exploration seismic lines of Petro-Canada. She stated, "I tried to use my compass but because of the bog and trees I couldn't follow a straight line. Without the seismic lines, I would have been lost."

She became very hot by noon but refused to remove the jacket as it was her best protection from the pesky bugs attacking her in a perpetual black buzzing cloud. I "couldn't take off my winter jacket because of the mosquitoes." Even with the insect repellent the mosquitoes and black flies were relentless, swarming about her all day.

"My clothes were soaking wet. I enclosed myself inside the little bag I brought to rest and decided then to walk at night."

Lydia's difficult survival trek gained only five miles in ten hours of negotiating the wild woods and tundra country. She knew she had her work cut out for her. At this rate it would take nine or ten days to reach her objective. Would her food hold out? Would her energy match her desire to live?

On her second day she encountered a bear. "I was reading my map when he appeared about five to 10 meters away. He got up on his haunches and sniffed twice." She told herself, Don't move! Don't even blink! "I stood very still and he left."

After the bear left, she continued on her journey. The constant threat of survival was in the forefront of her mind and she said, "I often thought I would never get out, but you can't think of that all the time or you'd never continue. I told myself if I got this far I can get the rest of the way."

She kept reminding herself to stay calm and to stay in control of her situation.

Daytime temperatures in the 80s turned cooler with nighttime temperatures in the 50s.

She struggled on, the flies and mosquitoes dining on her exposed flesh, attacking her eyes and boring into her hair. She was a flurry of constant swatting as she shuffled along the shoreline of Lake 766. An hour of nearly unbearable heat and bugs brought her to the realization that she was going the wrong direction. Her error in direction cost her in spent energy, wear and tear on her body and consumption of her sparse food supply. Soaked in perspiration and covered with bites, she retraced her steps to the cache to reorient herself.

Lydia applied more insect repellent before re-starting her trek, this time in the right direction. She left her sweater and departed.

Early in the afternoon she was nearing exhaustion, pushing herself unmercifully. She was reaching her limits and knew that she needed to regroup and control her destiny in order to stave off panic. She forced herself to stop, dropping to the ground beneath a tree where she removed the items from the nylon bag before pulling it over herself to fight off the flies and mosquitoes.

For several hours she endured fitful, semi-conscious sleep. During that time she dreamed of Jean-Jacques. Her dream was so real that it was as if he were there exhorting her to stick to her plan, continue on without delaying where she was. She knew that walking at night would reduce the hordes of insects, and she could rest by day. She willed herself to continue at all costs. I will not quit or give up.

Lydia arose and continued onward. During winter months when the water and ground surface area was frozen, huge machines had cut a swath through the forest. She followed the twenty feet wide path.

In places she met with obstacles in the form of ponds and swamp areas. At one point she encountered a lake blocking her pathway.

Whether she followed the seismic trail or diverted from it, her progress was constantly challenged. When she was forced to leave the trail, thick brush made it difficult for her to follow her compass course. On the trail she encountered more swamp or her compass necessitated an alternate route when the trail deviated from the course. Hour upon hour the difficulty never let up.

With the dropping of the temperature that evening, the insect attacks diminished. Lydia built a fire and ate a handful of rice. She was somewhat rejuvenated and felt hopeful for the first time.

In the early dawn the next morning at 3 o'clock she was up and walking. She determined that a steady, productive pace would accomplish her goal. Convinced that following her compass course would reduce the risk of getting lost, even at the inconvenience of barriers, she trudged on.

When she came to a wide stream, she followed the compass, took off her clothes, placed them in the bag with her other gear and stepped into the water, holding the nylon bag over her head. Within minutes she emerged from the cold, neck-deep water, shaking uncontrollably.

She took time to build a fire which dried and warmed her. Then she was off again, more confident than before. She remained hopeful but still wondered about her endurance.

Because of her knowledge of the human anatomy and the body's nutritional needs, she acknowledged her rice supply would only last so long.

She conserved her food, planning to eat as a reward at given points on the map. She ate unripe, sour berries that she found along her pathway. Water was plentiful and she frequently drank to lessen her hunger as much as to replenish her lost fluids.

Hour by hour she plodded on, developing a routine. When she was overcome by the insects, she robbed them of their objective by covering herself with her nylon bag before pressing on.

She met water barriers such as ponds and rivers with her steeled will to strip naked, carry her gear overhead and continue on the far shore. Swamps contained slimy goop into which she sank up to her ankles.

Light turned into dark. Dark became dawn. She moved resolutely onward. Day turned to day. The days slowly, painfully turned into nearly a week.

She held to her southeasterly course, always reassessing her route. She determined from the map that she was twenty miles from Colville Lake and another twenty-five to the Mission, her objective. Possibly a day away from Colville Lake and two more to the Mission.

With the possibility of reaching the Mission in three to four days, Lydia's condition included blistered and infected feet. And she had only a fraction of food left. But she chose to live. She pressed onward.

Euphoria embraced her as she identified Aubry Lake, only ten miles from Colville Lake.

The next morning tragedy struck. The day became unbearably hot. Lydia stopped time and again to drink water and to apply insect repellent. The flies and mosquitoes were relentless. The pesky bugs had taken their toll upon her physical and mental reserves. The lack of protein severely weakened her and she stumbled along on bloody feet. It was then that she discovered she had made another mistake in determining her exact whereabouts.

She was going in the wrong direction, north. She's mistaken this lake for Colville Lake. Lydia was near physical and emotional exhaustion. Although she took refuge with her nylon bag, she could not sleep. Lydia took solace in the faces of her family and friends as she studied their pictures. But she couldn't help wondering if she'd ever see them again.

The next morning, July 21, she retraced her steps. Dizziness nearly overwhelmed her. Eating more unripe berries, she stumbled onward hour after hour until at last she came to the shore of Colville Lake.

While resting on the shore and attending her feet, she experienced some stomach pain. Probably from the green berries.

She didn't think she could go on. Closing her eyes and resting momentarily, she suddenly reminded herself of Jean-Jacques and his exhortation. Lydia told herself to get up and to move.

At that point she opened her eyes and discovered what appeared to be a cabin. Is it real? She realized that it was.

She approached the dwelling and found the door unlocked. Though swathed in agony, she moved on bloody, swollen feet into the cabin. She found tea, rice and pancake mix. She prepared her first meal in nearly a week.

For twenty hours she slept, barely moving.

When she awoke, she saw a wolf standing near the cabin. Every day for the next four the wolf was there, almost as if awaiting her departure. But perhaps it was a positive omen which kept her at the cabin. On that fourth day, July 26, she did not see the wolf. That day as she prepared to leave the cabin after writing a note for the cabin's owner, a man arrived.

A deliverer in the form of Gene Marie Oudzie motored along the lake in his boat. He discovered Lydia at his father's cabin. And the manager of a cooperative who was duck hunting marveled that he had come upon the only person ever to walk on foot to this cabin.

He helped Lydia into his boat and rushed toward Our Lady of the Snows Mission, twenty miles across the lake. Lydia had covered over 70 miles in her solo trek from Lake 766, accomplishing one of the most courageous survival achievements in recent years.

The next day she accompanied the Royal Canadian Mounted Police in a helicopter to the site of the canoe accident. They recovered her boyfriend's body and discovered canisters of film at their charred campsite. The canisters contained pictures of the couple's last days.

Cpl. Malcolm MacKinnon of the Royal Canadian Mounted Police commented on Lydia's journey, "Most people couldn't have survived. She did because she's one tough lady."

SOURCE NOTES:

1. "Woman survives 10-day ordeal in Canada's wilds," *The Anchorage Times*, pp. A1 and A12, June 30, 1987

2. "One Woman's Wilderness Odyssey," Sheldon Kelly, *Reader's Digest*, September 1988, pp. 76-82

Sometimes the Gear Messes You Up

by Larry Kaniut

Ambitious trek ends in drowning

TRAGEDY: Juneau guide hoping to traverse St. Elias Range encounters weak ice.

DOUG O'HARRA, *Anchorage Daily News*, April 13, 2004

I condensed and re-wrote to *Sometimes the Gear Messes You Up* June 2021

Sometimes the gear saves you; sometimes it doesn't.

Rawboned, muscular guys, Mike Nelson and Mike Miller, planned a three to four week traverse from Yakutat, Alaska, to Haines Junction, British Columbia. They liked pioneering new routes through Alaska's coastal mountain ranges and were well known among Juneau climbers. The men expected to cross the ice fields. Their first leg included an ambitious bike, ski and climbing traverse over the St. Elias Range.

Mike Nelson, 30, was an aspiring photographer who loved glaciers. Considered a very good, prolific climber doing adventurous stuff, Nelson was known to think things out clearly. He moved to Juneau from Provo, Utah, in 2003, and worked in Juneau for six summers. He was a partner in Above & Beyond Alaska, with a specialty in glacier travel. He lived at the office of the guide service, played the guitar and mandolin, wrote songs, produced glacier photos and worked for Miller as a carpenter

Mike Miller, a contractor, had completed a 250-mile traverse from Atlin, British Columbia, up frozen lakes and over the Juneau Ice field to town.

Their journey ended tragically as they fought their way through the wilds. Thirty miles east of Yakutat lay Harlequin Lake about five miles from a snowed-in road to Yakut. They skied on the rotten ice a half mile from shore. Although they wore floatation devices, in an hour's time one or the other had fallen through the ice and into the water and been rescued by his partner. Each time they found solid ice and retreated to safety on shore. But the last time was a killer.

Because immersion in ice water shunts blood from arms and legs into the body core, those experiencing it, eventually lose the ability to move limbs or swim.

On the fourth time into the water, Mike Nelson, struggled to extricate himself from the ice hole. Pilot Les Hartley of Alsek Flying Service said, "Once Mike Nelson broke through the last time, and he couldn't get back out on his own, Mike Miller tried to get to him, but he kept breaking through himself. This water is extremely, extremely cold, and hypothermia was setting in extremely fast."

Even though Miller, 41, eventually pulled himself out, he could not reach Nelson and could no longer hear any sound from his friend. Miller squatted on his skis and pulled himself to land with his hands and a single ski pole, then hiked to a cabin near an airstrip at the southern end of the lake.

Hartley flew over the lake about 6:30 p.m. to check on their progress. When he didn't see any sign of the men, he flew toward the cabin. Miller signaled the pilot to land.

Nelson was presumed drowned after he and partner Mike Miller exhausted themselves in a horrifying scramble to climb from frigid water while wearing skis and backpacks, and tied to sleds carrying their gear and bikes, according to the Alaska State Troopers.

The sled was later reported on the ice. It was thought that Nelson remained tied to the sled just beneath the surface. The U.S. Forest Service will charter a helicopter to carry a recovery team to the scene this morning to attempt to recover Nelson's remains, Wilkinson said. "Basically, someone is going to have to be lowered down from the helicopter and go into the water with him."

He is survived by his parents and three brothers in Utah. And because he touched a lot of lives, he leaves behind a ton of Juneau friends.

Cornice Gives Way, Climber Plunges to Death

by Larry Kaniut

AVALANCHE: Partner, only 5 feet away, makes it down to Portage visitor center.

By LISA DEMER, *Anchorage Daily News*, March 1, 2004

In June 2021 I re-wrote this newspaper article by Lisa.

Joseph B. Neale, 23, and climbing partner Jesse "Bill" Billmeier, 24, skied toward Byron Glacier some fifty miles southeast of Anchorage, Alaska. Both men were outdoor studies students, had climbed together and acknowledged their outing could be an adventure or a misadventure. Billmeier had graduated with an outdoor studies degree the previous year from Alaska Pacific University. Their gear included helmets, crampons, avalanche beacons, probes and shovels. As they neared their destination, they stashed their skis and started climbing.

Their path climbed the outer edge of the ridge on a cornice, an accumulated mass of snow that evolved from winter's windblown snow or rain, often overhanging a ridge or mountain edge. Some cornices are a dozen or more feet thick and extend far beyond the mountain's side. They took turns leading. Billmeier warned Neale more than once that he was too close to the edge and Neale moved away and closer to the inside of the cornice.

Around 6 PM while nearing the summit, Billmeier trailed Neale. Bill heard a whumph and watched the cornice break lose beneath Neale and cascade off the mountain. Billmeier revealed he was about five-feet behind Neaale when he "just disappeared" with a thirty-feet wide by thirty-five to forty feet deep chunk of compacted snow and ice dropping into space and falling roughly 4,000 feet.

Billmeier approached the edge and saw his friend engulfed in a mass of snow, rock and debris. He called for Neale but heard nothing. Because the area was too steep and avalanche-prone to climb down to Neale, Billmeier descended the mountain to get help. A cleaning crew let him into the Begich, Boggs Visitor Center in Portage Valley, where he called troopers around 7:30 PM.

Troopers sent a helicopter from Muldoon with members of the Mountain Rescue Group. By the time they got to Byron Glacier, it was dark and too dangerous for a ground search. Returning Sunday the helicopter rescue crew spotted a dark spot below the cornice fault. It proved to be Neale and the rescuers roped together to reach his body. He had suffered massive injuries.

Joseph Neale was from Tulsa, Oklahoma, and a sophomore transfer to APU the previous fall. Many APU students knew Joseph as sweet, kind, good and helpful. Bill Watkin, a 20-year-old marine biology major, said, "He was the kind of guy who would do anything for you" and acknowledged that Neale was there to help a struggling student with a class project. Alaska Pacific University president Douglas North said Joseph was well-known and well-liked, an excellent student receiving "A's" in all classes. A memorial service was slated for later in the week.

Hopefully other adventurers will learn from the loss of this young man and take every step toward a safe return

Tragedy on the Mountain

by Larry Kaniut

An 11-year-old Anchorage boy encountered tragedy on Mount Alyeska Sunday night, December 8, 1991. Bart Rizer was an experienced skier who loved the sport. His younger sister Megan is also an avid skier. A 6th grade student at Bear Valley Elementary School on Rabbit Creek Road, he enjoyed skiing the mountain nearly every weekend with his family who has a condominium at Alyeska.

Bart skied with a friend on the mountain. He decided to ski powdered snow, but his friend chose to ski down the mountain alone. At 3:10 p.m. they separated just below the Roundhouse lift terminus.

Because of his experience and ability to ski even advanced runs, Bart confidently attacked the run.

Snows had accumulated as a result of a recent storm that dumped a foot of fresh snow on the mountain four days in a row. Snow depth at the base of the mountain measured 39 inches while at mid-mountain and an elevation of 1,500 feet, the snow measured 62 inches. The recent snowfall made un-groomed areas more difficult to navigate. Although the snow didn't slow down Bart's enthusiasm, he may not have expected the conditions he encountered. Once off the groomed area Bart skied over a ledge and into powder 5-feet deep.

When Bart didn't show up at the base of the mountain, his friend notified Bart's family as they were also skiing that day.

Shortly before 5 p.m. the Alyeska Ski Patrol received word of Bart's disappearance. A very brief time after his disappearance officials closed the run due to darkness.

News of Bart's situation launched thirty professional ski patrol members and volunteers who combed the 140-acre area. Six searchers at a time departed down the mountain in a grid pattern. Searchers followed off-trail tracks in hopes of finding Bart. Just before Alaska State Troopers joined the search effort around 7:30 p.m. searchers located tracks about 90 feet off the main trail.

Bart had been missing more than 4 hours when ski patrol members skied the tracks and found him. He was unconscious and under deep snow. Bart was placed into a sled and whisked off the mountain.

Two patrol officials who began cardiopulmonary resuscitation while another guided the sled down the mountain to a waiting ambulance. The Girdwood ambulance transported Bart to Providence Hospital in Anchorage.

Alyeska Ski Resort spokeswoman Laure Hite said, "The area he was in was on open ground within boundaries. As far as we can tell, he did nothing wrong. It was a freak accident." 2

Hite said, "His friend stayed on the groomed trail, while (Bart) went off into the powder and they lost touch with each other. We don't know if the friend lost sight of him or if he skied to the bottom to wait." 2

Unfortunately all the efforts of the family, officials, volunteers and medical professionals after several hours expended to revive him failed to bring back Bart, and he was declared dead at 11:39 p.m. at Providence Hospital

Some people speculated that Bart suffocated under the deep snow. The official reason given for his death was hypothermia...not suffocation.

It is always unfortunate to lose a loved one and Bart's departure will never be forgotten. This tragic event points out the need to use the buddy system in order to keep track of your partner in the outdoor setting. More than likely if Bart hadn't been alone, he would be alive today.

In 1989 a Florida tourist took the chair up Mount Alyeska sightseeing and fell from a chair lift. The lift stopped and the man tried to get out of the chair after discovering that his wife had not boarded a chair. The 76-year-old man fell in an area beyond the safety net and died

SOURCE NOTES:

1. "11-year-old skier dies after fall," (Hypothermia claims boy stuck in snow for 4 hours), Gail Boxrud, *The Anchorage Times*, December 9, 1991, pg. B5

2. "Eleven-year-old skier's death called 'freak accident,'" Diana Elliott, *The Anchorage Times*, Tuesday, December 10, 1991, pp. A1 & A12

Snowing Inside Me

by Verna Pleasure

"I was holding onto my heart and trying to push it back into my chest..."

Verna Pleasure lay upon the ground beneath the plane's spinning propeller, wondering, hoping, fearing. The gusting wind pounded the bush plane on the Yukon River ice, bouncing it from right to left. Her eyes scrutinized the propeller just inches from her face, and she wondered if a wind gust would lift the tail of the plane enough to allow the prop to rip her mangled body again. Her torso looked like a side of beef hanging at a slaughter house.

The date was December 18, 1980. The place was Pilot Station, Alaska. The situation was a woman fighting for her life. Sometime later I met Verna and she told me about her experience.

We were to take off when the pilot discovered the plane had a flat tire. Because of the extreme cold, the engine needed to be left running. The pilot said, "Stay in the plane. I'll go to the village to get help." The wind was blowing the Cessna 180, buffeting it about severely. I was concerned the plane might flip over and break into flames with me in it, so I got out.

I walked diagonally until I was far enough from the prop to turn back to the river bank leading up to the village. I turned. That's when I felt excruciating pain in the back of my head, right in the middle. Everything went black. Then the pain left.

What I didn't realize was that I had cleared the prop, but that the prop wash had sucked my scarf back into the propeller and was slowly pulling me back into the spinner.

I kept walking. The pain returned. Something hit me in the back of my head every now and then.

It hurt so badly. It was like something sucking out my brain. It was just a nauseating, sucking feeling. I kept getting sleepy as I walked. It was a sweet and sinking kind of sleep that pulled me deeper into the darkness of my mind.

I heard a humming noise like bees all around me, and I smelled some kind of oil. I didn't realize the sound and smell were from the engine.

Then I must have blacked out because I felt like dreaming. I heard tearing and splintering. I tried to imagine why these sounds were so vivid in my dreams, but that sinking, peaceful darkness forced me to give up all thought. My head felt heavy and my body was oh so lazy. I gave in.

Something would hit me in my head every now and then, and I would go back to sleep and see all of my family when they were little and my grandmother who was dead. We were all standing around the old bath tub listening to grandmother in north Philadelphia. One of us kids was sick and grandmother was telling my mother what to do for us. We were all so little. I must have been about four or five. I remember thinking...what a cute picture. But I also remember asking myself, "Verna, why aren't you working?"

Even in this dream I wondered why I had this sickening sensation in my head.

As I woke up, I realized the pilot was crying. I heard him screaming, "Oh, my God! Oh, no! Oh, my God!" I heard him gagging and throwing up over and over again.

My left hip was killing me. I didn't feel any pain in my left arm and shoulder...the propeller was grinding around inside there, up by my ear. I was thinking, "Oh, my gosh! I'm asleep inside the propeller." I forced myself to stand on my leg and tried to get my arm out of the propeller.

The propeller had gouged my hip, and my left upper thigh was cut from one end all around to the other. I was afraid to fall down, because I knew I'd hurt my body more if I fell. I thought I had my arm—I didn't know the propeller had amputated it. I knew I'd hurt my leg or my hip, and I was afraid it was broken. I was wondering how I could maneuver over the hard ice on the river without falling.

I assumed my ribs were broken. A voice said, "Close your eyes, Verna. Remember your First Aid course in Cantwell...never allow the victim to see his injuries." I kept my eyes closed.

As I lay on the ground with the propeller spinning inches from my face, I thought that I was going to die..."I'm on the ground. This propeller is going to finish me off. Nobody's going to come and cut this propeller off. The wind is blowing the plane up and down, and the propeller is dipping down into my face.

"I'll try to turn away from the propeller. My head is all the way back inside my parka hood...I'll try to just move it back a little bit more. I love my Eddie Bauer parka. They don't even make coats like this anymore. It's a beautiful coat...beautiful, foxy, satin, shiny and I love beautiful things."

Something came over me while I was thinking this, and I looked up at the sky. I was holding onto my heart and trying to push it back into my chest. But I didn't know where it was supposed to be, so I was kind of hoping that I had the right spot. It was all soft and squishy, and I was freaking out on the beats of my heart because it was like a big bass drum (I used to teach music in San Francisco and it's weird that the rhythm reminded me of a drum). My ribs and the muscle and the tissue and the skin...there was nothing there but this big, powerful sound...like something from an amplifier. I'm freaking out on my heart beats, trying to deal with it and saying, "Wow, this is a neat rhythm."

Meanwhile the other side of my head was saying, "Gee, my papers. The students' papers. How will anyone from the college know that they have finally finished their incompletes? They'll need documentation. I hope the propeller didn't shred them. How am I going to convince the teachers that these students finished their courses?"

My involvement with the village people was such a joy. I was a field center coordinator for the University of Alaska with the branch in Bethel, Kuskokwim Community College. I was the college. I traveled to villages, canvassing the community to discover what courses they wanted. I registered students, and then I facilitated classes and sent their work back on the plane to the instructor of records. It was really exciting. Many of the native people didn't want to leave their families to go into town to go to college, so why not bring the college to them?

In addition to the school incompletes my sister Cindy and her little boy were coming to the bush for the first time to visit. Who will tell them where I am? How will I be able to make them love the village people as I do if I'm splattered here on the Yukon holding on to my heart and unable to move? What about my son Keith? I'm glad I left him back in the village with a good family.

I experienced this beautiful feeling, a natural high. The sky got really blue—it was the most beautiful blue I had ever seen. I started smiling to myself and just feeling so good about the world and about everything, and life was wonderful. Everything was just so bright and beautiful and I felt better than I ever had.

I'm talking to myself, "Gee, Verna, how can you be thinking like this when you're about to die?" I had three conversations going on. One was, of course, the good feeling that was exhilarating, a feeling of ecstasy. I was feeling good because something had placed me on the ground. I was wondering, "There's not supposed to be angels around anymore; and I didn't put myself on the ground because I couldn't. I didn't fall to the ground. I stood up and something pulled me gently to the ground." I was kinda going over how I had gotten to the position without hitting my head on the Yukon River and all of a sudden something moved the plane away.

The other one was the drum beats of my heart and how my rhythm was so interesting. I wanted to harness that rhythm and use it to write a song.

And then I was worried about the propeller in my face—I wondered how I would ever be able to tell the college which students had finished their incompletes.

It was thirty to forty degrees below zero Fahrenheit and the winds were gusting about fifty, sixty miles an hour. I tried to cover my heart up so snow wouldn't blow into my chest cavity. The wind raged. My life's blood oozed. I lay there bleeding to death with a growing patch of blood creeping across the snow in all directions, staining it red. Village people stood and stared. *They're all over there looking at me. I'm going to die.*

The people were blaming themselves; and from what the pilot was saying, I knew he shouldered the blame. That made me sad to hear a dear friend pouring out his guts. The native guys were quiet. I thought about the contrast and said, "Oh, the poor pilot. I think some of them are going to blame him. They're not gonna understand. And maybe I'll never be able to tell them what really happened." I was really wanting to live because I needed to tell people what happened, as I knew they were going to get the wrong story.

Two hundred feet away, they were motionless. I realized they were in shock. I heard them talking. They were saying, "Is she dead?"

Somebody said, "Why don't we cut the plane off?"

The pilot said, "She's already dead. It's no use. It's not going to make any difference all the damage and everything's done." He freaked out.

If they think I'm dead, they're not going to come over and try to help me. Nobody can look into my parka. They're all over there on the side of me, and they'd have to be right over the plane to see that my eyes are open...that I am very much alive. I was afraid that if they didn't come soon enough and if the wind tipped the plane down again, the propeller might kill me.

The propeller was bent. Two or three times people fought through the gusting wind to cover me up. They'd get to me, get sick, return to the others and cry. They couldn't do it. It was a bloody mess. Finally somebody came over and threw a sled cover over me so he wouldn't have to look at me. At the same time somebody cut off the propeller. Then I relaxed.

But then I couldn't breathe because they had me covered up for dead. I could only hear mumbling.

I moved the cover so I could breathe. Somebody noticed and said, "She's still moving."

Then they came a little closer.

One young female approached me and asked, "Verna, is there anything you want to say?"

I nodded my head. She said, "What do you want to say?"

I said, "Take care of Keith."

She asked, "Where is he?"

That's when I realized I couldn't say too many words because I was losing all the air from my lungs. I wanted to say, "My sister's coming in. Please meet her. Let her know what happened. Keith's at such and such a house. Please take care of him."

The pilot could do nothing. He was still crying. I never heard a man cry. And he was crying and screaming and vomiting all at the same time. I was so worried about him. I was trying to get up and go to him and tell him that everything was going to be okay; but I was scared to move. All I could hope was that maybe somebody would console him, but he got no consolation.

I started praying for him because I felt it was my fault. I shouldn't have gotten out of the plane. It wasn't his fault. My thoughts apologized for the pilot...*I'm sorry, Larry.*

I had been on the ice for twenty-five minutes...uncovered. Snow had been blowing inside me. The pain in my chest intensified. However it helped that everything froze and slowed down the bleeding, assisting my body in its life saving struggle.

When I first went to the villages, I wanted to live with the native families. I didn't want to stay in the school, so I asked if there was a family that I could pay a little money to stay with. The family I was staying with embraced me as their daughter. I got myself adopted and had an Eskimo mother and father in Pilot Station—my adopted father's name was Fred Nick. They started telling people that I was their daughter.

After my accident Fred Nick went up to his house and called Kuskokwim Community College to tell them I was coming. He told them that one of their workers had had an accident and was probably dead. But he wasn't sure.

There was a mail plane coming over, but it wasn't scheduled to stop at Pilot Station. Somebody called on their CB (citizens band radio) and signaled to the mail plane to stop.

When the mail plane landed, the villagers loaded me onto a dog sled and strapped me down. They drug the dog sled across the ice to the plane which hurt because it was real bumpy with icy ridges all the way. I cried for the first time.

Once they had the mail out of the plane, they put me on board. Fred Nick was a neat father to me. When they were putting me on the plane and nobody else looked at me, he came over, pulled the canvas back, looked at me then covered me up again. When the canvas from the dog sled was placed over me, I had a little bit of air left from my nose. I realized I could move my hand and I pushed the canvas up so I could breathe.

The nearest medical facility was in Bethel, a village of 4,000 people, an hour and a half away by plane. Although the Pilot Station health aide didn't want to go, they forced her to accompany me. She was so scared somebody had to go with her.

When we got to the airport in Bethel, the ambulance was there. They knew I was coming in because the college had called the hospital. The president of the college and my supervisor met me.

A number of doctors were with the ambulance. They looked into the plane and took over. The last words I remember hearing were, "Drive fast and don't mind the bumps."

"We have no blood pressure," the emergency room nurse informed the staff. "Her pulse is all but non-existent." How was this mutilated female patient capable of drawing a breath?

They wanted to start an IV but they couldn't find a vein. The veins didn't work because they had retracted, so the doctors cut into my body to locate them. They figured my blood pressure must have been forty over zero because they couldn't get a bottom number—they found very little blood in my body. So they did cut downs (a procedure involving cutting into the tissue to locate a vein) on my wrist at the bend of my right arm just above the elbow and on my right leg just above the ankle.

Later I was told a call went out for blood donations. All kinds of people from the Bethel community heard about me over the radio and came to give their blood: from the seasonal worker to the housewife, from the professional worker to those struggling for sobriety, people from all ethnic groups and all faiths to those curious and searching for a faith.

I later heard that the blood donor line was so long it stretched out of the hospital and into the road. Some still get teary eyed as they tell me these events that transpired as they prepared me for surgery.

The medical staff didn't know that because of my religious convictions as one of Jehovah's witnesses, I wouldn't accept a blood transfusion. We govern ourselves by God's word, the Bible, and Acts 15:28 and 29 says we should abstain from blood. Only sacrificial use of blood has ever been approved by God (Leviticus and Hebrews 9).

When there is severe blood loss, the greatest need is to restore the fluid volume. Blood is actually 50% water and there are the red and white blood cells and so forth. When much blood is lost, the body itself pours large reserves of blood cells into the system and speeds up the production of new ones. But fluid volume is needed. Plasma volume expanders that contain no blood can be used to fulfill that need, and we are permitted to accept these.

They started pouring blood into me. Later they found out that they had the wrong type—my medical records read "uncrossed mismatched blood." Luckily my body would not retain the blood, and I kept bleeding.

I kept waking up. The medical staff kept drugging me because I was real stubborn. The doctor said that I kept calling Jehovah's name. That's what I had been doing when I was in the propeller. As soon as I started calling His name, I started getting out. I couldn't really pray— all I could say was, "Jehovah God in Jesus' name." That's all I said.

I woke up one time, and they were all working below the pelvis. To myself I said, "Those fresh guys. What in the world are they doing?" I realized I had been hurt in my hip, but I didn't know my leg was only hanging on. I said, "Those guys are so fresh, they're looking at my body." And I was rolling my eyes and looking at them. They realized I was awake and said, "Give her some so and so and so." And they knocked me out again and everything went black.

I woke up again later and they were pressing my nose flat, and I had tried for years to build a bridge. The mask flattened my nose all the way out. Caring about the way I look, even in the emergency room, I kept saying, "You're flattening my nose. I've been working for a long time to get it...would you please move the mask up."

"What is she saying?" The doctor would give me something, and I would sink into blackness again. That was the last time I woke up. They kept saying, "When she wakes up, give her lots of something." I was over drugged.

They had never done this type surgery and after five hours the medical staff flew me by Lear jet to Anchorage for more medical help. Just about all the doctors from the Bethel hospital came on the plane with me. I heard them saying, "There's nobody left in the hospital. You gotta get back."

Once I woke up inside the Lear jet and was amazed to see so many medical personnel so close to me. Someone said, "She's coming to again!" Then blackness shot into my head and I never came to for a long time.

I was still concerned about missing my sister Cindy. I was to have met her in St. Mary's at the same time of my accident. That's the reason I fought so hard to get through the anesthesia. I had so much to tell them and they never gave me the opportunity...they just kept giving more anesthesia to knock me out and keep me quiet...

At Providence Hospital in Anchorage I was feeling badly because I wasn't getting any phone calls, nobody was coming to see me. I was feeling real sad because I thought I was dead. Then one day I opened my eyes and looked on the wall. My sister had arrived and had put up all these cards around my room to encourage me. I saw all these cards. It was just wonderful. I thought, "Hey, I'm not dead yet."

I had to undergo five more hours of surgery at Providence Hospital which included wiring my ribs, giving me more blood and making me a shoulder. Dr. Anderson used my own muscle and tissue and wrapped it around my remaining clavicle portion to make me a shoulder. He was proud of his work and excited about my astounding recuperative powers.

The medical staff told me I had lost my arm. The propeller had amputated it. They'd found it hanging inside my coat by a sliver of skin. There was no neatness about the propeller's amputation, and because of the blades the doctors had to go inside my chest and shoulder and de-bride blackened tissue and muscle. So I lost part of my shoulder and chest and pieces of my ribs. Later I saw pictures from the coroner's office. Even now, I can still see my arm and hand in a box inside a plastic bag...it is all swollen and blackened. I can see trails of perspiration glistening on my poor arm. I believe it is really in a lot of pain. I look at my arm in the photograph and I feel sad.

They called a priest to deliver last rites. But my sister said, "She's Jehovah's Witness. You can't have a priest do that." The priest agreed, "When somebody is this close to death, they deserve to have somebody of their own faith come and give them last rites." He looked in the phone book and called the Kingdom Hall of Jehovah's Witnesses. It was very neat that one religion would defer to another like that. I don't know who that priest was, but I appreciated his decision.

There was a meeting being held that night at the Kingdom Hall. The brothers who were there realized that there was a sister in the hospital that desperately needed their spiritual support, and a few of them left the meeting right then and came straight to the hospital.

Yet I found myself wondering about my accident, "Why did all this happen to me?" I got angry. I decided to turn my back on Jehovah, "I'm not going to pray to You anymore."

I was talking to Jehovah about how He had caused this to happen. I felt that He had led me on. Why was I feeling so beautiful about everything, and then have to be rigged up to all this equipment? The pain was now unbearable. They had me on as much morphine as I could possibly take. They were worried about kidney damage but nothing would stop the pain.

I was angry at Him because I had believed He wouldn't cause me to have a life of discomfort and pain. I was angry about the pain and I was angry that I'd been given blood transfusions

My hip was hurting—I was lying on the stitches in my hip. My arm was just killing me—my arm still feels like it's there. All these painful sensations like needles were going through it. It was hurting and contracting with feelings, like something would squeeze it into a vice then let it go.

It was painful every time I took a breath. My lung had been slashed. They had a tube going into my mouth and the tube going down into my lungs...and that was very painful. The tube inside my nasal passage created a great deal of pain. Everything was hurting, one big hurt.

When I woke up and smiled at my family they did not smile back at me but instead they looked afraid...afraid to come too close.

I was also angry because I had wanted to be so close to Jehovah that I even had gone to bed every night with a Bible under my pillow. When I traveled, I had my Bible with me. Whenever I went to a student's home, I had my Bible with me. I touch my Bible sometimes, and I would say a few prayers.

I always prayed at night and counted my blessings before I went to bed. I had personal Bible studies every night and sometimes in the morning.

I never consumed any alcohol. I never consumed drugs. I didn't go out to parties. I was not immoral in any way. I was doing everything right; I was where I was supposed to be. I was working. I had given glory to Him, I was giving glory to Him and thanking Him every night.

I was happy being in the village. I had always wanted to work with the natives. I was expressing my happiness to Him daily.

Then this happened to me. Why?

I really felt like my faith was shattered. I felt like I had believed in Something that had let me down. For three days and nights that went on because I was so angry.

But because praying had become such a habit for me, I realized when I couldn't pray, that I felt empty. I got bored. My mind and my heart felt empty because there was nothing. So after three days I said, "Oh, I'm sorry. Gosh, I'm so glad You understand. In Your loving kindness and mercy please forgive me."

I started praying again. I wanted to believe and my faith was restored.

EPILOGUE:

I was in the hospital three and a half to four weeks when they sent me to Our Lady of Compassion nursing home. They felt after ten days to maybe three weeks I'd get stabilized.

As I started healing, I was overwhelmed by the love shown to me by the Jehovah's Witnesses and people from a number of communities. My travels around Alaska exposed me to a lot of people, and their coming to visit was real important. It encouraged me because I was scared. The teachers at Kuskokwim Community College in Bethel showed that they cared.

I felt they would be angry with me and I was still concerned about records. Next to the Christian community, my strongest support came from the native people. They had prayer lines in different homes for the nights I was supposed to die. I had groups of natives in my room en masse telling me about the prayer support. I thought I looked so bad that they wouldn't want to see me, so their presence was reassuring, and made me feel good.

In Pilot Station they closed the school and everybody went home. They closed the schools and went home and prayed. When I went back to the village, I was afraid of how I would be treated even by the little kids. But they all looked up to me like I was something like maybe out of a miracle. They treated me with reverence. I realize there were a lot of things that happened behind the scenes. There were prayer lines in Bethel and my three villages—St. Mary's, Mountain Village and Pilot Station.

People in the villages got together to support me. In Pilot Station villagers packed up my stuff and the city manager Tim Troll had my phone cut off and watched out for my wellbeing.

I had lived in different villages for a total of six years.

I got calls from every village I had ever taught in. Some had been four or five years earlier, but they all came to see me or called me. And they kept coming to see me. I learned and gained from them—more like strength and courage and stoicism and just kind of keeping quiet and not ever treating a person in a way that would make them lose face. That's taken me a long ways.

I hardly work with any native people at all now, and I really, really miss that because there's a beauty that they have about them that even the alcoholism does not cloud. But you have to live in the village in order to see what that is. They possess a beauty, strength, resourcefulness, dignity and pride. I picked up quiet strength from them.

I have a lot of phantom pain and painful sensations which no drugs can eradicate. I didn't think I could concentrate, stay on task and function with continual pain. When the pain was the worst, I considered suicide.

Today I have a lot of trouble breathing because of the uncrossed, mismatched blood I was given.

The pilot of my accident owned the company. I didn't sue him—I could have gotten millions of dollars. He was my very good friend. There were no romantic entanglements. It wasn't like that out in the village. People are just nice to you; and they help you if they see that you are really trying to help yourself. They were admiring you for your strength and your courage, and they saw me going out every day and hop in the planes going here and there. The pilot had given me free trips here and there.

He was the first one to talk to me when I hit Pilot Station. He told me a lot about the native people, a few do's and don'ts. I think he moved to the Lower 48 States. I have never held any negative feelings toward him throughout my ordeal. He eventually started drinking really badly and he did lose the company.

Later the doctors at the Bethel hospital, Dr. Dunn and the whole team, got a special commendation award for the emergency support that they gave me.

Verna lay beneath the throbbing plane propeller...

holding her heart with her right hand,

feeling its squishy tissue and its rhythm,

to put it back into her chest without knowing exactly where it went or how to do it,

wondering about writing a song to the rhythm,

fearing the propeller's proximity to her face,

feeling ecstasy about the blueness of the sky and her feelings of peace,

wondering if Jehovah would take her home and

dreading death because she had a job to do--students' papers to verify and grades to validate,

and a pilot to reassure that this accident was not his fault.

Verna did not give up. She had a job to do and a God to worship.

Seward Sinking Kills Two

by Larry Kaniut

RESCUED: Tour boat pulls survivors from bay after an hour in water.

PETER PORCO, *Anchorage Daily News*, September 5, 2004

I re-wrote Porco's piece June 2021 and titled it *Water Bound Rodeo*.

The first inkling something was wrong came about 12:30 p.m. when the skipper of a boat in the Seward harbor picked up a Mayday call on a non-emergency channel, authorities said. The call was brief and gave no indication of what vessel was in trouble or where. Nothing further was heard from whoever made the call, and authorities could not trace it.

An hour later Coastal Explorer skipper Tim Fleming, 51-year-old and a tour boat worker of fifteen years, completing a six-hour excursion for Kenai Fjords Tours, slugged his way back to Seward with winds at 25 miles per hour, gusting to 35, and wind-blown seas at 3 to 4-foot chop...sometimes 5-feet. While rounding the southern end of Rugged Island a quarter mile off shore and 20 miles south of Seward, early Saturday afternoon, crew members spotted something white in the water.

Turned out the white objects were coolers from a sunken 22-foot boat. The five occupants had left Anchorage homes to fish, not knowing water would crash over the stern killing the engine, leaving them dead in the water and swamping the boat. If they had anchored in the wind, with the seas rolling, the boat could have easily gone down fast.

In retrieval mode, Fleming steered the Coastal Explorer closer and members of his crew saw a man bobbing in the waves amongst the debris on the water. A man's head popped up. As the boat slowed, his hand rose above the surface and Fleming heard a yell. Fleming said, "He was just about ready to give up."

Once the crew pulled the man aboard, Fleming alerted his 86 passengers and crew to watch for others in the water and in a few minutes they saw a woman in the distance, evidently alive, and spun the vessel around.

On the way to her, they noticed two others, face down and unmoving. Soon they would see a fifth person, a man shouting at them from an eighth of a mile away. Fleming said, "They were scattered from here to Kansas, because the wind was blowing so hard. It was just an act of God that we came across those guys." He acknowledged that those in the water were "in a world of hurt" before the Coastal Explorer showed up.

They spotted the older of the two male survivors, Lim, barely alive, and Fleming notified the Coast Guard. The agency issued a call for other vessels to help.

Kenai Fjords Tours crews are trained for man-overboard scenarios, said Fleming, so his crew tossed a sling to Lim and got him up.

One of the unconscious men floating in the water had wrapped an arm through the strap on a cooler, Fleming said. The other lay face down with his body curled, he said. No life vest was visible. They decided to pass the two and bring in Seo.

After pulling her aboard, they went for Kim. The three survivors had used life vests to help them stay afloat, but only one was wearing the vest, and it was on backward, said Fleming. The others merely held fast to them.

Meanwhile, although Fleming's crew understood how to treat hypothermia, he located a doctor aboard the vessel, who supervised treatment of the survivors. Fleming said he was surprised on leaving the bridge and descending to find that several passengers had removed their clothes and gotten under blankets with the victims, whose wet clothes had been removed.

Two other vessels had come along, the Kenai Star, operated by Major Marine Tours in Seward, and the Alaskan Summer, a 31-foot charter fishing boat, also from Seward. The Alaskan Summer maneuvered quickly to pick up Lee and the other unconscious man while the Kenai Star let off two tourists to board the Alaskan Summer and start CPR. Troopers identified them as respiratory therapist Ruth Howser of Milwaukee, Wisconsin, and registered nurse Shirley Betz of North Liberty, Indiana.

Because of the wind, a fourth boat led the Alaskan Summer up the bay, breaking the waves for it, said Fleming.

Halfway to Seward, Anderson and three medical technicians aboard another boat met the Alaskan Summer, boarded it and used defibrillators and other techniques on the two unconscious men. But the men never revived and were pronounced dead at the hospital, troopers said.

Since only one of the survivors could speak any English, Troopers had some difficulty piecing events together. In the end, three people survived. Troopers identified one of the dead men as Jong Sil Lee, 48. By Saturday night they still had not reached the family of the other man, aged 53, and did not release his name. The boat was owned by one of the two dead men, troopers said. The survivors were Sung Seo, a 28-year-old woman; Yu Kim, a 30-year-old man; and Sam Lim, a 58-year-old man, said troopers Sgt. Brandon Anderson in Seward.

Boat size, inexperience and lack of communication created this situation.

When Ice Fishing Gets Hot

by Larry Kaniut

Flames poured from the shack. Steve Frith awakened and yelled at his buddy then fled out the door, away from the flaming building and into the night. They were on an ice fishing trip which turned nasty.

On December 12, 1990, the two Fairbanks buddies left their homes for an 80-mile trip to Quartz Lake. Steve Frith, 23-year-old university student, and Tom Villa, 35-year-old family man, looked forward to spending the night and fishing for rainbow trout and salmon.

The two swimming instructors reached the lake, pulled Tom's pickup up to the ice fishing shack and carried their gear into the empty 8x8-foot building where they would spend the night.

Villa caught three fish before the men decided to stop fishing for the night. They set up their propane stove and went to bed.

During the night, Frith awoke to fire in the shack. He said, "I woke up and there was flame everywhere. It spewed like a blowtorch." 1

He yelled to alert Tom. Then he fled the flaming building.

Villa said, "I did not think of being burned. I was thinking about all the equipment we had in the shack or leaning against the shack. That's what I was thinking, 'What are we going to do for warmth?'" 1

Once clear of the building, they rolled in the snow to put out the fire that burned their clothes.

Neither man knew what caused the 20-pound propane bottle to explode, but they theorize that it was too close to the heat. Evidently the tank's pressure valve released gas which eventually ignited.

The men were not fully aware of the tissue damage they'd suffered. Villa had second- and third-degree burns on 60 percent of his body, including his chest, waist and arms. Frith was burned on 50 percent of his body including his face, back, arms and right leg.

Standing in the snow clad only in their underwear, the buddies knew they needed to find clothes and shelter to increase their chances of survival.

The most sensible solution for their problem was to seek refuge in Villa's vehicle.

Fortunately he had not locked it with his key which burned up in the conflagration. Enduring indescribable pain from their burns and knowing they faced the possibility of freezing to death, they climbed into the truck. They found a sweat suit. Villa put on the pants and Frith wore the shirt.

Without Villa's keys they couldn't start the engine. Their time in the unheated truck was frigid. He said, "We kind of assessed the situation and it looked pretty bleak. We decided that we wanted to live." 1

The pain of the burned skin was compounded by the freezing temperatures. The men lay on the truck seat agonizing the night away. Every bump or touch irritated the skin. Hours dragged away.

They could only hope that help would arrive. They continued to reassure each other of their desire to live. Villa continued to coach himself to persevere, "I want to live. I want to live. I want to live. I have a wife and two children. I want to live." 1

Villa and Frith clutched each other for warmth. Their shivering encouraged them because they knew that it was a sign that their bodies were automatically trying to keep warm. They knew that once they stopped shivering, they were in trouble from serious hypothermia, where the body's core temperature drops because the body isn't producing enough heat to keep warm. Hypothermia untreated causes death.

They kept hoping for the dawn. Hoping for someone to come to their aid. For four hours they waited, clinging to hope.

Late that morning Dick McManus of North Pole and a friend arrived at the lake to fish. When they drove into the fishing area, they saw Villa's truck parked in the roadway. The two men were somewhat puzzled, thinking the truck had been abandoned. But then Villa opened the door, stuck his head out and screamed for help.

McManus was startled by the sight of the men. He said later, "I didn't think they were dying, but boy, I knew they were in pain. They begged us not to leave, but there was nothing I could do for them." 1

Rescue required McManus' departure to find a phone. The nearest one was about ten miles away at the general store. McManus reached it and called officials. Medics arrived and transported the burned buddies to Fort Greeley.

Villa and Frith were near death. In addition to their burns the men suffered frostbite and hypothermia.

From Fort Greeley a Lear jet zipped them to Anchorage's

Providence Hospital.

Recovering from burns in separate rooms at Providence Hospital both men agreed that they would have died had it not been for the constant encouragement that each provided the other. "If either one of us had given up, lost consciousness or panicked, neither would have made it," said Frith. 1

Villa spent two months at Anchorage's burn unit with second-degree burns over 60 percent of his body. Surgeons operated four times to replace flesh lost from his feet, arms and hands.

Both men wear pressure suits which are designed to protect the tender young flesh of burn victims. Frith said, "It's like wearing Spandex over your whole body." 2 The material is uncomfortable and itchy. However it helps minimize scarring. They expected to wear the suits at least a year.

A year later, the men say they are doing well, thanks to family, friends and a strong will to live.

Villa admitted that even though he knew hundreds of kids from his swimming instruction days, he was surprised at how many people remembered him and chose to assist in his medical bills (he and his family, including wife Kimberly, and their two infant children was uninsured).

He stated later that, "For three weeks I didn't know what was going on, and for another three (weeks) I didn't know much. When I was able to read the mail it was just amazing." 2

He admits that both mentally and physically, there is much to cope with, "I was talking with my wife about it and crying on her shoulder. I think it's important to talk about it.

"My body looks pretty trashed, my arms, my chest. Getting used to this new body is a little bit different." 2

However he proudly admits, "We are not burn victims, we are burn survivors. Steve and I went out to have a good time. We had an accident…My doctor says you don't get burned twice." 1

A year after their ice fishing shanty caught fire and burned them badly, Steve Frith and Tom Villa have returned to life. However life will never be the same for them.

Frith said that the choice to live was easy, "You either bounce back or you don't, and given that choice, it was pretty cut-and-dried for me." 2

Frith lost his left foot which was replaced with an artificial one.

He has adjusted to it and gets around well. He admits that his burned hands are more of a problem. He said, "A lot of people said I'd never use them again. I wouldn't accept that." 2

He discontinued going to physical therapy a month after he started in Anchorage. He types 50 words a minute. He hopes to go fishing again as soon as he sheds his pressure suit.

Frith was a University of Alaska Fairbanks student who wrote for the campus alternative newspaper. He did not experience the financial problems that Villa had with his medical coverage.

Both men chronicled their year of recovery by writing about it. Frith hopes someday his account will be published.

Villa busies himself these days watching the children, cleaning the house and chopping wood. Although he's not 100% he says, "I just think it's important to look back at where you started so you know how far you've come."

SOURCE NOTES:

1. "'There was flame everywhere,'" Pamela Doto, pp. B1 & B2, *Anchorage Daily News*, January 24, 1991

2. "Men struggle back from burns," AP, *Anchorage Daily News*, pp. B1 & B3, November 30, 1991

3. "Fire survivors' recovery sure but slow," AP, *The Anchorage Times*, pg. B4, November 30, 1991

APPENDIX 1

SURVIVAL BOOKS OF NOTE

Almost Too Late—family faces survival after boat's sinking; Alaska

Hey, I'm Alive!—pilot and passenger crash in Yukon; fight fear, freezing and starvation

Pirate, Pawnee and Mountain Man: The Saga of Hugh Glass— 1800's grizzly mauling,   subsequent survival trek

Into Thin Air—man falls into crevasse; survival trek

The Long Walk—escapees from Siberian prison camp; goal is to reach India

Alive and Miracle in the Andes—rugby team crashes into Andes Mountains; 72 days on the mountain

APPENDIX 2
NEWSPAPER HEADLINES

All these events took place in Alaska unless otherwise noted.

Boy, 14, kills himself after fatally shooting brother (Wisconsin), June, 225, 1989

Family's first outing has somber ending, July 7, 1987

Turtle saves sinking survivors (Philippines), May 21, 1989

Fisherman may have fallen overboard, July 6, 1989

Search party uncovers missing hunter's body, February 20, 1990

Woman pinned under snow machine dies, January 18, 1991

Hunter shot, killed, November 6, 1991

Teen twins killed after ATVs collide (Florida), November 12, 1991

Father kills himself after shooting son in hunting accident (New York), November 27, 1991

Eight-year-old boy killed in snowmobile collision, March 1992

Emmonak villager found dead in snow cave, March 5, 1992

Snowboarders die in powder (California), January 4, 1993

Girl dies in sled accident, January 5, 1993

Moose won't yield right-of-way, February 1, 1993

Two women hurt by crashing wave, June 25, 1993

Nobody answers door; woman freezes outside, February 17, 1994

Climbers found dead on mountain (New Hampshire), March 1, 1994

Man dies reeling in a fish, June 8, 1994

Moose collision kills 19-year-old, August 16, 1994

Breaching whale lands on boat, July 14, 1995

Collision with moose kills snowmachiner, January 30, 1997

Pet peacock attacks, kills master (Thailand), April 1997

Ice yields body; likely lost climber's, February 19 1998

Troopers search for hunter, August 17, 1998

Stranded boatman found after 3 days, May 12, 1999

Moose drowns entangled in net, September 17, 1999

APPENDIX 3

KANIUT TITLES

KANIUT TITLES
website: www.kaniut.com
email: kaniut@alaska.net

Bear books:

Alaska Bear Tales
More Alaska Bear Tales
Some Bears Kill
Bear Tales for the Ages
SAFE with Bears

Adventure-Misadventure books:

Cheating Death
Danger Stalks the Land
Alaska Air Tales
Swallowed Alive, Fighting for Life in Alaska Volumes 1 and 2

Novels:

Trapped
Brachan
The B.G

Coloring-activity book:

Alaska's Fun Bears

Alaska terminology:

Instant Sourdough

Memoir:

Heavenly Rose, Angel in Disguise

Forthcoming:

What's Bruin?
Charlie's Tails
Snatched from Death
Alaska...comin' atcha

www.ingramcontent.com/pod-product-compliance
Lightning Source LLC
Chambersburg PA
CBHW070106030426
42335CB00016B/2030